GEOLOGY

Andrew McLeish

Blackie

ISBN 0 216 90447 1

First published 1978

Published by Blackie and Son Limited,
Bishopbriggs, Glasgow G64 2NZ
and 450/452 Edgware Road, London W2 1EG

Filmset by
Willmer Brothers Limited, Birkenhead,
Merseyside
and Printed by
Thomson Litho Ltd., East Kilbride, Scotland.

PREFACE

his book covers the requirements of the various ted Kingdom CSE, O Level and O Grade abuses in geology. These syllabuses contain a siderable element of common ground, and the hor's main aim has been to present this core terial in as simple a manner as possible. The k will also be of use to pupils following non-mination courses.

he text adopts a modern, scientific approach to subject and is enhanced by a large number of grams and photographs. Experiments have n suggested where possible. Full treatment is en to basic topics such as minerals and rocks, ace processes, earthquakes, Earth movements and fossils. Topics briefly considered include the Earth in space, isostasy and palaeomagnetism. A simple treatment of plate tectonics is included, and the stratigraphy of Britain is described partly in terms of plate movements. The importance of an appreciation of the environment is emphasized; the finite nature of the Earth's reserves and future trends in the use of resources are discussed. Special reference is made to fuels and ores and an account of the development of North Sea oil and gas production is included.

Geology is an admirable subject for both able and less able pupils because of its inter-relationships with the other sciences and with geography. Its environmental relevance and its practical, outdoor nature give it added significance. The future of geology as part of the school curriculum seems assured.

The author accepts full responsibility for any errors which may appear in the book and he will be pleased to receive helpful comments from teachers, particularly suggestions for additional experiments. Finally, the author would like to thank the many people and organizations who have helped him with this work.

Andrew McLeish

The author and publishers would like to thank the following for permission to reproduce photographs:

National Aeronautics and Space Administration 2, 6
NERC Copyright, by permission of the Director, Institute of Geological Sciences 12, 13, 32, 33, 40, 49 (top), 62 (top), 101, 111
New Zealand High Commission 20, 53 (left)
United States Travel Service 21, 48
E. K. Walton 17, 25 (top), 43, 103
M. R. W. Johnson 25 (bottom), 26, 27, 28, 64
Aerofilms 35, 41, 42, 47, 49 (bottom), 61
G. N. Wright 36, 46, 59, 62 (bottom), 63
Royal Danish Embassy 45
Kyodo News Service 53 (right)
E. Dunsmore 66
British Museum (Natural History) 88, 90, 98
National Coal Board 122
Shell Photographic Service 124, 125, 128
British Gas Corporation 129
Phelps Dodge Corporation 133

CONTENTS

UNIT
1
Planet Earth

hat is geology?

Geology is the part of science which deals with e study of the Earth. So, as we learn about ology, we shall be asking ourselves such things What is the Earth made of? What kinds of things ppen on the inside and on the outside of the rth? and: What has happened to the Earth in past es?

To help answer questions like these the ologist, a scientist who studies geology, makes e of parts of chemistry, physics, biology and ography. One thing that makes geology such an eresting subject is that it covers a wide range of bjects. Something else which makes geology eresting is that it is largely an outdoor science. und about you, you can always see things ich tell you something about the Earth. At the ach you can see sand and pebbles being moved the waves and you can see shells being buried.

In the countryside you can see evidence that rivers and streams slowly wear away the land. Perhaps, too, you have seen films of volcanoes, glaciers and desert sand dunes. Study of all these things tells us that the Earth is a very active place where changes are constantly taking place (although these changes are usually very slow).

Besides being interesting, geology, like other sciences, can be very useful to man. Study of geology can help us to find materials such as coal, oil and metals. Geology may also be useful to the engineer because it can tell him the best places to build bridges and dams.

What is the Earth?

The Earth is one of the planets of the **Solar System**. The Solar System is made up of the Sun, which is a star, and nine planets. From the Sun outwards, the planets are Mercury, Venus, Earth, Mars, Jupiter, Saturn, Uranus, Neptune and Pluto. Figure 1.1 will give you an idea of the sizes of the planets compared to the size of the Sun.

The planets all move around the Sun in nearly circular paths called **orbits**. The Earth travels round the Sun once every year. Mercury and Venus, which are nearer to the Sun, take less than 365 days to orbit the Sun, whereas the planets from Mars outwards take longer than 365 days.

Besides orbiting or revolving around the Sun, the planets also spin or **rotate** like tops. The Earth rotates once every 24 hours. Some planets rotate very quickly; for example, Jupiter, the largest planet, completes a rotation in just under 10 hours. On the other hand, Venus takes 243 days to rotate once.

In table 1.1 you will find some information about the planets. The photographs on pages 2 and 6 will show you some of the main features of the planets.

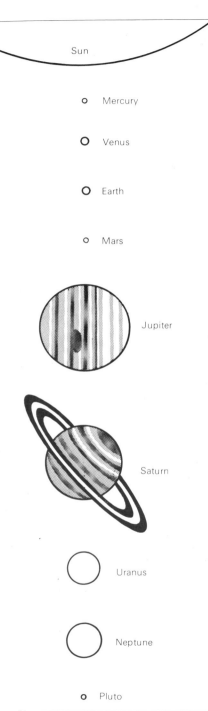

Sun

Mercury

Venus

Earth

Mars

Jupiter

Saturn

Uranus

Neptune

Pluto

1.1 The Solar System. Note that the distances between the planets have not been drawn to scale; use the information in Table 1.1 to make a diagram with the spacings properly represented. You will be surprised by what you find.

This photograph of Jupiter was taken by the Pioneer II spacecraft as it approached the giant planet from below its south pole. At this point the planet was 2 300 000 kilometres away from Pioneer II.

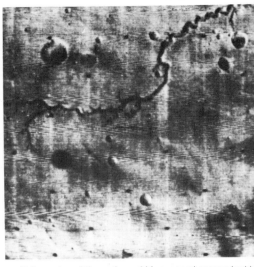

This portion of the surface of Mars was photographed by the spacecraft Mariner 9 from 1 666 kilometres away. The sinuous valley which can be seen is 400 kilometres long and about 5 kilometres wide, and is rather like a giant version of water-cut gulleys found on parts of the Earth. However, scientists believe that there is not enough water on Mars at present to allow rivers to form.

This view of the Earth was seen by the Apollo 8 astronauts as they came from behind the Moon in a lunar orbit.

Planet	Distance from Sun (millions of km)	Time taken to revolve around Sun	Time taken to rotate	Diameter (km)	Mass relative to Earth	Density (grams per cubic cm)	Main gases of atmosphere	Surface temperature (°C)	Number of moons
MERCURY	58	88 days	59 days	4880	0.06	5.4	no atmosphere	350	0
VENUS	108	225 days	243 days	12 104	0.8	5.2	carbon dioxide	480	0
EARTH	150	365 days	24 hours	12 756	1	5.5	nitrogen and oxygen	22	1
MARS	228	687 days	24.5 hours	6787	0.1	3.9	carbon dioxide, argon, nitrogen	—23	2
JUPITER	778	12 years	10 hours	142 800	318	1.3	hydrogen and helium	—150	13
SATURN	1427	29 years	10 hours	120 000	95	0.7		—180	10
URANUS	2870	84 years	16 hours	51 800	15	1.2	hydrogen, helium and methane	—210	5
NEPTUNE	4497	165 years	16 hours	49 500	17	1.7		—220	2
PLUTO	5900	248 years	6.5 days	3000	0.002	0.9	no atmosphere	—230	1

Table 1.1 (a) The main features of the planets.

MERCURY	Looks very like the Moon.
VENUS	Pale yellow in colour. Surface is obscured by thick clouds which may be made up of sulphuric acid droplets. Swirling motions of the clouds indicates strong winds in the upper atmosphere. Radar photographs have shown the presence of craters and the landing site of the Russian spacecraft Venera 9 had a surface covering of jagged boulders.
MARS	Orange in colour. In places cratered like the Moon but also has huge volcanoes, enormous gorges and ancient valleys which seem to have been cut by running water. Dust storms sometimes stirred up by strong winds. The Martian polar ice caps grow large and small with the seasons. The permanent ice is frozen water; the seasonal ice may be solid carbon dioxide.
JUPITER	Pale orange in colour. Mostly liquid with a small solid centre. The thick atmosphere is banded pale yellow and red-brown.
SATURN	Yellowish in colour. Deep cloudy atmosphere. Saturn's rings are made up of lumps of ice up to about 1 metre in diameter.
URANUS	No visible surface markings. It may have a deep atmosphere. Surrounded by eight narrow rings.
NEPTUNE	Discovered in 1846. It seems to have a deep, clear atmosphere.
PLUTO	Discovered in 1930. It began as a moon of Neptune.

Table 1.1 (b) More details about the planets.

Where did the Earth come from?

It is thought that the Solar System formed about 4600 million years ago from the material of a spinning cloud of cold dust and gas called a **nebula**. The dust grains and condensed gases collided and formed bigger and bigger masses which eventually came together to form the planets (figure 1.2). Between Mars and Jupiter there are objects called **asteroids** (the largest is about 1000 kilometres in diameter) consisting of material which did not come together to form a planet.

In its early stages the Earth would have looked quite like a larger version of the Moon because it was cratered by falling objects of asteroid size (figure 1.3). Eventually, the Earth heated up and melted. At this time its surface was completely changed and gases which had been held within the Earth were pushed out to form an atmosphere made up of water vapour, carbon dioxide and methane. (Methane is commonly known as 'natural gas'.) As the Earth cooled the oceans began to form by the condensation of water vapour, and the earliest land began to appear about 4000 million years ago. Since these early days the surface of the Earth has been slowly changing so that today, the geography of the world is very different compared with its geography in past ages.

The original rotating dust cloud or nebula.

The spinning nebula flattens to a disc shape.

The dust particles collect to form objects of asteroid size. The primitive Sun appears in the centre.

The asteroids collect to form planets.

1.2   Stages in the formation of the Solar System.

4600 million years ago: the newly formed Earth was cratered by infalling objects of asteroid size.

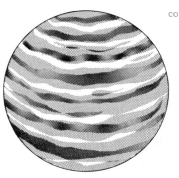

4500 million years ago: the Earth melted.

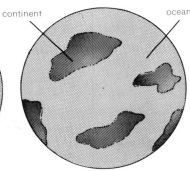

continent   ocean

4000 million years ago: the oceans and continents began to form.

1.3   The early development of the Earth.

The Earth today

If you look at a globe or an atlas you will that most of the Earth's surface is covered water. Land makes up only about 30% of surface area. The main features of the contine are the long **mountain chains**, such as Himalayas and Andes, the low plateaus **shields**, such as the Canadian and Baltic Shie and the plains or **platforms** such as the lowla of western Russia and the Great Plains of N America (figure 1.4).

At first sight the sea looks quite uninteres but if the oceans were to dry up we would many surprising features. First of all, near centres of the oceans we would find enorm

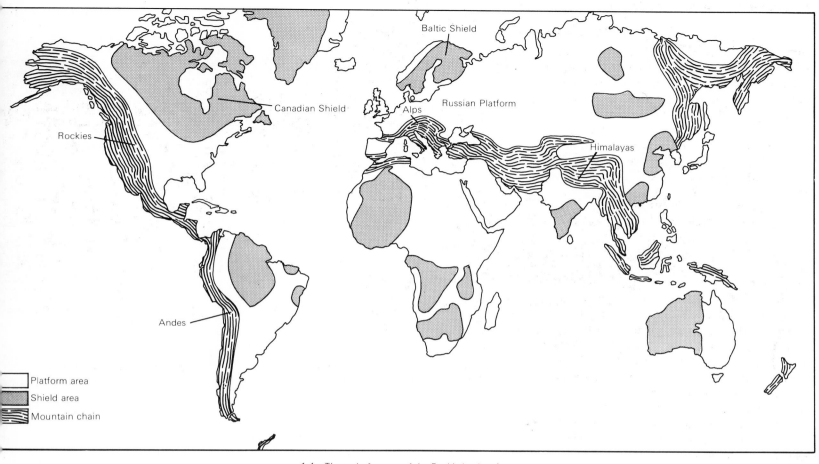

Platform area
Shield area
Mountain chain

1.4   *The main features of the Earth's land surface.*

ountain ranges called **oceanic ridges**. On the
es of the ridges are flat **ocean basins**. The
ean floor rises from the basins towards the
ntinents. Around parts of the continents there
 areas covered by shallow seas called
ntinental shelves. The North Sea is part of the
ntinental shelf of Europe. Other features of
eans are very deep valleys called **oceanic**
nches; these are found most commonly
und the Pacific. Figure 1.5 will give you some
ormation on continents and oceans.

e on Earth

One thing which makes the Earth so very
ferent from the other planets of the Solar
stem is the abundance of plants and animals.

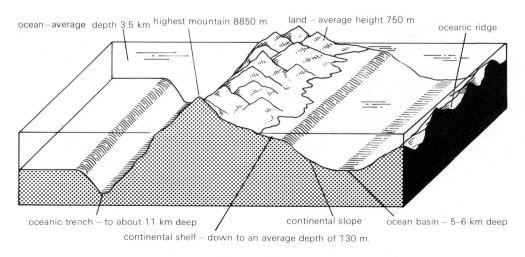

ocean – average depth 3.5 km   highest mountain 8850 m   land – average height 750 m   oceanic ridge

oceanic trench – to about 11 km deep   continental slope   ocean basin – 5–6 km deep
continental shelf – down to an average depth of 130 m.

1.5   *Land and sea.*

This photograph of Venus is made up of several superimposed photographs taken by Mariner 10. The thick cloud cover of Venus can be seen.

The first living things were very simple organisms which formed about 3500 million years ago, perhaps in the sea. Since then, plants and animals have gone through many slow changes and man, the most intelligent animal, appeared within the last 5 million years.

The living things of the Earth are very important geologically. For example, coal was formed from the trees which grew in ancient forests and oil was formed by the decay of small organisms which lived in the sea. Also, the oxygen which we breathe has been produced over long ages by green plants.

Climate

The type of weather which an area has can greatly affect the processes which change the shape of the land surface. For example, in areas of heavy rainfall there are large rivers wearing away the land. In desert areas changes in the land surface may partly be caused by wind-blown sand. In Greenland and Antarctica thick ice sheets grind away the land.

This photograph of Mercury is made up of eighteen superimposed photographs taken by the spacecraft Mariner 10 from 200 000 kilometres away. The cratered surface is similar to the cratered highlands on the Moon.

UNIT
2
Earth Chemistry

What is the Earth made of?

All substances, whether solid, liquid or gas, are made up of tiny particles called **atoms**. In substances such as copper and sulphur all the atoms are of the same kind; such substances are called **elements**. When elements join together they form new substances called **compounds**. For example, when copper atoms join with sulphur atoms a compound called copper sulphide results.

Elements and compounds found in the Earth are called **minerals**. Copper, sulphur and copper sulphide are all minerals. Most minerals are compounds; see if you can find out which elements, besides copper and sulphur, occur in the

Earth. Although there are nearly 2000 minerals, less than thirty are common. We can identify these minerals by using a few simple tests.

Identifying minerals

To identify minerals we have to look for differences between them. Here are some of the ways in which minerals differ from each other.

Colour

Some minerals can be identified fairly easily just by looking at their colours. For example, galena is always lead-grey. Unfortunately, however, some minerals can have different colours; quartz can be clear like glass or it can be white, pink, purple, red, brown or yellow. As a general rule, common dark-coloured minerals contain iron while light-coloured minerals contain no iron.

Streak

This is the colour of the mineral when it is powdered. You can find the streak of a mineral by rubbing it on a piece of white, unglazed porcelain called a streak plate. This test is only useful for coloured minerals; white or transparent minerals always give a white streak. Also, minerals which are harder than the plate will not give a streak.

Lustre

This describes the way in which the mineral reflects light. Some minerals shine like metal (i.e. they have a metallic lustre), some look glassy and some are dull.

Hardness

Some minerals are very soft whereas others are very hard. For example, diamond will easily scratch glass while graphite (a substance contained in pencil 'lead') rubs off onto paper. Minerals are given hardness values on a scale called **Mohs' Scale of Hardness**. This scale goes from talc, the softest mineral (hardness 1) to diamond, the hardest mineral (hardness 10). You

8

will see from table 2.1 that by using your fingernail, an untarnished twopence piece and a knife blade you can get a good idea of the hardness of any mineral you want to identify. You should note that harder minerals will scratch softer minerals.

Density

The density of a substance is a measure of its heaviness. If you pick up a water bottle and a similar bottle filled to the same depth with mercury you will get a good idea of how substances can differ in density. To find the density of a mineral specimen you have to measure two things.

Firstly, find the mass of the specimen in grams. Secondly, measure the volume of the specimen in cubic centimetres. Partly fill a measuring cylinder with water and read the volume. Hang the mineral specimen in the water and take the new reading. You will find that the water has risen by an amount equal to the volume of the specimen.

If you divide the mass of the specimen by its volume you will have the value of the density of the mineral in grams per cubic centimetre (g/cm^3). Remember that when measuring densities you must only use pure specimens, and the specimen must contain no air bubbles. Can you see why?

Most minerals have densities of about $3 \ g/cm^3$. Minerals with densities above $5 \ g/cm^3$ feel distinctly heavy in the hand.

Sometimes you will find the heaviness of minerals given in terms of **specific gravity**. All this means is that a mineral with a specific gravity of 4 has a density of $4 \ g/cm^3$, that is, the specific gravity is equal to the number value of the density when the density is given in grams per cubic centimetre.

Reaction with acid

Some minerals react with dilute hydrochloric acid. Calcite fizzes strongly and gives off carbon dioxide (this is the gas in lemonade). Galena gives off a smell like rotten eggs.

Crystal shape

Minerals form **crystals** whose shapes can sometimes help to identify the mineral. Crystal shapes can be grouped into the seven simple types shown in figure 2.1.

Shape		Minerals with shapes based on those shown
	cube	magnetite, iron pyrites, galena, sphalerite, fluorite, halite, garnet
	square prism (tea packet or packet of 'Spangles' shape)	cassiterite chalcopyrite
	rectangular prism (matchbox shape)	sulphur barytes olivine
	parallelogram prism (squashed matchbox shape)	malachite, gypsum, augite, hornblende, mica, talc, orthoclase feldspar
	triangular prism ('Toblerone' shape)	quartz haematite calcite dolomite
	hexagonal prism (shape of some pencils and pens)	graphite
	all sides parallelograms— no right angles. To make this shape cut the outside of a matchbox as shown then squash it	plagioclase feldspar

2.1 *Basic crystal shapes.*

Some minerals, for example, iron pyrites (fool's gold), form cubic crystals. You can grow cubic crystals of your own if you dissolve some table salt (sodium chloride) in warm water in a shallow dish. If you leave the water to evaporate for a few days cubic sodium chloride crystals will form. See if you can grow alum crystals on a thread dipped in strong alum solution which has been left to evaporate. The shape of an alum crystal does not look like a cube but it is based on a cube and you can easily see this. Make a cube of plasticine then cut off the corners a bit at a time. Make drawings of the shapes produced as you go along (figure 2.2). Compare your final shape with an alum crystal (figure 2.3)–this shape is called an octahedron. You can continue the above process with plasticine cubes by cutting off the edges, or the corners and the edges. Again you can produce a number of shapes based on a cube (figure 2.2). You will see from this that crystal shapes, although based on something as simple as a cube, can look quite different from each other. In the same way, the different crystal shapes found among minerals can be produced from the simple shapes in figure 2.1 by cutting away corners and edges.

Cleavage and fracture

Many minerals split easily along well-marked planes inside the crystals. These planes are called **cleavage planes** and they commonly run in one, two, three or four directions through the mineral (figure 2.4). Sometimes, the cleavage planes are parallel to the crystal faces. For example, galena crystallizes in cubes with cleavage planes parallel to the sides of the cube. Frequently, however, the cleavage planes are not parallel to the crystal faces. Fluorite forms cubic crystals with the cleavage along planes which cut off the corners of the crystals (figure 2.5). You should be careful not to confuse cleavage planes and crystal faces; they are not the same. As you examine many mineral specimens you will find that cleavage planes can be seen more often than crystal faces. Some minerals have no planes of weakness in the crystals so they break in any direction along surfaces called **fractures**.

1 TALC	⎫	Scratched by fingernail
2 GYPSUM	⎭	
3 CALCITE		Scratched by untarnished twopence piece
4 FLUORITE	⎫	Easily scratched by knife blade
5 APATITE	⎭	
6 FELDSPAR		Just scratched by a good knife blade
7 QUARTZ	⎫	
8 TOPAZ	⎪	
9 CORUNDUM	⎬	Scratch knife blade easily. Quartz may be scratched by a file.
10 DIAMOND	⎭	

Table 2.1 Mohs' scale of hardness.

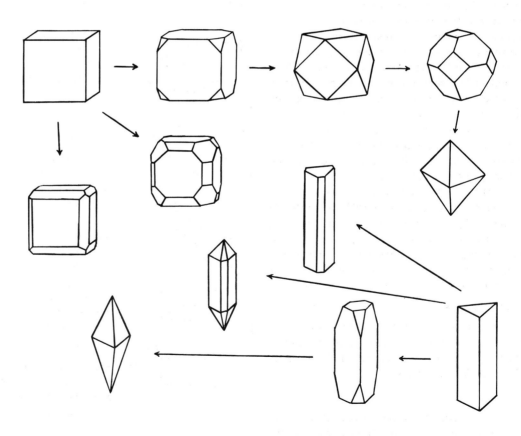

2.2   Showing how complex crystal shapes can be derived from simple forms by cutting away corners and edges.

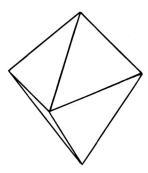

2.3 *An alum crystal – this shape is an octahedron.*

Twinning

Crystals sometimes grow together like Siamese twins (figure 2.6). Such crystals are said to be **twinned**. Twinning is common in minerals called feldspars and can sometimes be seen as dull and shiny strips on the specimen. In fact, the different parts of the specimen may look quite like the strips on a newly-mown lawn.

The main mineral types

We can divide minerals into groups simply by looking at their chemical compositions. Some of these groups are as follows:

Elements

Besides **copper** and **sulphur**, which we have mentioned already, elements such as **gold**, **silver** and **carbon** are found in the Earth.

Copper, gold and silver are well-known metals usually found in variously shaped masses including lumps, small grains, sheets, threads and moss-like forms. These metals are soft (hardness 3) and very dense (gold 19 g/cm³; silver 10.5 g/cm³; copper 9 g/cm³). Unlike most other minerals copper, gold and silver can be hammered into thin sheets.

You can make sulphur crystals by dissolving some powdered sulphur in xylene. Filter the

mixture and leave the filtrate aside for some of the xylene to evaporate. Examine and describe the crystals which form. Sulphur is non-metallic and its yellow colour and low density (2 g/cm³) make it easy to recognize. Also, it is one of the few minerals which burns. Heat a small quantity of sulphur powder on a tin-lid. What happens to it before it burns? What colour is the flame? Do you recognize the gas which is given off?

Carbon occurs in the forms of **diamond** and **graphite**. What qualities does diamond possess that make it useful as a gemstone? Can you find out what use is made of diamonds which are not of gem quality? Graphite is a very soft (hardness 1), shiny, black or dark-grey mineral which is used to make pencil leads.

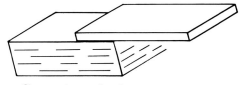

Cleavage in one direction – the mineral splits into flakes.

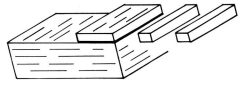

Cleavage in two directions – the mineral breaks into long fragments.

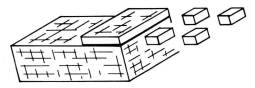

Cleavage in three or four directions – the mineral breaks into pieces with sides all about the same length.

2.4 *Cleavage.*

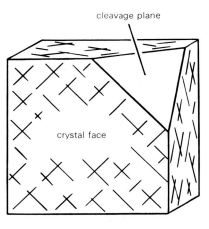

2.5 *Cleavage in fluorite. The cleavage planes run in four directions.*

You should note that the mineral elements are all rare.

Oxides

An oxide is a compound made up of oxygen and another element.

Quartz (silicon dioxide or silica) is an extremely common mineral. It is very hard (hardness 7), it has no cleavage planes and it breaks like glass along a curving, shelly-looking surface. This is called a **conchoidal fracture**. Quartz often looks quite like glass but it also occurs as coloured varieties such as **rose quartz** (pink), **amethyst** (purple), **smoky quartz** (brown) and the common **milky quartz** (white). **Rock crystal** is water-clear quartz.

Opal is composed of silica combined with water. It does not form crystals: Opal is usually white but its colours are very variable and include brown, red, orange, grey and yellow. **Precious opal** shows a great variety of rich colour within one specimen. Opal displays a property known as opalescence; that is, it appears milky or cloudy when light is shone through it. You can produce a similar effect by passing a beam of light through soapy water or through water containing a few drops of milk. With a hardness of 6, opal is softer than quartz.

Chalcedony is a form of silica made up of numerous microscopic grains of quartz along with

fluorite

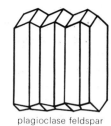
plagioclase feldspar

orthoclase feldspar

gypsum

2.6 Twinned crystals.

some opal. The mineral is commonly white or grey but it may also be blue-grey, brown, red, green or black. **Agate** is a form of chalcedony showing rings of colour banding; **onyx** shows flat banding.

Magnetite, haematite and **limonite** are all forms of iron oxide. Since iron is extracted from these minerals they are examples of **ore minerals**; an ore mineral is a mineral from which a useful metal can be economically obtained. Magnetite is grey-black and it looks quite like iron. It can easily be recognized because it is strongly magnetic. Haematite occurs as **specular iron ore** which consists of very shiny, black crystals and as **kidney ore** which is made up of red-brown, lumpy masses which are grey-black on the inside. Limonite contains water in addition to iron and oxygen. It is brown or yellow-brown and, since it does not form crystals, it occurs as lumpy or earthy masses. The three iron oxide ores can be distinguished easily by their streaks; magnetite has a black streak, haematite has a red-brown or cherry-red streak, and limonite has a yellow-brown streak. Haematite and limonite are non-magnetic.

Cassiterite (tin oxide) is the chief ore mineral of tin. It is a hard, black, glassy-looking mineral of high density (hardness 6.5; density 7 g/cm³). If cassiterite and zinc are added to dilute hydrochloric acid the cassiterite becomes coated with grey or silvery metallic tin.

Sulphides

Sulphides result from the combination of metals with sulphur.

Iron pyrites (iron sulphide) looks like brass and it often occurs as cubes with lined faces. Iron pyrites is also known as **fool's gold** because it resembles gold. However, gold (hardness 3) can easily be cut with a knife whereas iron pyrites (hardness 6) is only scratched by good quality steel. Also, pyrites shatters on hammering whereas gold flattens out. **Marcasite** is a white form of iron pyrites.

Chalcopyrite (iron and copper sulphide) is similar in appearance to iron pyrites but it is less brassy and often has a many-coloured shine (tarnish) on its surface. Also, since the hardness of chalcopyrite is only 4 it can be scratched more

easily than iron pyrites.

Galena (lead sulphide) is easily recognized because it looks like shiny lead. It forms cubic crystals with three good cleavages parallel to the crystal faces. It also has a distinctive lead-grey streak.

Sphalerite (zinc sulphide) is the only common sulphide which does not look metallic. It is usually brown or black although it may be yellow. It has a glassy or plastic lustre and it cleaves in six directions with the cleavage planes meeting each other at angles of 60°.

Chalcopyrite, galena and sphalerite are the main ore minerals of copper, lead and zinc, respectively. Iron pyrites is not used as a source of iron.

Chlorides and fluorides

A chloride is formed when a metal combines with chlorine. **Halite** (sodium chloride) is the most common chloride. It is well known for its use as table salt and can be easily recognized by its taste. It forms cubic crystals which can readily be grown from solution. Halite has three good cleavage planes which run parallel to the crystal faces. It is colourless or white when pure, but when impure it may exhibit a variety of colours including yellow, red, blue and purple.

A fluoride is formed when fluorine combines with a metal. **Fluorite** (calcium fluoride) is the only common fluoride mineral. It often occurs as cubic crystals with four good cleavage planes cutting the corners of the cubes (figure 2.5). Fluorite is commonly colourless or white, but it may have many colours including yellow, blue, purple, green, brown and black.

Carbonates

The compounds formed when a metal combines with carbon and oxygen are called carbonates.

Calcite (calcium carbonate) is a very common mineral. It often looks like quartz, but the two minerals can be distinguished because calcite is much softer (hardness 3) and it cleaves easily in three directions. Calcite also fizzes strongly when placed in dilute hydrochloric acid. You can identify the gas given off by testing with lime water. Calcite is usually white or colourless but it may show pale

12

Quartz crystals – the shapes of these crystals are based on triangular prisms.

A conchoidal (shell-like) fracture in quartz.

Agate – a form of chalcedony showing rings of variable colour.

Kidney iron ore – a form of haematite consisting of lumpy masses.

nts of other colours. It often occurs as six-sided cleavage fragments which look something like squashed cubes. Calcite also occurs as blunt-ended crystals called **nail-head spar** and as sharp-ended crystals called **dog-tooth spar**. **Iceland spar** is a pure, transparent form of calcite.

Dolomite (calcium and magnesium carbonate) is quite like calcite but it may be honey-coloured. Also, it shows little or no reaction with cold, dilute hydrochloric acid but it reacts readily if the acid is heated. **Pearl spar** is a pearly-looking form of dolomite.

Malachite (copper carbonate) is easily recognized by its bright green colour. It reacts with cold, dilute hydrochloric acid and it turns black on heating. Malachite is an important ore mineral of copper.

Sulphates

Sulphates are compounds of metals with sulphur and oxygen.

Gypsum (calcium sulphate) is the most common sulphate. When pure it is colourless or white, but when impure it may be pink, yellow or grey. Gypsum usually has a pearly or silky lustre. It possesses one very good cleavage plane so it tends to break into thin flakes. Since its hardness is only 2, it can easily be scratched with a fingernail. Gypsum occurs as clear crystals of **selenite** and as silky, thread-like crystals of **satin spar**. **Alabaster** is a fine-grained form of gypsum.

Barytes (barium sulphate) is sometimes called **heavy spar** because it is the only white mineral with a high density (4.5 g/cm^3). Barytes is usually white or colourless but it may be pale yellow or pale brown. It has good cleavage planes in three directions and its lustre is usually glassy or pearly.

Silicates

Silicates are very common minerals formed by the combination of metals with silicon and oxygen. Silicates are usually either pale-coloured (pink or white) or dark-coloured (green, brown or black). In general, the dark silicates contain iron and the pale silicates do not contain iron.

Feldspars are the most common of all minerals. The two main types of feldspar are **orthoclase** which contains potassium and is usually pink, and **plagioclase** which contains sodium and calcium and is usually white or grey. Both feldspars are opaque with pearly or glassy lustre and both have hardnesses of 6. Orthoclase sometimes forms box-shaped crystals and it has two cleavage planes at right angles to each other. Plagioclase also has two cleavage planes but they are not quite at right angles. Twinning is common in both feldspars; in plagioclase it often makes the specimen look stripy.

The **pyroxenes** and **amphiboles** are common silicates which are usually green or black in colour. **Augite** is a common pyroxene often occurring as stumpy, dull-black crystals. It has a glassy or plastic lustre, and two indistinct cleavage planes at right angles to each other. **Hornblende** is a common amphibole. It usually forms long, very dark green crystals. Hornblende is shinier than augite and it has two fairly distinct cleavage planes at 60° to each other. Augite and hornblende are not easy to tell apart; figure 2.7 shows some of the differences between the minerals. Some types of **asbestos** are thread-like varieties of amphibole.

Olivine is a silicate which often looks like green glass, although it may also be yellowish or brownish. It has no cleavage planes and breaks with a conchoidal fracture. It is never found

Two forms of calcite crystals based on triangular prisms:

(a) sharp-ended dog-tooth spar

(b) blunt-ended nail-head spar

14

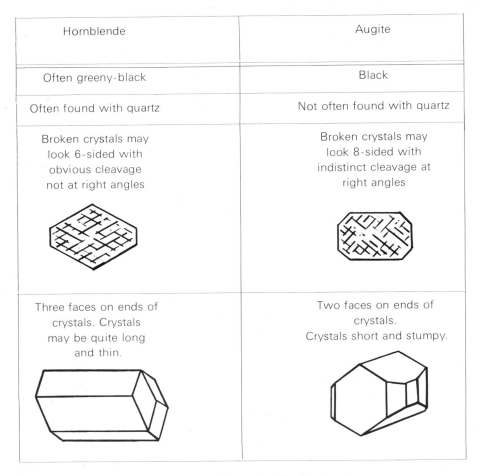

Hornblende	Augite
Often greeny-black	Black
Often found with quartz	Not often found with quartz
Broken crystals may look 6-sided with obvious cleavage not at right angles	Broken crystals may look 8-sided with indistinct cleavage at right angles
Three faces on ends of crystals. Crystals may be quite long and thin.	Two faces on ends of crystals. Crystals short and stumpy.

2.7   The differences between hornblende and augite.

occurring with quartz. **Peridot** is gem quality olivine.

Garnet is a silicate which is usually red, brown or green in colour. It has no cleavage planes and it often occurs as nearly round crystals based on cubic shapes. Garnet has a glassy lustre and a hardness of 7.

Mica is a common silicate which can easily be recognized because it has a single very good cleavage plane which allows it to be split into springy sheets. It has a lustre like pearl or plastic. The two common forms of mica are **biotite** (**black mica**) and **muscovite** (**white mica**).

Talc is a very soft (hardness 1), silvery-white silicate. Like mica, talc has one very good cleavage plane which allows it to be split into very thin flakes. These flakes can be bent but they are not springy and elastic like those of mica. A fairly distinctive feature of talc is that it feels slippery or greasy between the fingers. Talc is not very common.

In table 2.2 you will find details of most of the minerals mentioned above. On page 15 you will find a key which should help you to identify mineral specimens. Remember that this key has been put together using only a few properties of a small number of minerals. If you cannot identify your specimen from the key use the other properties given in the table; for example, measure the density and hardness of your specimen.

Rocks

Look carefully at a piece of granite. What is made up of? You will see that granite is made up of minerals. Can you recognize the minerals present A natural material which is made up of minerals called a **rock**.

As with minerals, we can identify rocks by looking at the differences between them. Here are some of the ways in which rocks differ from each other:

Mineral content

Some rocks can be identified by looking at the types of minerals present in them. For example **granite** is made up of quartz and feldspar, usually with biotite, and **marble** may be made up almost entirely of calcite. The colour of a rock will sometimes give you a good idea of its mineral content. Light-coloured rocks often consist largely of quartz, feldspar or calcite while dark rocks may contain quite a lot of augite, hornblende or olivine.

Grain arrangement

In some rocks the mineral grains form a tight interlocking mass; such rocks are described as **crystalline**. On the other hand, some rocks are made up of separate grains which do not lock together - these are sometimes called **fragmental** rocks.

Grain size

Rocks may be made up of large or small mineral grains. If the grains are bigger than 5 mm in diameter the rock is described as **coarse grained**. **Medium-grained** rocks have grain sizes between 1 mm and 5 mm and **fine-grained** rocks are made up of grains less than 1 mm in diameter. As a general rule the grains of a coarse grained rock can be seen easily without being magnified; if the grains can be seen quite easily with a hand lens the rock is medium-grained and if the grains cannot easily be seen with a lens the rock is fine-grained.

Grain direction

In some rocks the mineral grains lie together

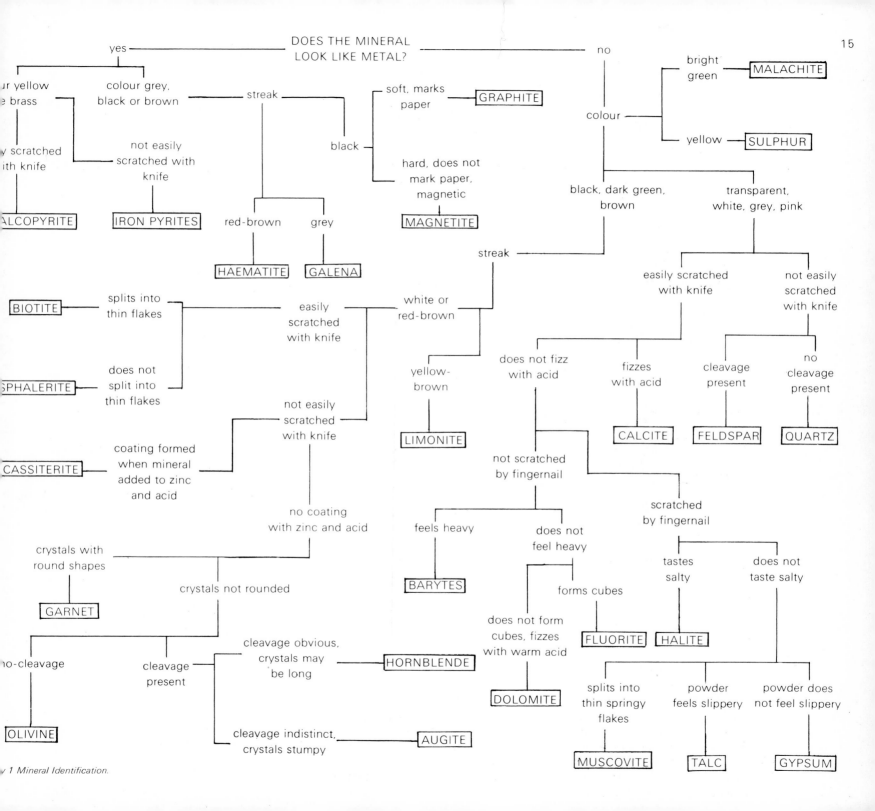

DOES THE MINERAL LOOK LIKE METAL?

1 Mineral Identification.

MINERAL	COLOUR	STREAK	LUSTRE	HARDNESS	DENSITY (g/cm³)	CLEAVAGE PLANES	OTHER DETAILS
GRAPHITE	Black	Shiny black	Metallic	1	2.1	One good set	May feel greasy. Writes on paper.
SULPHUR	Yellow	Yellow	Like plastic	2	2.1	Not usually seen	Yellow, non-metallic
QUARTZ	Usually transparent or white	White	Glassy	7	2.7	None-fracture surfaces curved	Can form good six-sided crystals. Usually found as shapeless lumps. Crystals may have horizontal lines
CASSITERITE	Black	White or grey	Glassy	6.5	7	None or indistinct	Add to zinc and dilute hydrochloric acid—becomes coated with metallic tin
HAEMATITE	Black or dark red	Red-brown	Metallic	5.5	5	None	Distinctive red-brown streak
MAGNETITE	Black	Black	Metallic	5.5	5	None	Magnetic
LIMONITE	Brown	Yellow-brown	Usually dull	3 to 5.5	4	None	Distinctive yellow-brown streak
IRON PYRITES (PYRITE)	Brassy yellow	Green-black	Metallic	6	5	None	Often found as cubes with lined faces
CHALCOPYRITE (COPPER PYRITES)	Brassy yellow	Green-black	Metallic	4	4.2	None	Often has many coloured shine on surface. Softer than iron pyrites
GALENA	Lead-grey	Grey	Metallic	2.5	7.5	3 sets parallel to crystal faces	Often found as cubes. Lead-coloured
SPHALERITE (ZINC BLENDE)	Black or brown	White or red-brown	Glassy or like plastic	4	4.1	6 sets at 60° to each other	Only glassy mineral to give smell of rotten eggs with dilute hydrochloric acid
FLUORITE (FLUOR SPAR)	Transparent, white, yellow, blue or purple	White	Glassy	4	3.2	Good cleavage cutting corners	Often forms good cubic crystals
HALITE (ROCK SALT)	Transparent or white	White	Glassy	2.5	2.2	3 sets at right angles	Salty taste
CALCITE	Usually white	White	Glassy	3	2.7	Obvious in 3 directions	Fizzes with dilute hydrochloric acid
DOLOMITE	White or pale yellow	White	Glassy or dull	4	2.9	Very obvious in 3 directions	Fizzes with heated dilute hydrochloric acid
MALACHITE	Bright green	Pale green	Like silk or dull	4	4	None	Turns black on heating. Fizzes with dilute hydrochloric acid
GYPSUM	Usually white	White	Like pearl or silk	2	2.3	One good set	Sometimes forms good crystals. Also found as groups of shiny thread-like crystals (satin spar)
BARYTES (BARITE)	Usually white	White	Glassy	3	4.5	3 good sets at right angles	Only white mineral which feels heavy in the hand

Table 2.2 Mineral properties

MINERAL		COLOUR	STREAK	LUSTRE	HARDNESS	DENSITY (g/cm³)	CLEAVAGE PLANES	OTHER DETAILS
GARNET		Usually dark red or brown	White	Glassy	7	4	None	Crystals often look nearly round
OLIVINE		Green	Colourless	Glassy	6.5	4	None	May look like green glass. Never found with quartz
PYROXENE-AUGITE		Black	White	Glassy	6	3.4	2 sets at right angles	Difficult to tell apart (see figure 2.7)
AMPHIBOLE-HORNBLENDE		Dark green or black	White	Glassy	5.5	3.2	2 sets not at right angles	
MICA	BIOTITE	Black	White	Glassy or like shiny plastic	2.5	3	One very good set	Splits very easily into thin springy flakes
	MUSCOVITE	White						
TALC		White	White	Like pearl	1	2.7	One very good set	Very soft. Feels greasy
FELDSPAR	ORTHOCLASE	Usually pink	White	Glassy	6	2.6	2 sets at right angles	Twinning may show as strips on some cleavage surfaces in plagioclase. Both are opaque
	PLAGIOCLASE	White, pink or grey					Not always easily seen	

Table 2.2 (continued)

Dolerite seen under a microscope – this rock has a crystalline texture.

Sandstone seen under a microscope – this rock has a fragmental texture.

...ile of books; that is, the grains are lined up in the ...ne general plane. A crystalline rock with its ...nerals lined up like this is said to be **foliated**.

Method of formation

There are three groups of rocks differing from each other in the way in which they form. The groups are called **igneous**, **sedimentary** and **metamorphic rocks**. We will now look at these three different rock types.

Igneous rocks

Melt some acetamide or salol on a slide. Watch the acetamide through a microscope as it cools. What happens? This experiment will give you a good idea of how igneous rocks form. They are formed by the solidification of molten rock material called **magma**. Magma forms deep within the Earth and as it rises it cools. Mineral crystals grow in the cooling magma until solidification is complete. As the crystals grow they lock together to form a crystalline rock. Sometimes the magma crystallizes before it reaches the Earth's surface and it forms a body called an **intrusion** within the Earth. Igneous rocks found in intrusions are often called **intrusive** rocks. Sometimes the magma reaches the surface of the Earth and it flows from **volcanoes** as **lava** which solidifies on the surface. Lavas are **extrusive** igneous rocks.

When naming igneous rocks two properties can be used. Firstly, we can look at the sizes of the mineral grains in the rock, and secondly at the types of minerals present.

Grain size

Compare a piece of granite with a piece of rhyolite. What do you observe? Although these two rocks are made up of the same minerals you will see that the grains in the granite are large and quite easily seen whereas in the rhyolite you will probably not be able to see any crystals at all. How can we account for the difference in the grain size of these two rocks?

Make a hot solution of copper sulphate. (Do this by adding copper sulphate crystals to hot water until no more will dissolve.) Pour half of the solution into a metal tray and leave the rest to cool slowly in the beaker. Compare the crystals you obtain in both cases. Can you explain your findings? What you have found with the copper sulphate crystals also applies to igneous rocks; that is, slow cooling allows large crystals to grow while rapid cooling causes rocks to be fine-grained. Can you suggest where coarse-grained and fine-grained igneous rocks might form? If magma crystallizes deep within the Earth will it cool slowly or quickly? What size of grains will result? Lavas solidify on the Earth's suface. Do you think they will cool slowly or quickly? Would you expect them to be coarse or fine-grained? Sometimes, magma cools so quickly that crystals have no time to form. When this happens the rock which results is called **glass**.

Minerals present

Besides grain size we can use the types of minerals present and their amounts to name igneous rocks. The minerals most commonly found are quartz, feldspar, hornblende and augite. In table 2.3 you will find the names of some common igneous rocks along with their grain sizes and mineral content. Rocks such as **granite** which contain quite a lot of quartz are sometimes called **acid** igneous rocks. Rocks with no quartz, **gabbro** being an example, are **basic. Diorite** is

Table 2.3 Igneous rocks.

GRAIN SIZE		MINERALS PRESENT		
		feldspar + about 30% quartz	feldspar + about 30% hornblende	feldspar + about 50% augite
	Coarse — diameter greater than 5mm	granite	diorite	gabbro
	Medium — diameter between 1 and 5mm	microgranite	microdiorite	dolerite
	Fine — diameter less than 1mm	rhyolite	andesite	basalt
	Glassy	obsidian		
COLOUR	Light ⟶ Dark But note: obsidian is usually black			

an **intermediate** rock. Intermediate rocks have less than 10% quartz.

You should note that besides the minerals used in naming the rocks other minerals are always present; for instance, granite often contains about 10% mica and hornblende along with the quartz and feldspar. Sometimes. additional minerals present are added to the rock names; for example, a gabbro containing quite a lot of olivine would be called an olivine-gabbro and a diorite with obvious quartz would be described as quartz-diorite. Some igneous rocks have a few large crystals called **phenocrysts** dotted about among the smaller grains. Such rocks are described as **porphyritic**; for example, a porphyritic basalt would be fine-grained except for a few large crystals of augite or feldspar.

Intrusions

You will remember that igneous intrusions are masses of igneous rock which have crystallized

beneath the Earth's surface. We can nar intrusions by looking at their shapes and sizes

The largest intrusion is called a **batholit** Batholiths are usually shaped like upturned boa and they are so large that they seem to bottomless. They are commonly found mountainous areas and seem to have bee intruded at great depth when the mountains we being pushed up. The rocks forming batholiths a always coarse-grained (can you see why?) and a often called **plutonic rocks**. Granite is the mo common plutonic rock. A well-known batholi occurs in south-west England where the granit from Dartmoor to the Scilly Isles are all known be part of a single very large intrusion (figure 2.8 A **stock** is the name given to a small batholith. T Galloway granites of south-west Scotland occ as stocks.

A **sheet** is an intrusion shaped something lik piece of cardboard. Vertical or nearly vertic sheets are called **dykes** (figure 2.9). **Sills** a sheets intruded between layers of other ro

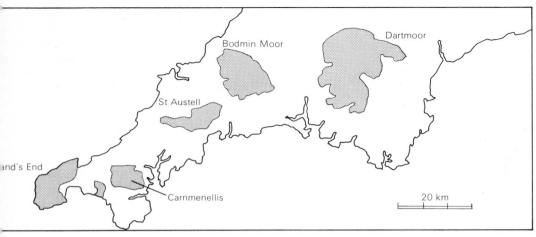

2.8 *(a) The granites of south-west England. These granites, with those of the Scilly Isles, are part of a single batholith.*

(b) The granite batholith shown with its overlying rocks stripped off.

ure 2.9). Dykes are common in north-west otland and a well-known sill is the Great Whin of northern England. Whinstone is another ne for dolerite. Since sheets are much smaller n batholiths they are usually made up of dium-grained rocks. Can you tell why this uld be so?

trusive igneous rocks

xtrusive igneous rocks result from the idification of magma which has come to the th's surface through **volcanoes**. If the magma nes from a round opening the volcano is scribed as being of **central type**. If the magma nes from a long crack in the Earth's surface the cano is of **fissure type**.

When a volcano of central type erupts, the products of the eruption rise through a tube-like channel called a **volcanic pipe** and escape to the surface through an opening called a **vent**. As well as lava, volcanoes produce showers of solid fragments broken off from inside the pipe. The finest material, made up of fragments less than 4 mm in diameter, is called **ash**. **Lapilli** are between 4 and 32 mm in diameter and fragments larger than 32 mm are called **bombs** if they are rounded and **blocks** if they are angular. A hard rock made up of ash or lapilli is called a **tuff**; **agglomerate** is made up mostly of bombs, and **volcanic breccia** consists largely of blocks. With repeated eruptions lavas and ashes get piled up around the vent and a **volcanic cone** is formed (figure 2.10). The top of the cone has a round depression called a **crater** formed by the explosive blowing out and collapse of material around the vent. The shapes of volcanic cones largely depend on how runny the lava is. Basaltic lava flows very easily so it forms flat, wide cones like those of the Hawaiian Islands. Andesites and rhyolites are lavas which do not flow easily, and they therefore form steep volcanic cones. Rhyolites are often so sticky when they flow that the minerals in them get lined up in the direction of flow. When this happens the rhyolite may show a layering known as **flow banding**.

Some central type volcanoes have huge craters called **calderas**. Small calderas, up to about 2 km in diameter, can be formed by the top of the

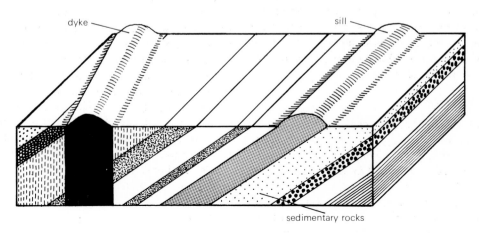

2.9 *A dyke and a sill.*

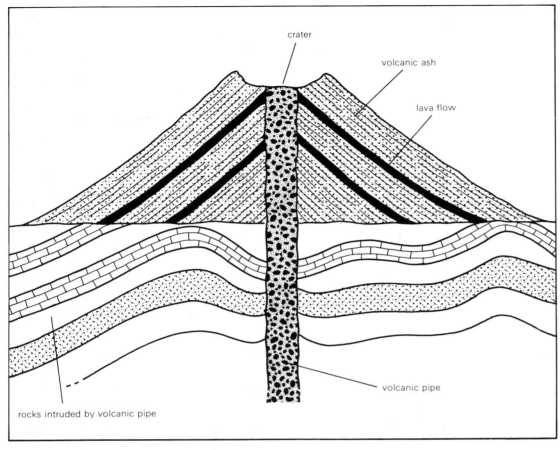

2.10 A section through a volcanic cone.

A steep-sided volcanic cone – Mount Nguaruhoe, New Zealand.

volcanic cone being blown off. Calderas of [this] type are not common. The magma which supp[lies] volcanoes is held before eruption in underly[ing] storage spaces called **magma chambers** [and] large calderas are formed by the sinking [of] volcanoes into their magma chambers (fig[ure] 2.11). The largest caldera in the world, 50 km l[ong] and 20 km wide, is in north-west Sumatra. [The] best known caldera is Crater Lake in Oreg[on] U.S.A.; it is 10 km in diameter.

When lava flows from a fissure type volcan[o it] does not build large cones. The lava, which [is] always basaltic and very runny, floods out over [the] Earth's surface as horizontal flows which o[ften] cover a very large area. In Britain, lavas of this t[ype] form the Antrim Plateau in Northern Ireland, [and] the hills around Glasgow are the remains of w[hat] was once a large area of such lavas. In 178[3 a] famous fissure eruption took place at Laki [in] Iceland. From a crack about 30 km long, stream[s of] lava poured out and buried the surround[ing] countryside.

Volcanoes can also be described in terms of t[heir] environment, that is, whether they occur on [the] continents or in the oceans. Contine[ntal] volcanoes are mostly of central type and t[hey] usually produce andesitic lavas. Oce[anic] volcanoes may be of central type (the isl[and of] Hawaii is the tip of such a volcano), but m[uch] more often, oceanic volcanoes are of fiss[ure] type. The oceanic ridges running up the middl[e of] the oceans are produced by large-scale fiss[ure] eruptions. In fact, the floors of the oceans are m[ade] up of basaltic rock given out by such erupti[ons.] When lava is extruded under water the coo[ling] effect of the water causes the lava to solidif[y as] distorted, rounded masses. Lava of this typ[e is] called **pillow lava**.

What makes lava come to the surface?

You can get a good idea of how an erupt[ion] takes place from a bottle of lemonade. Give [the] bottle a good hard shake then quickly remove [the] top. What happens? Can you explain why [this] happens? The lemonade does not froth up w[hile] the bottle-top is on because the gas cannot esc[ape]

en the lemonade is kept under pressure.
moving the bottle-top releases the pressure and
ws the gas to escape. The gas rises and carries
me of the lemonade with it.

The upper parts of the Earth, although solid, are
ught to contain very small amounts of liquid
persed among the grains of rocks lying roughly
a zone between depths of 50 and 250 km. If the
th's surface develops a weakness the pressure
this deep-lying molten material is released and
liquid (magma) can escape to the surface. As it
es it loses gas, mostly steam, to the atmosphere.
metimes the gas does not escape completely
d the lava coming from the volcano may be full
bubbles called **vesicles**. Frothy volcanic rock
ich looks like hard sponge is called **pumice**.

A caldera – Crater Lake in Oregon, U.S.A. In the centre is the small cone of Wizard Island.

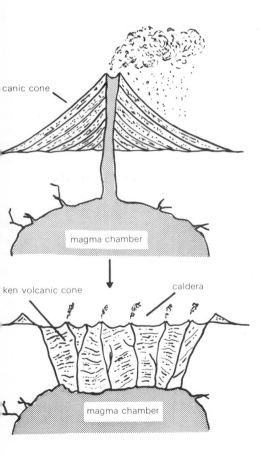

2.11 Caldera formation.

Solidified basaltic lava in Hawaii.

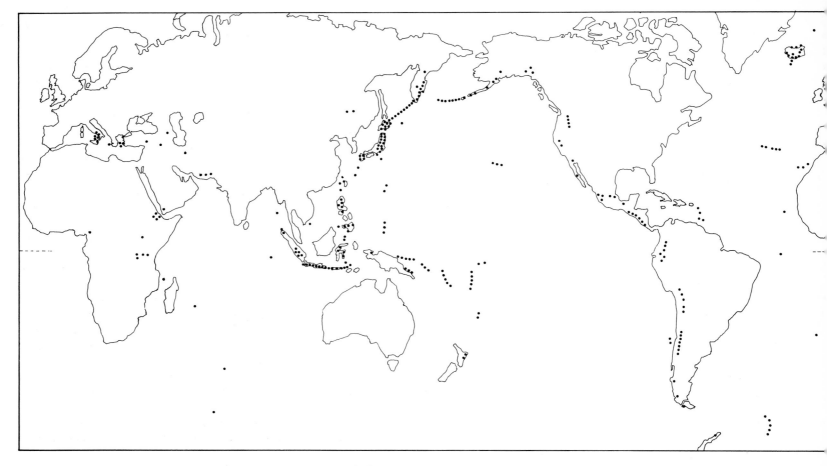

2.12 Distribution of active volcanoes.

Extinct and active volcanoes

Volcanoes become **extinct** when they cease to erupt. Long-extinct volcanoes are common in central Scotland where Arthur's Seat and the Castle Rock in Edinburgh are well-known examples.

Active or erupting volcanoes are not found all over the Earth. From figure 2.12 you will see that active volcanoes are found in areas where there are high mountains, particularly around the Pacific. You will also see that volcanoes are active in bands near the centres of the oceans.

Some volcanoes have had disastrous effects on the people living near them. The Roman towns of Pompeii and Herculaneum were buried by an eruption of Vesuvius in A.D. 79. In 1883, Krakatoa, a volcano between Java and Sumatra, blew up and produced an explosion which was heard 5000 km away in Australia. The explosion caused a wave which drowned 36 000 people on the surrounding islands. In 1902, Mount Pelée on the island of Martinique in the West Indies gave off a dense cloud of hot, ash-laden gas which rolled over the nearby town of St. Pierre and killed its 30 000 inhabitants. However, volcanoes are not always destructive. Volcanic districts often have fertile soils which can be richly cultivated and in places such as Italy and New Zealand electricity is generated from natural steam in geothermal power stations.

Sedimentary rocks

Examine some sand with a hand-lens or microscope. What is it made up of? You will ha found that sand is mostly made up of mine particles. Can you suggest how sand is formed? what kinds of places is sand found? How doe get to these places?

Materials such as sand, mud and gravel produced by the break-up of rocks at the Eart surface under the action of such things as frost a rain. The broken material may then be moved **transported** by water and wind to be laid do or **deposited** in beaches or dunes. The deposit material is called **sediment**. But how does a ha rock form from loose sediment? Mix some th 'Polyfilla' paste with your sand and leave

...xture to harden. What you have made is rather ...e a sedimentary rock called a **sandstone**. ...dimentary rocks are therefore formed from ...ostances such as sand, mud and gravel by ...ocesses taking place after deposition which ...use hardening of these materials to form rocks.

...ming sedimentary rocks

As with igneous rocks, we can use grain size and ...neral content to name sedimentary rocks.

...ain size

...Examine gravel, sand and mud in as much detail ...possible. Are these materials similar to each ...er in any respect? How many differences can ...u see? The most obvious difference is that their ...rticles are of different sizes. Since many ...dimentary rocks are made up of rock and mineral ...gments like those of gravel, sand and mud, this ...e difference can be used to describe ...dimentary rocks. Rock and mineral fragments ...classified by size according to the following ...heme:

...me of particle	Diameter of particle
boulder	greater than 256 mm
cobble	64 – 256 mm
pebble	4 – 64 mm
gravel	2 – 4 mm
sand	1/16 – 2 mm
silt	1/256 – 1/16 mm
clay or mud	less than 1/256 mm

...Where possible, examine and classify particles ...various sizes. Note that clay-sized particles can ...ly be seen with a very good microscope. ...Sedimentary rocks which consist mostly of ...rticles larger than 2 mm in diameter are called ...nglomerates if the particles have rounded ...apes, and **breccias** if the particles are sharp and ...inted like road chips. Rocks with grains (usually ...artz) smaller than 2 mm but larger than 1/16 mm ...diameter are called **sandstones**. **Grit** is a ...ndstone made up of angular grains. **Siltstones** ...nsist mostly of particles of silt size (1/256 – ...16 mm in diameter) and **mudstones** are mostly

made up of clay-sized particles (less than 1/256 mm in diameter). **Clay** is a soft mudstone which behaves like plasticine when wet and **shale** is a flaky mudstone.

Mineral content

Some sedimentary rocks are described in terms of the minerals present. For example, **limestones** consist mostly of carbonate minerals. The carbonate present is normally calcite, so limestone can be easily recognized because it fizzes strongly when added to cold, dilute hydrochloric acid. (Note that limestones which contain a high proportion of dolomite will show a weaker reaction with the acid.) If a sandstone contains more than 25% feldspar it is called an **arkose**. **Marl** is a mudstone which contains quite a lot of calcite.

You will remember from the previous section that you mixed some sand with 'Polyfilla' to make an imitation sandstone. What did the 'Polyfilla' do to the sand grains? In a similar way, sedimentary rocks can be formed from loose materials by sticking the particles together. Material which holds the particles of sedimentary rocks together is called **cement**. Cement can consist of various materials but it is often iron oxide, calcite or quartz. Sometimes the cement is used in naming the rock; for example, a sandstone with a quartz cement is called a **sedimentary quartzite** while a sandstone with a calcite cement may be described as a **calcareous sandstone** ('calcareous' means 'calcite rich'). The colour of a sandstone is largely determined by the nature of the cement. Quartzites and calcareous sandstones are usually pale-coloured while sandstones with iron oxide cement are brown or red. Cement is material which has come into the sediment after it has been laid down. Sometimes, larger particles such as pebbles or sand grains may be deposited along with the mud, and the hardened mud holds the larger particles together. In a case like this, the muddy material is called the **matrix**. A **greywacke** is a black or grey sandstone made up of angular rock fragments set in a muddy matrix.

Figure 2.13 shows the main sedimentary rocks along with some related types.

Mix some mud with some aquarium gravel. Put the mixture at the top of a slightly tilted board then slowly pour water onto it. What happens? Which substance, mud or gravel, is moved more easily? Can you separate the mud from the gravel? During transport, rock and mineral fragments are often separated into their different sizes. Small particles of sand and mud are often moved away, leaving the larger pebbles and boulders behind.

Pour equal amounts of dry, powdered mud and aquarium gravel into water in separate measuring cylinders. Pour them both in at the same time. What happens? Which substance settles more quickly? In the same way, during sediment formation the large fragments may sink and be deposited while the small fragments are still undergoing transport. In general, we can say that pebbles are only moved and deposited by strong currents. Mud can easily be moved even by weak currents, and it will only settle out where currents are very weak. Remembering this, can you suggest places where conglomerates and mudstones will be formed?

Pour some dry sand into water in a measuring cylinder. Now add some gravel. Then put in more sand followed by more gravel, and describe what happens. In this experiment you have seen how sediments can be laid down. They are deposited in layers called **beds** or **strata** (singular **stratum**). The layers are usually laid down parallel to each other like the slices of bread in a loaf; layering of this type is sometimes called **regular bedding**. Where water currents or wind have been active during deposition the sediment, usually sand, may be laid down on sloping surfaces (figure 2.14). Bedding of this type is called **cross-** or **current bedding**. Sometimes beds have large particles near the bottom and progressively smaller ones towards the top. Bedding like this is called **graded bedding**. Can you suggest how grading develops? Add some dry, powdered soil to water in a measuring cylinder. Allow the soil to settle then repeat the process three or four times. Make drawings of what you see. Have you managed to produce layers which show grading? Graded bedding results from the settling in water of

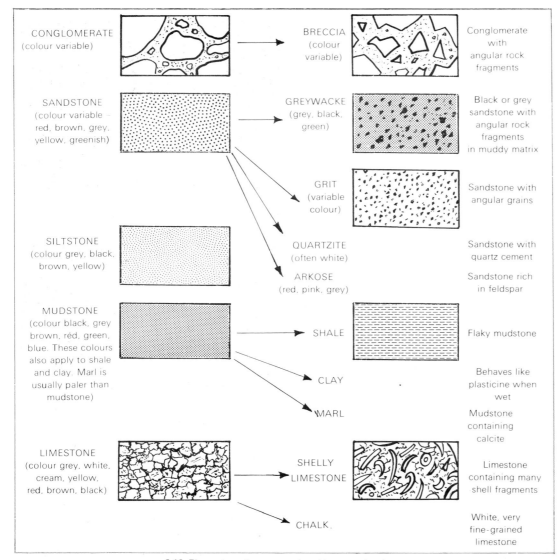

2.13 The main sedimentary rocks with some related types.

Regular bedding – the beds lie in parallel layers.

Cross bedding – the sediment has been laid down o[n]
sloping surfaces.

mixtures of large and small fragments. The various types of bedding are shown in figure 2.15.

As well as the structures seen inside beds, the surfaces of beds often show the marks of processes which have taken place during deposition. The commonest surface structures are **ripple marks**. These are produced by the movement of wind or water over loose sand.

So far we have said that sedimentary rocks result from the deposition of rock and mineral fragments. However, sedimentary rocks can form by other methods.

Some sediments result from the activities of plants and animals. In marshy conditions dead plants do not rot away completely and their remains form peat. If the peat is buried by

sediments it becomes compressed and eventua[lly] **coal** is formed. Some marine animals, particula[rly] corals, have skeletons or shells made from calci[um] carbonate taken from the sea water. When th[e] animals die their remains may accumulate to fo[rm] various kinds of limestone. **Shelly limesto[ne]** contains large numbers of shell fragments wh[ile] **coral limestone** is made up of coral fragmen[ts.] **Chalk** is a white, fine-grained limestone larg[ely] made up of the skeletons of microscopic pla[nts] (these are called coccoliths).

Sediments can also result from chemi[cal] processes. Leave some strong salt solution i[n a] shallow dish. What is left when the water h[as] evaporated? In the same way, when sea wa[ter] evaporates the salts in it can be deposited as ro[ck]

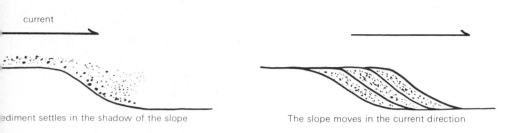

current

ediment settles in the shadow of the slope

The slope moves in the current direction

2.14 The development of cross bedding.

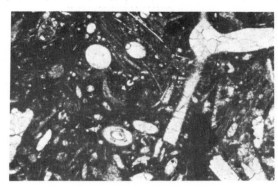

Shelly limestone seen under a microscope. The regularly shaped fragments are the preserved remains of animal shells.

ed **evaporites**. As the water evaporates, the s in it separate out. The least soluble salts such calcite and dolomite are the first to be osited, followed by gypsum and then by halite, ch is the most soluble salt. Present-day orites form in hot, dry regions such as on the es of the Persian Gulf and the Red Sea. In some s, for example near the Bahamas, calcite arates from the sea water because the shallow er is warmed by the Sun and is partly orated. Wave action causes the calcite to form round grains called **ooliths**. A limestone le up of ooliths is called an **oolitic limestone**.

Changes in sediments after deposition

The two main processes which change loose sediment into hard sedimentary rock are **cementation** and **compaction**. Cementation is the process by which cementing minerals (already mentioned on page 23) are introduced into the sediment. Compaction results from the squeezing of the sediment under the weight of the layers above. During compaction water is partly removed from the sediment and the rock and mineral fragments are pushed closer together. The effects

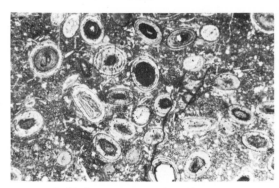

Oolitic limestone seen under a microscope.

of compaction can be seen very clearly in mudstones; deep burial can reduce them to about half of their original thickness. The flakiness of shales is partly produced during compaction by pressure which causes flat mineral grains to be pushed into parallel alignment with each other.

Sedimentary rocks sometimes contain lumps of material which are formed by the coming together of mineral matter which was originally spread throughout the rock. Such lumps are called **concretions**. Rounded concretions are called **nodules**, well-known examples of which are the **flints** which often occur in chalk. Flint consists of microscopic quartz crystals. It is usually brown or black and, like glass, it breaks with a conchoidal fracture into pieces with sharp edges. Because of this property it was much used by Stone Age Man for making cutting tools. **Chert** is a substance similar to flint which occurs as concretions in limestones. Chert tends to break along flat surfaces.

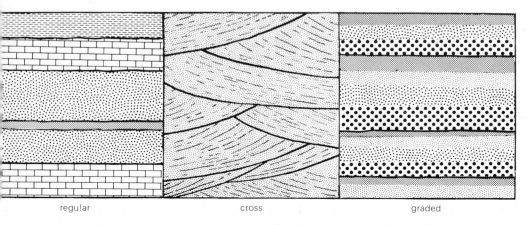

regular

cross

graded

2.15 Types of bedding.

Metamorphic rocks

Make two flat shapes from modelling clay. Leave them to dry and then have one fired in an oven. After firing compare the two pieces of clay. How has firing changed the clay? What you have seen is a change similar to that which produces metamorphic rocks. When rocks are heated or squeezed inside the Earth they recrystallize while remaining solid and metamorphic rocks result. Like most igneous rocks, metamorphic rocks are crystalline.

Naming metamorphic rocks

Most metamorphic rocks have been formed under the action of heat and pressure acting together. Because of the squeezing the minerals in the rocks are lined up in the same direction; that is, these rocks are foliated. The three main foliated rocks are **slate**, **schist** and **gneiss**. Slate is a very fine-grained rock which splits easily into thin sheets along planes called cleavage planes. (Note that this cleavage is not the same as mineral cleavage.) Most slates are dark grey in colour. For what purpose is slate commonly used? Schist is a medium- or coarse-grained rock in which mica flakes can easily be seen lying in the foliation. Quartz and feldspar are also usually present, perhaps with hornblende and garnet. Gneiss is usually coarse-grained with the foliation taking the form of obvious banding. The minerals present are commonly quartz, feldspar, mica and hornblende.

Some metamorphic rocks are produced by the action of heat alone. Since these rocks have not been squeezed during formation they are not foliated. An example of a metamorphic rock formed in this way is **hornfels**. Hornfelses are fine- or medium-grained rocks which sometimes look like igneous rocks because their minerals are not lined up. The main minerals present are usually quartz and feldspar; other minerals may include mica, hornblende, pyroxene or garnet. Someti[mes] larger crystals have grown among the smaller c[rystals] and this gives the hornfels a spotted appeara[nce].

Metamorphic rocks named from the mine[rals] present are **marble** which consists of calcite [and] results from the recrystallization of limestone, [and] **metamorphic quartzite** which consists [of] quartz and results from the heating of [pure] sandstones.

Table 2.4 gives details of the main metamor[phic] rocks.

Gneiss showing well-developed foliation.

	ROCK NAME	COLOUR	GRAIN SIZE	MAIN MINERALS	ORIGINA[L] ROCK
FOLIATED ROCKS	slate	black, dark grey, brown, greenish, bluish	very fine	mica quartz feldspar	mudston[e] tuff
	schist	usually pale and shiny	medium-coarse	mica quartz feldspar garnet	mudston[e] greywac[ke] tuff
	gneiss	usually pale with bands of different colours	medium-coarse	quartz feldspar mica hornblende	difficul[t] to say — could b[e] mudston[e] greywac[ke] granite
FOLIATED OR UNFOLIATED ROCKS	marble	white, grey, black, red, green, yellow	medium	calcite	limeston[e]
	metamorphic quartzite	white grey	medium	quartz	sandston[e]
UNFOLIATED ROCK	hornfels	grey, black, bluish, greenish	fine-medium	quartz feldspar pyroxene	mudston[e] or other fi[ne] grained ro[ck]

Table 2.4 Metamorphic rocks.

formation of metamorphic rocks

ou will recall that metamorphic rocks are
ned by the recrystallization of already existing
ks. This process of rock change is called
tamorphism. Let us look at the ways in which
amorphism can take place.

ocks baked by the heat given off by igneous
usions are said to have been metamorphosed
thermal or contact metamorphism. The
unt of heat given off by an intrusion depends
s size; small intrusions may change only a few
imetres of the surrounding rock while large
usions such as batholiths may be surrounded
is much as 2 km of metamorphic rocks. The
e of metamorphic rocks around an igneous
usion is called a **metamorphic aureole**
ire 2.16). On the outer edge of an aureole the
cts of metamorphism are slight with
ystallization only weakly developed; close to
intrusion the rocks are completely changed.
rmal metamorphism leads to the formation of
oliated rocks such as hornfels.

hen mountains are being built the rocks deep
de them are metamorphosed by the combined
cts of heat and pressure so that foliated rocks
as schists and gneisses are formed.
amorphism of this type is called **regional**
amorphism because it affects rocks over
large areas. For example, the Scottish

Highlands are mostly made up of regionally
metamorphosed rocks.

When rocks are metamorphosed they may go
through a number of changes. When a sediment is
metamorphosed it changes from being fragmental
to being crystalline; for example, the quartz grains
of a sandstone may recrystallize to form a
metamorphic quartzite.

During metamorphism new rocks are formed
which usually have minerals differing from those
of the original rock. The new mineral groupings
which are produced depend very much on the
temperature and pressure conditions during
metamorphism. For example, if a gabbro (feldspar
and augite) is recrystallized at fairly high
temperature and pressure, it gives rise to a rock
made up of feldspar and hornblende; at very high
temperature and pressure it gives a rock made up
of garnet and pyroxene; and at high temperature
and low pressure it gives a feldspar-pyroxene rock.

In the course of metamorphism new minerals
may grow over and erase many features of the
original rock. For instance, the bedding of
sediments may be wholly or partly destroyed. In
sediments, too, the remains of plants and animals
(these are called **fossils**) are almost always
removed.

The squeezing of rocks which is part of regional
metamorphism very often leads to the formation of
foliated rocks. The type of foliation which
develops depends largely on temperature. Slates

Oolitic limestone deformed during low-temperature
metamorphism. Compare this rock with the undeformed
oolitic limestone shown on page 25.

form at low temperature from fine-grained rocks
such as mudstones. The foliation of slates is called
slaty cleavage. At higher temperature schists are
formed with foliation called **schistosity**. At still
higher temperature gneisses are produced; their
foliation is called **gneissose banding**.
Sometimes during the movements which
accompany regional metamorphism, narrow
zones of very intense squeezing are developed.
The rocks produced in these zones are called
mylonites. Mylonites are fine-grained rocks
which often show fine banding produced by the
streaking out of earlier foliation or bedding.

The rock cycle

So far we have seen how sedimentary and
metamorphic rocks are produced from other rocks
by break-up or recrystallization. But during
regional metamorphism rocks may be heated so
much that they melt to form magma, which may
then rise and solidify to form igneous rocks. So we
can see that over very long periods of time, the
materials of the Earth undergo repeated or cyclic
changes through the stages of igneous,
sedimentary and metamorphic rocks. The
sequence of changes showing how all the rock
types are related to each other is called the **rock
cycle**. Some of the processes involved in this
cycle are shown in figure 2.17.

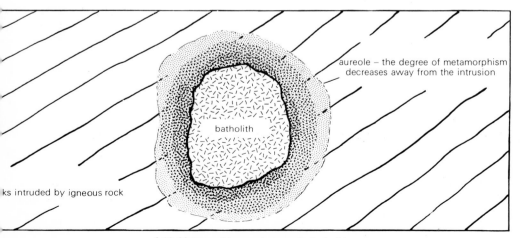

aureole – the degree of metamorphism
decreases away from the intrusion

batholith

ks intruded by igneous rock

2.16 Metamorphic aureole around a batholith.

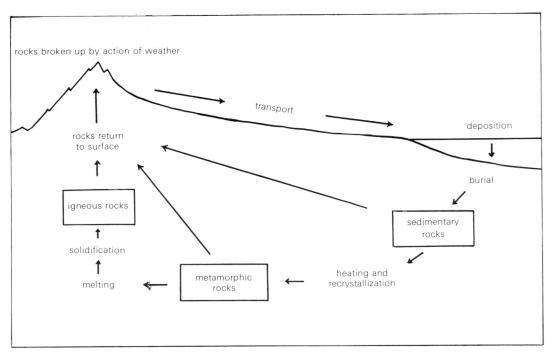

rocks broken up by action of weather

transport

deposition

rocks return to surface

burial

igneous rocks

solidification

melting

metamorphic rocks

heating and recrystallization

sedimentary rocks

2.17 The rock cycle.

Secondly, you can study the rocks in countryside or **field**. In the field you can usu see if a rock occurs, for example, as beds, foli layers or intrusions and this can tell you how rock formed and perhaps give you an indicatio the name of the rock. In small specimens ro formed in different ways can often look similar. For example, a piece of weakly foli gneiss can often look like an igneous rock, a specimen of black mudstone which shows layering might look like basalt. In the field v evidence would you look for to help you distinguish between such similar-looking roc

You can use the key on page 30 to to help yc identify rock specimens. As with the key for mir identification, you should realize that this key uses a few properties of a few rocks. As a furthe to identification the main features of igne sedimentary and metamorphic rocks are give table 2.5.

Finely banded and folded mylonite shot through by veins of coarser material. The mylonite has been formed by the intense squeezing of gneiss.

Rock identification

Now that we have looked at igneous, sedimentary and metamorphic rocks you will realize that there are two main approaches to rock identification.

Firstly, you can look at rocks in small specimens. In a specimen you can see the rock **texture** which is a description of the relationships between the grains. Texture includes such things as whether the rock is made up of interlocking crystals or separate grains, along with the sizes, shapes and arrangement of the grains. In a specimen, too, you may be able to determine the types and amounts of the minerals present. In general, coarse-grained rocks can be identified much more easily than fine-grained rocks; for example, a gabbro can easily be seen to be made up of about equal parts of feldspar and augite whereas in a basalt, which has the same minerals as a gabbro, you may not be able to see any crystals at all.

	IGNEOUS	SEDIMENTARY	METAMORPHIC
GRAIN RELATIONS	crystalline	fragmental	crystalline
GRAIN DIRECTION	grains not usually lined up		grains usually lined up
MAIN MINERALS	quartz feldspar augite hornblende olivine	quartz feldspar calcite + rock fragments	quartz feldspar mica hornblende garnet
FORMATION	crystallized from magma	deposition of rock and mineral particles	recrystallization of other rocks
FOSSILS (PLANT AND ANIMAL REMAINS)	absent	may be present	absent
APPEARANCE WHEN BROKEN	shiny	usually dull	shiny
EASE OF BREAKING	Hard — not easily split. May be crumbly when rotted by weather	May be soft and crumbly but some sedimentary rocks are difficult to break	Hard — but may split in layers. As with igneous rocks may be crumbly when rotted by weather

Table 2.5 Igneous, sedimentary and metamorphic rocks.

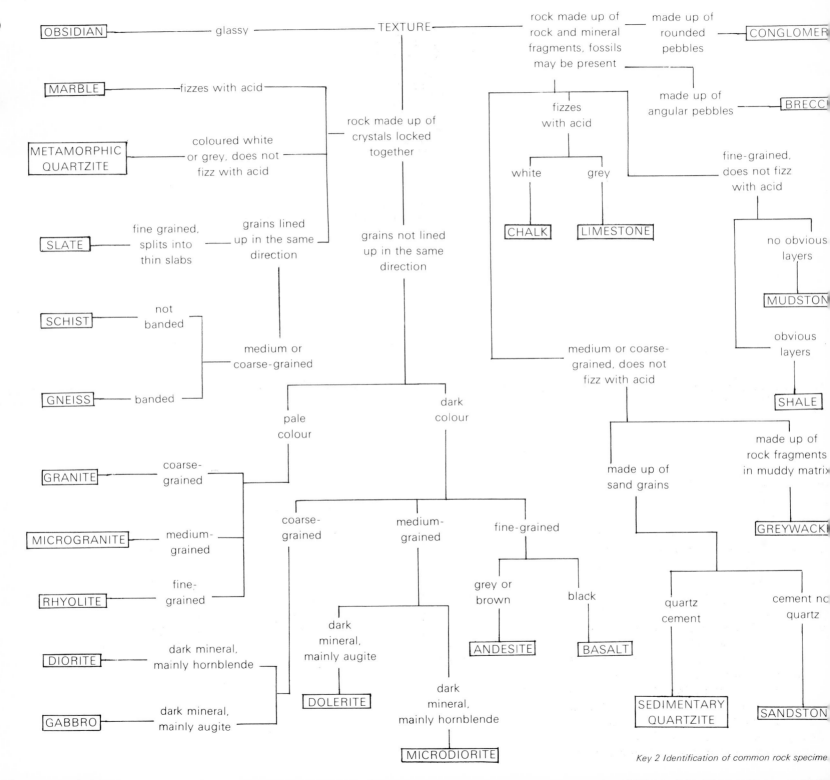

OBSIDIAN — glassy — TEXTURE

MARBLE — fizzes with acid

METAMORPHIC QUARTZITE — coloured white or grey, does not fizz with acid

rock made up of crystals locked together

SLATE — fine grained, splits into thin slabs — grains lined up in the same direction

SCHIST — not banded

GNEISS — banded

medium or coarse-grained

grains not lined up in the same direction

pale colour

dark colour

GRANITE — coarse-grained

MICROGRANITE — medium-grained

RHYOLITE — fine-grained

coarse-grained

medium-grained

fine-grained

DIORITE — dark mineral, mainly hornblende

GABBRO — dark mineral, mainly augite

dark mineral, mainly augite

DOLERITE

dark mineral, mainly hornblende

MICRODIORITE

grey or brown

black

ANDESITE

BASALT

rock made up of rock and mineral fragments, fossils may be present

made up of rounded pebbles — CONGLOMER

made up of angular pebbles — BRECC

fizzes with acid

white — CHALK

grey — LIMESTONE

fine-grained, does not fizz with acid

no obvious layers

MUDSTON

obvious layers

SHALE

medium or coarse-grained, does not fizz with acid

made up of sand grains

made up of rock fragments in muddy matrix — GREYWACK

quartz cement

cement no quartz

SEDIMENTARY QUARTZITE

SANDSTON

Key 2 Identification of common rock specime

UNIT 3

Shaping the Earth's Surface

Weathering

If you look carefully at old buildings, grave-stones or walls you will see that the rocks making them up seem to be rotting away or breaking up. This very slow process is called **weathering**.

What happens to iron when it rusts? Set up three test-tubes as shown in figure 3.1. Leave them aside for a few days. Do the nails all rust to the same extent? Can you account for the difference which you see? In a similar way, some minerals can be altered during weathering by chemical changes into other minerals. Weathering of this type is called **chemical weathering**. Rust is iron oxide and you saw from the above experiment that water must be present before iron will combine with oxygen from the air. Similarly, chemical weathering always requires the presence of water,

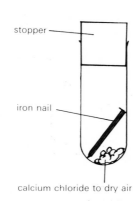
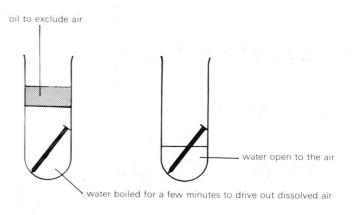

stopper

oil to exclude air

iron nail

water open to the air

calcium chloride to dry air

water boiled for a few minutes to drive out dissolved air

3.1   Studying the rusting of iron.

either as the medium in which weathering reactions take place or as one of the substances actually taking part in the weathering reactions. The chemical weathering of iron-containing minerals results in the formation of a brown, red or yellow surface crust on the weathered rock.

Place pieces of limestone in water and in dilute hydrochloric acid. You will see that the limestone does not change in the water but it reacts with the acid. When rain water falls, carbon dioxide from the air dissolves in it to form a weak acid called carbonic acid. This acid has two effects—it dissolves limestone very slowly, and also speeds up the chemical weathering of feldspars by allowing them to combine with water. When this happens the feldspar is converted to a type of mineral called a **clay mineral**. Clay minerals are water-containing silicates which occur as tiny, platy crystals only visible under very high magnification. **Kaolinite** is a common clay mineral; it is the main constituent of **china clay**.

Chemical weathering does not affect all minerals to the same extent. Quartz is virtually unaffected, but minerals such as olivine, pyroxene, amphibole and feldspar are rapidly altered. Can you suggest why quartz should be much more common in sedimentary rocks than any of these other minerals?

Climate plays an important part in determining the rate at which chemical weathering takes place. The fact that water is necessary means that chemical weathering does not take place to any great extent in arid climates. On the other hand, the reactions of chemical weathering are speeded up by high temperatures. Chemical weathering therefore takes place at maximum speed in hot, wet climates.

When a rock is broken into small pieces without being changed chemically the weathering is described as **mechanical**. Why do water pipes burst in frosty weather? When water freezes its volume increases. If water freezes in cracks in rocks it pushes out with enormous force and breaks the rock in the same way that it bursts a water pipe. This breaking process is called **frost wedging**. You can study the effects of frost by repeatedly freezing and thawing a variety of rocks which you have soaked in water. Frost wedging is most effective in wet climates where the temperature daily rises and falls around freezing point. In such areas water soaks into the rocks by day and freezes at night, producing huge quantities of frost-shattered rock. In hot desert areas rocks are heated strongly by the Sun during the day and cooled to very low temperatures at night. This causes repeated expansion and contraction which can break the rocks apart.

Landscapes

Rock or mineral particles produced by weathering may be transported by gravity, water, wind or ice. The moving water, wind or ice along with the transported materials wear away or **erode** the land. Erosion is quite like the action of sandpaper on wood. Overall, then, there are three processes—weathering, transport and erosion—which act to make land surfaces lower. These three processes together are called **denudation**. Eventually, the transported rock and mineral fragments are deposited in places such as lakes and deltas. So, in places, the land is being built up.

The processes of denudation and deposition are continuously acting to change and reshape the surface of the Earth. The land features produced, which include such things as hills, valleys and deltas, are called **landforms**. Landforms can result from either erosion or deposition. **Landscapes** are made up of many landforms; for example, a coastal landscape could be made up of landforms such as cliffs, beaches and sand bars. Landscapes change very slowly through time and the way in which they develop depends on such things as the type of weathering, the type of erosion or deposition taking place and the type of rock on which the landscape is formed.

We will now look at gravity, water, ice and wind and see how they affect or change landscapes.

Weathered dolerite at North Queensferry, Fife. Weathering has taken place most rapidly along cracks in the rock leaving rounded blocks in between – this is sometimes called spheroidal weathering.

Gravity

The downward movement of weathered rock material under the action of gravity is called **mass wasting**. **Creep** is a form of mass wasting in which downhill movement is very slow. Signs of creep include cracked roads and pavements, tilted walls and telegraph poles, and bent trees (figure 3.2). Can you find out why the trees are bent?

If the soil is thoroughly soaked with water it behaves like dough and it may move downhill at a rate of a few metres per day. This movement is called **solifluction** ('soil flow'). Solifluction is very common in sub-polar regions where the soil in summer is saturated with water from melted ice. The water is retained by the soil because it cannot drain away through the permanently frozen layers beneath. Occasionally, after very heavy rain soil may become so wet that it behaves like thick paint and moves rapidly downhill as a **mudflow**.

Material can also move downhill by **sliding**. **Slumping** is a type of sliding movement which occurs when weak material on a hillside collapses under its own weight and slides down on curved slip planes. **Landslides** are rapid movements on planes of weakness such as water-lubricated bedding planes. They can block roads and valleys and cause considerable damage. For example, in northern Italy in 1963 a huge landslide filled the Vaiont Reservoir for 2 km above the dam. The water was pushed out over the dam and caused a flood which killed 3000 people in the valley below the reservoir.

In mountainous areas, rock fragments produced by frost wedging fall from cliffs and steep slopes and accumulate as landforms called **screes**. The slope angle is usually about 30°. The material in a scree is constantly moving downwards because as material is being added at the top, it is being removed from the base. In this way, the scree can retain its characteristic shape for long periods.

Water

Water affects the land in two ways. Firstly, as it flows over the land it erodes rocks and carries material downstream, perhaps to deposit it in lakes or in the sea; and, secondly, ocean waves and

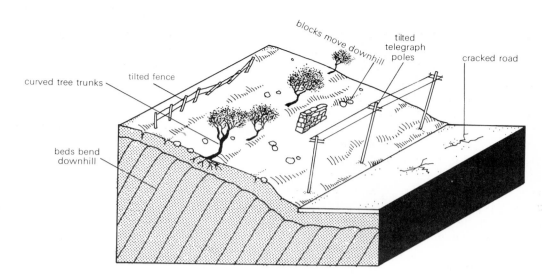

3.2 *Some of the effects of creep.*

Screes at Wastwater in the Lake District.

currents erode and deposit material around the coast.

The work of rivers

Rivers act on the land through the processes of transport, erosion and deposition. Trickle some water onto sand in a tilted tray until a small stream of water runs across the sand. If you look closely you will be able to see sand grains being moved along by the water. How do the sand grains move? Do they roll or bounce along or are they carried by the water without touching the bottom? Now put some mud in your model stream. Can you see how the mud particles are carried along? In rivers, boulders, pebbles and sand grains move along the river bed by sliding, rolling or bouncing. The very small mineral particles are carried along without touching the river bed; the swirling motion of the water prevents them from sinking (figure 3.3). How does the appearance of a river in flood compare with that of a normal river? Flood water looks muddy because it is carrying more material than usual. A river in flood can also move larger fragments along its bed.

Erosion causes the banks and bed of a river to wear away. Some of this wearing away is brought about by the action of the moving water. By itself, water does not have much erosive effect on hard rocks, but it can erode loose material such as gravel. Sometimes a river will undercut its banks and the unsupported bank material then falls into the river to be transported away. Water can also erode soluble rocks by dissolving them. Most river erosion takes place by the grinding action of the transported fragments on the bed and banks. As the fragments are moved along they bump into the rocks the river is flowing over and slowly wear into them. In hard rocks, round **potholes** are sometimes carved by the rubbing action of small boulders being swirled around by the water. In the river bed the transported fragments are continuously bumping into each other. How will this affect the sizes and shapes of boulders, pebbles and sand grains? Examine some river gravel. How would you describe the shapes of the pebbles? In general, transport causes rock and mineral fragments to become smaller and more rounded.

Since erosion is mostly downwards, you would expect a river valley to be shaped like the cut made by a saw in a block of wood. However, river valleys are V-shaped because as the river erodes downwards, mass wasting acts to carry material into the river and it is then transported by the water.

When a river runs onto flat land it slows down, and as a result many of the transported fragments are deposited as material called **alluvium**. The alluvium often fills the bottom of the valley and the river may run over its own sediment. If a river suddenly runs onto flat land the rapid drop in speed may cause the sediment to be deposited in a heap called an **alluvial fan**.

River courses

When rain falls on land the water which does not drain into the soil collects in tiny trickles. If the soil is not protected by a layer of vegetation the trickling water can cut out small channels called **rills**. As the water flows downhill the trickles come together to form tiny streams which can erode the soil more deeply to form deep, narrow channels called **gullies**. With the continued coming together of small streams a small river results. Rivers which rise in mountain areas run down steep slopes, and in doing so actively erode steep-sided valleys. Mountain rivers tend to move downhill in zig-zag paths. Between the twists and turns of the river are sharp-edged landforms called **spurs**.

In their upper courses rivers often flow over waterfalls and rapids, and lakes are formed when rivers flow into hollows. Can you suggest why waterfalls exist? Through time, the hard rocks causing the waterfalls are cut away. The lakes may be filled in with sediment or the rocks damming back the lakes may be eroded away. In this way the irregularities in the course of a river are slowly but surely smoothed out.

When a river leaves the mountains and begins on its middle course it flows down shallow slopes through wide valleys among rounded hills. In its lower course a river may flow over a flat area called a **flood plain** which has been built up by the deposition of sediment carried from upstream. The slope is very gentle and, as the river flows, it wanders from side to side in large loops called **meanders**. Since the river now runs in sand and gravel its course often changes, and sometimes it cuts off its own meanders to leave loop-shaped lakes called **ox-bow lakes**. In times of flood the river is liable to overrun its banks. When it does this the heaviest particles are deposited right beside the river, and these deposits can build up to form embankments called **levees**. This building-up process can result in the river flowing at a higher level than its flood plain.

water surface

mud particles

current

sand grain

boulder

pebble

river bed

3.3   Transport of material by a river.

Meanders and ox-bow lakes in the River Jordan.

Underground water

We have already said that some of the rain which falls on the land drains into the soil and underlying rocks. This water is called **ground water**. Pour some water into a beaker full of marbles or glass beads. What do you find? The spaces between the marbles at the top are occupied by air but the spaces at the bottom are water-filled. The water in soil and rocks behaves in the same way. Near the surface, the water does not fill up the spaces among the soil particles but deeper down every space is filled. The level at which the spaces are filled is called the **water table**. The water table tends to follow the shapes of landforms; it curves up under the hills and down under valleys. Can you work out what will happen when the water table meets the ground surface? Make piles of marbles at opposite ends of a tank then pour in some water. If the marble heaps represent hills then the water in the middle could represent a lake, marsh or river. How is the level of the water between the piles of marbles related to the level of the model water table? The water table can move up or down depending on the weather. Can you see why this should be so?

The amount of water which a rock can hold depends on the amount of pore space which exists between the grains. **Porosity** is a measure of this intergranular space. Drop pieces of dry sandstone and basalt into water. What happens? What does this tell you about the porosities of these rocks? How porous are crystalline rocks likely to be? The porosity of a rock depends on the shapes of its grains and how they are packed together. Porosity is reduced if there is a mixture of grain sizes because the small grains can fill up the spaces between the large grains. Ground water can flow slowly from pore space to pore space. A measure of how easily it can flow is given by the **permeability** of the material. Insert small cotton wool plugs into the necks of three filter funnels and add equal volumes of aquarium gravel, sand and powdered clay. Make sure that the gravel, sand and clay are all dry. Now run 100 cm³ of water through each sample and see how quickly the water flows through. Which material is the most

When a river flows into the sea its sediment may be carried away by waves and currents. However, if tides and currents are weak, the sediment may be deposited as a **delta** at the river mouth. Deltas are best developed in enclosed seas such as the Mediterranean and the Gulf of Mexico where well-known deltas such as those of the Nile and Mississippi have been built out into the sea.

It sometimes happens that because of the land rising or the sea falling a river may cut a new course at a lower level than its old one. When this happens parts of the old flood plain are left as **terraces** on the valley sides (figure 3.4). A river which has cut a new course at a level below the old course is said to have been **rejuvenated**. Sometimes, rejuvenation allows a meander to cut itself down into hard rock. The loop of the Wear Gorge in Durham has been formed in this way.

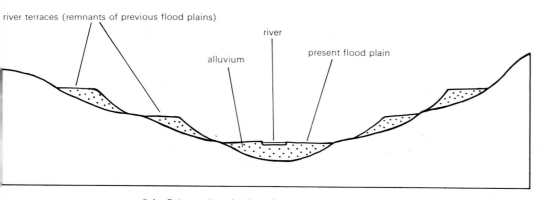

river terraces (remnants of previous flood plains)

river

alluvium

present flood plain

3.4   Rejuvenation of a river allows it to cut down through its former flood plains leaving river terraces on the valley sides.

Limestone pavement above Malham Cove in Yorkshire. The enlarged cracks are grikes and the ridges between them are clints.

Ingleborough in the Pennines; it is about 120 metre deep. Running water which enters a limestone mas attacks the rock along cracks by erosion as well a solution so that the limestone becomes riddled wit underground caverns and passages. If there i impervious rock under the limestone, the wate eventually emerges from a **spring** at the base of th limestone.

When water drips from a cave roof it lose carbon dioxide to the air, and this makes the wate less able to hold the carbonate dissolved in it. As result calcium carbonate is precipitated a **dripstone**, forming **stalactites** hanging fror the roof and **stalagmites** growing up from th floor. Where water rich in dissolved calciur carbonate emerges at the surface, spongy **cal tufa** may form as a crusty deposit around th spring.

Limestone areas which have their landform produced mainly by solution are said to hav **karst landscapes** (figure 3.5).

permeable? Which is the least permeable? In general, the larger the pore spaces the more permeable the material. A permeable rock is one through which water can flow; an impermeable rock is one which will not allow water to pass through it. Remembering the results of the experiment, how do you think the permeabilities of sandstone and mudstone will compare?

With the exception of evaporites, rocks do not dissolve to any great extent in pure water. Can you think of any rocks which will dissolve in acid? You will remember that rain water dissolves carbon dioxide in the air, forming carbonic acid. Limestone is soluble in this weak acid. Solution of the limestone may leave behind insoluble impurities as a thin soil. Where no soil remains the bare rock forms **limestone pavement**. On this surface, cracks enlarged by solution are called **grikes** and the ridges between the cracks are **clints**. Continued solution and collapse of material along the cracks may form an opening which penetrates deeply as a vertical **sink** or **swallow-hole** into which surface water flows. A well-known swallow-hole is Gaping Ghyll near

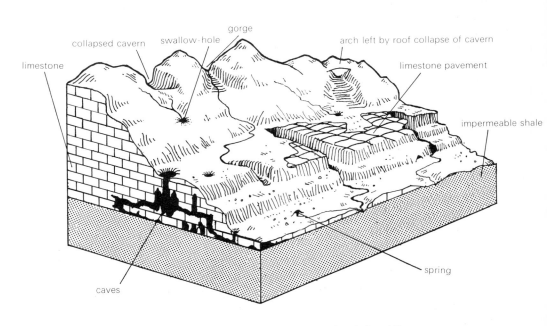

3.5 Some features of a karst landscape produced by solution of limestone.

Springs and wells

Where the water table meets the ground surface water may emerge by slow seepage or it may run from **springs**. Springs are commonly found where a permeable bed lies on top of an impermeable bed which prevents the ground water from moving to a lower level. Springs may also arise where the water table is brought to the surface by the damming effect of igneous rocks, or where rocks have been broken and moved along a **fault** so that permeable and impermeable beds are brought into contact. Water may also run from springs at the bases of limestone masses or gravel deposits, and from cracks in broken igneous rock. Some types of spring site are shown in figure 3.6.

Wells are holes dug or drilled to meet the water table. You can make a model well by putting a glass tube into some marbles in a beaker. Pour water onto the marbles. How does the level of water in the tube compare to the level between the marbles? In the same way, the water in a well is at the same level as the water table. An **artesian well** is a well from which water gushes out on to the surface. Artesian wells are drilled into water-containing strata called **aquifers**. You can make a model artesian well as shown in figure 3.7. Put your finger over the end of the well tube while your neighbour fills the aquifer tube with water. Remove your finger and watch what happens. When does water stop flowing from the model well tube?

The sea

What happens when you move your finger along a piano keyboard? As your finger moves it produces a ripple which moves in the same direction. But how do the piano keys move? Do they move in the same direction as the ripple? In a somewhat similar way, when wind blows over the sea it produces **waves** in the surface water. You can get a good idea of how water particles move in ocean waves if you watch aniline drops in salt water. Aniline is slightly more dense than water. Why must some salt be added to the water? (Note that aniline should only be handled by your teacher.) When the tank has been set up make

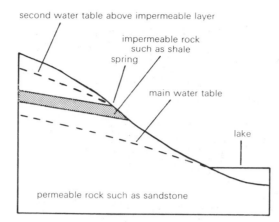
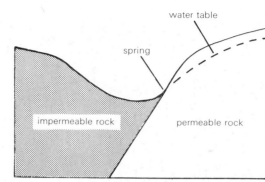
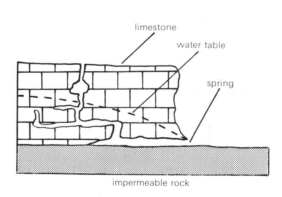
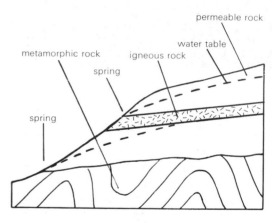
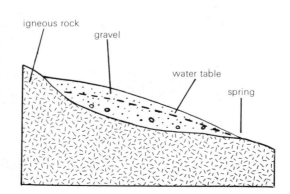
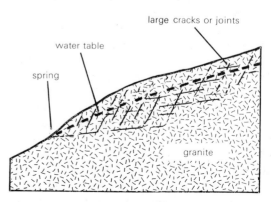

3.6 Spring sites.

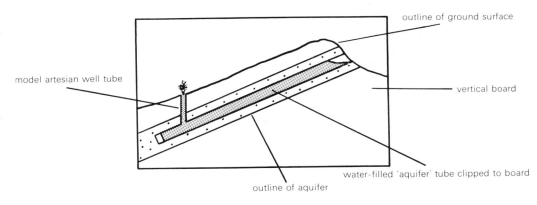

model artesian well tube

outline of ground surface

vertical board

outline of aquifer

water-filled 'aquifer' tube clipped to board

3.7   A model artesian well.

water particle moves A to D
as wave moves 1 to 4

wave moves 1

path of circular motion
decreases rapidly with depth

3.8   The movement of water particles in waves.

waves by moving a piece of wood backwards and forwards. Observe carefully the movements of the aniline drops. How do they move? What happens to the amount of movement as the depth of a drop increases? You should see that the aniline drops (and therefore the water particles) move in circles which become smaller as the depth increases (figure 3.8). So, like a ripple on a piano keyboard, a **wave shape** moves through the water but the water particles, like the piano keys, do not move along with the wave.

When waves come into shallow water the bottoms of the waves catch on the sea floor and the tops of the waves fall over. When this happens the waves are called **breakers**. If you have seen films of people surf-riding you will realize that the water in breakers moves forward. Would it be possible to go surf-riding in the middle of an ocean? If not, why not?

Sea water can also move in **currents**. You can find out how currents are formed on a shoreline by doing simple experiments with a ripple tank, using a weighted block of wood to represent the shoreline. Surface currents can be shown with chalk dust and bottom currents can be shown with the aid of small crystals of potassium permanganate. **Bottom currents** flow along the bottom of the sea bed. **Surface currents** flow on the surface and to some depth below it. Set up the apparatus shown in figure 3.9. Copy the diagram into your notebook and draw in the current

directions shown by the purple trails of potassium permanganate. You should find that a current flows along the side of the wooden block and that some of the current curves round the end of the block. This experiment shows what happens on a real shore when the waves strike it at an angle. The current which runs along the shore is called a **longshore current**.

You can repeat this type of experiment varying the shape of the model shore to include such features as headlands and bays. You can also use pieces of plasticine to show the effects of islands and reefs. One of the interesting things that your experiments should show is that surface and

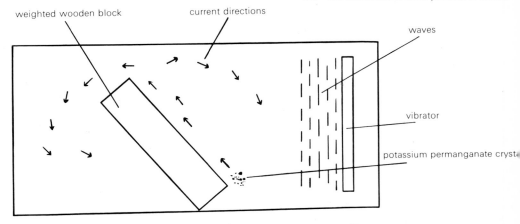

weighted wooden block

current directions

waves

vibrator

potassium permanganate crystal

3.9   Studying currents using a ripple tank. The current directions are shown by purple trails of potassium permanganate solution.

ttom currents often differ in direction and speed. metimes they are opposite in direction, or there y be a fast surface current when there is no ttom current.

Tides are twice-daily changes in sea level. See if u can find out how tides are formed. When the e is coming in or going out **tidal currents** flow wards or away from the land. Where the tidal rents are forced into narrow channels they may very strong. For example, the Bristol Channel nels incoming tidal water which sometimes hes up the River Severn as a wall of surf called ore.

insport, erosion and deposition the sea

'ut some sand and gravel into the top of a ing tank. Run water into the tank until it ches the bottom of your model beach and make es by moving a piece of wood. Observe efully the movement of the sand and gravel n try to answer these questions. In what ctions do the particles move? Are the different ticle sizes separated or do they remain mixed? at happens as you increase the size of the es? What particle sizes in the sea do you think be moved by small breakers? What sizes of icles will be moved in severe storms? How will continuous movement of beach particles affect r sizes and shapes?

the above experiment you saw what pened when the waves came straight in ards the beach. You should have found that sand and small pebbles were moved up and n the model beach. What would happen if the es came onto the beach at an angle? Use the e apparatus as before but put the sand and el at an angle to the waves. Tilt the aquarium e side so that the water's edge is parallel to the del beach. Look carefully at the effect of the es on the movement of the particles. How the movement differ from the movement duced by waves coming straight onto the e? This time you should find that the particles e up the model beach at an angle in the same ction as the waves, but that they tend to roll ght back down. In this way particles are

transported along a beach, moving in a series of loops (figure 3.10). This process of sediment transport is called **beach drift**. Some seaside resorts have structures called **groynes** built out across their beaches. For what reason do you think groynes have been built? How do they help to slow down beach drift?

Besides the movement of sediment as beach drift, material is carried parallel to the shore by longshore currents. This sediment movement is called **longshore drift** (figure 3.11). Note that beach drift and longshore drift both take place in the same direction.

The sea erodes the land in two ways. Firstly, the continuous beating of the waves on the shore slowly wears away the land. Wave erosion is at its most active during storms when the waves can exert enormous forces on the shore. The effects of wave erosion are best seen where the shoreline is made up of soft material such as gravel or clay. Secondly, breakers can pick up sand, pebbles and boulders and their movement produces a grinding effect on the land.

Deposition in the sea takes place where the motion of the currents and breakers is too weak for transport to occur. For example, deposition commonly takes place in the sheltered bays between eroding headlands. The type of material deposited depends on the strength of currents or breakers. Strong currents may deposit pebbles but

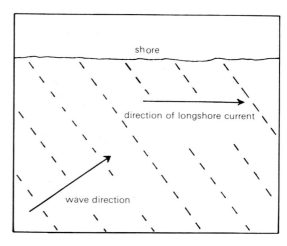

3.11 Longshore drift: sediment movement caused by longshore currents.

continue to transport sand. Mud is only deposited where currents and waves are at their weakest.

Coastal landforms resulting from erosion and deposition

The most obvious landforms of eroding coasts are cliffs and their related features. The process of cliff development is shown in figure 3.12. Here you will see that the waves first of all cut a notch, then a **wave-cut platform** backed by a cliff. On the seaward edge of the wave-cut platform

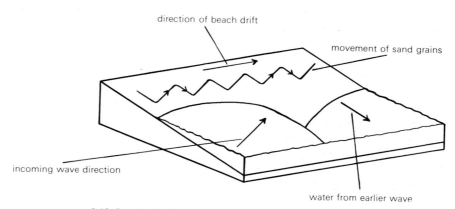

3.10 Beach drift. When a wave strikes the beach at any angle it moves the sand in the direction of the wave motion. When the water runs back off the beach it moves the sand in a downwards direction. In this way the sand grains move in loops along the beach.

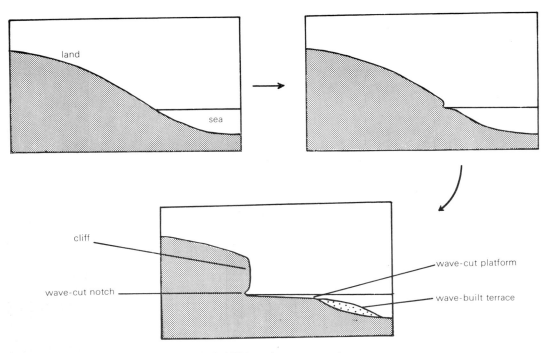

3.12 Cliff formation on a steep shore.

Deep-sea deposits

Most parts of the deep ocean floor are so far from the land that even the finest sediment from the land cannot reach them. Instead, the deposits of the deep sea are formed from organic remains and atmospheric dust. The commonest deep-sea deposit is **calcareous ooze** which is derived mostly from the skeletons of a microscopic animal called *Globigerina*. Another common deposit is **siliceous ooze** which is made up of the skeletons

A natural arch, 'The Green Bridge of Wales' in South Pembrokeshire.

The Old Man of Hoy, Orkney. This stack is about 140 metres high.

sediment may be deposited as a **wave-built terrace**. On an eroding shore, weak zones in the rocks are cut away to form bays and inlets while stronger rocks form jutting headlands. Eventually even the resistant headlands are broken up in the way shown in figure 3.13. First of all, slight weaknesses in the rock are attacked by the waves and caves are formed. If the cave works its way right through the headland it leaves an **arch**. Sometimes a cave opens at the top of a cliff through a hole called a **blow-hole** which emits spray during stormy weather. Continued erosion causes the arch to collapse and an isolated **stack** is left.

Where the coast is flat cliffs do not develop. Instead, the dominant features of the shore are produced by deposition. Sand and pebbles are often laid down by waves and longshore currents in long **bars** running parallel to the shore. The best known bar in Britain is Chesil Beach in Dorset. Between a bar and the inner shore a marsh or lagoon forms; for example, Chesil Beach encloses the Fleet. **Spits** are bars which run outwards from

the land and end in open water. Remembering the result of your experiment on longshore currents using a ripple tank, can you explain why spits often have hook-shaped ends? Spurn Head in Yorkshire is a well-known curved spit. In areas sheltered from wave action, perhaps at the head of a bay or behind a spit, currents may be very weak. As a result of this, fine-grained sediment is deposited and **mud flats** are formed. Some of the features of flat coasts are shown in figure 3.14.

Sinking and rising coasts

Sometimes, as a result of processes which will be described later, the land slowly sinks or rises. When the land sinks its margins are flooded by the sea to give an irregular coast line with islands, bays, headlands and drowned river valleys or **rias**. The coast at Falmouth in Cornwall shows many excellent examples of rias. When the land rises, cliffs and beaches may be raised well above sea level and parts of the sea floor may emerge to form flat coastal plains covered by marine sediment.'

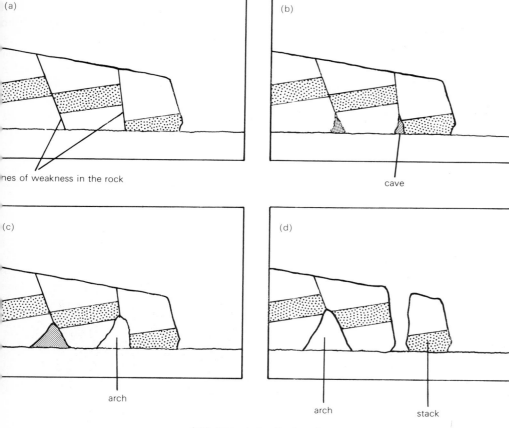

Chesil Beach in Dorset, a well-known shingle bar. The Fleet is on the left and the Isle of Portland is at the top of the photograph.

lines of weakness in the rock

cave

arch

arch

stack

3.13 Stages in headland erosion.

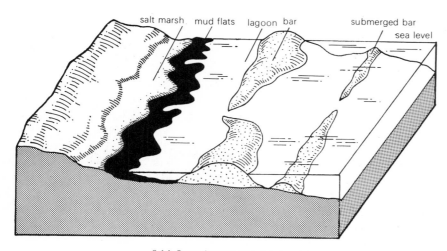

salt marsh   mud flats   lagoon   bar   submerged bar   sea level

3.14 Some features of a flat shore.

of diatoms (microscopic plants) and *Radiolaria* (microscopic animals). Calcareous ooze is mostly found in tropical and temperate regions while siliceous ooze occurs mostly in polar regions. However, calcareous ooze is not found at depths greater than 4000 metres and siliceous ooze does not occur below about 5000 metres because as the skeletons sink they dissolve slowly in the sea water. At depths greater than 5000 metres the deposit formed is **red clay** which results from the accumulation of dust from volcanoes and sand storms. Red clay forms at the rate of about 1 millimetre every thousand years; oozes are deposited about ten times faster than this.

Although you might expect that all deep-sea deposits would be fine oozes or clays, this is not always the case. In places coarse material is found.

of calcium carbonate. As the coral colonies d
new ones can grow on top of them to build up
rock-like mass called a **coral reef**. Coral reefs a
only found in shallow, clean, tropical or su
tropical seas. There are three types of re
fringing reefs are continuous with the sho
barrier reefs are some distance off-shore a
atolls are circular reefs enclosing lagoons (figu
3.15). **Coral limestone** is the rock formed fr
the remains of coral reefs.

A strongly recurved spit – Spurn Head in Yorkshire.

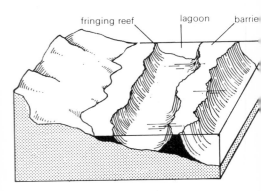

How can material like this reach the deep sea? Mix some fine calcium carbonate in cold water until the mixture looks like milk then pour it into still water in a tilted tank. What happens? What you should have found is that the mixture flows along the bottom of the tank in a current called a **turbidity** or **density current** ('turbid' means 'cloudy'). In the same way, it is thought that turbidity currents, heavily laden with sediment, can flow down the continental slope out onto the deep-sea floor. Some turbidity currents seem to be continuous with rivers; sediment-laden river water seems to be able to flow along the sea bed. The presence of **submarine canyons** on the continental shelves may even indicate that turbidity currents can erode channels. Other turbidity currents may be the result of loose sediment, perhaps dislodged by earthquakes, sliding down the continental slope.

Where ocean trenches exist they act as traps for turbidity current sediment and so prevent material from reaching the floor of the open ocean. When turbidity currents come to rest the sediment settles out on the sea floor. Will the large or small transported particles be deposited first? What kind of bedding will this produce? Rocks deposited by turbidity currents are called **turbidites**. Greywackes, which often show graded bedding, are examples of turbidites.

Coral reefs

Many organisms which live in the sea can extract dissolved substances from the water and use them to build their skeletons or shells. Corals are animals related to jellyfish which live in large groups called colonies. Their skeletons are made

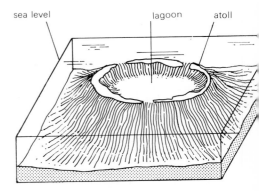

3.15 Coral reefs.

Since most sedimentary rocks are formed in the
, it is useful to look at the kinds of structures
ning in present-day sediments. If we then
nd similar features in ancient rocks, this might
us the kind of conditions under which the
ient rock was formed.

Probably the most common beach structures are
ples in the sand. You can find out how ripples
formed by running fast-flowing, shallow water
er sand in a tilted tank. If you only have a deep
k you can keep the water shallow by running it
through siphons. In this experiment you
uld be able to see ripples forming against the
ss sides of the tank. Can you see how the
ples form? What shape are the ripples? How do
y move? When water flows over sand, ripples
velop (commonly about 1 centimetre high and
centimetres apart) which travel in the same
ection as the current. The ripples move because
d is driven up the shallow slope and then falls
er the steep slope (figure 3.16(a)).

When waves move through water, the water
rticles in contact with the sea floor move
ckwards and forwards rather than in circles. You
y have seen just such a movement in your
periment with aniline drops in water. When this
ppens sand is formed into ripples with sharp
sts and round, shallow troughs (figure
6(b)). These ripples do not move with the
ves but remain in the same position.

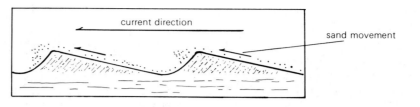

3.16 (a) The formation of ripples in sand. The ripples move
slowly forward in the same direction as the current.

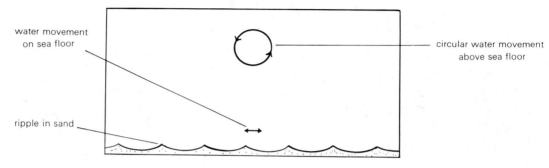

(b) Ripples in sand produced by the water movement of
waves. These ripples do not move with the waves but
remain in the same position.

Cross bedding (described on page 23) is a
common feature of present-day deltas and sand
bars. As these structures grow and move under the
action of strong currents, sand is continuously
tipped off their sloping edges into the deeper
water round about. **Graded bedding** is thought
to result from deposition by turbidity currents, as
previously described.

Animals also leave their marks on sediment. The
sediment is continuously being mixed by the
burrowing of marine worms, shell-fish and sea
urchins. On the surface the tracks of marine snails
and the footprints of birds are common.

Ice

When snow falls in Britain during winter it melts
by summer. At higher latitudes or in high
mountains the summers are not warm enough to
melt all the winter snow, and because of this the
snow accumulates. Fresh snow is made up of soft,
fluffy flakes which enclose a great deal of air.
During summer melting the flakes may partially
melt and then refreeze. In this way, the snowflakes

lose their original shapes and become firm,
rounded grains. This type of snow which has
survived summer melting is called **firn** or **névé**. As
layers accumulate annually the firn is buried and
compacted, air is squeezed out, and the ice grains
freeze together to form solid ice. The ice cannot
build up indefinitely because ice is a very weak
solid which slowly flows or creeps downhill.
These masses of slowly moving ice are called
glaciers. The main types of glaciers are **valley
glaciers** which, as the name suggests, are river-
like ice masses flowing in valleys, and **ice sheets**
such as those of Antarctica and Greenland which
cover very large areas. **Ice caps** are small ice-
sheets of the type found in places such as Iceland
and Spitzbergen.

Transport, erosion and deposition by ice

Because of the enormous force which ice can
exert on the rock over which it flows, huge lumps
of rock can be broken off and carried away. These
pieces of rock become embedded in the ice and
they greatly increase the erosive power of the
glacier as they are scraped along the rock under

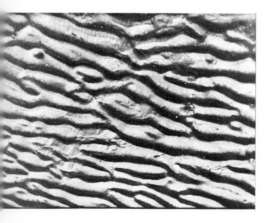

Ripples in beach sand.

44 the ice. Can you explain why boulders carried by ice often have flattened, polished surfaces? Can you also explain why the rock over which the ice has moved is often scratched? Ice also erodes material by a process called **plucking** in which the ice carries away blocks of rock which have been loosened by water freezing in cracks in the rock (figure 3.17).

Material carried by glaciers is picked up largely by erosion. However, in valley glaciers a good deal of material broken off by frost wedging falls into the glacier from the valley sides. The glacier continuously grinds away at its transported material, and as a result it carries rock fragments of all sizes from huge boulders to finely powdered material sometimes called **rock flour**.

At the melting edges of glaciers the ice can no longer transport material so deposition takes place, both from the ice itself and from the melt water which runs from the glacier. This deposited material is called **drift**.

Valley glaciers

Can you remember the type of landscape developed in mountainous areas by the action of rivers? Let us see what happens in such an area if the climate cools and snow and ice begin to collect on the mountain sides. Ice tends to collect in valleys and hollows on the mountains, and as accumulation continues the ice moves down and erodes the valleys. Erosion begins right at the top of the valleys where the ice is accumulating. In these places the ice cuts steep-walled, bowl-shaped depressions which in the Alps are called **cirques**. In Scotland these depressions are called **corries** and in Wales they are called **cwms**. The walls of a cirque are continuously cut back by plucking and frost wedging and the floor of the cirque is deepened by the moving ice. By these processes cirques become larger and adjacent cirques may meet along jagged ridges called **aretes**. Where three or more cirques intersect, a sharp-edged mountain called a **horn** is formed. Because of its enormous bulk, ice in a valley erodes over a very large surface and the valley is changed from a river-cut V-shape to a U-shaped **glacial trough**. These features are illustrated in figure 3.18.

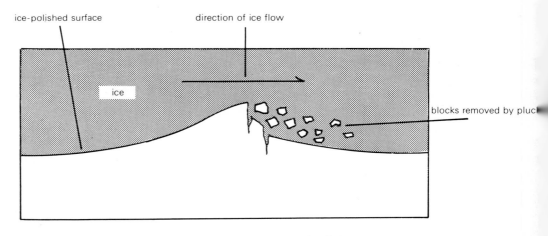

3.17 Glacial erosion by plucking.

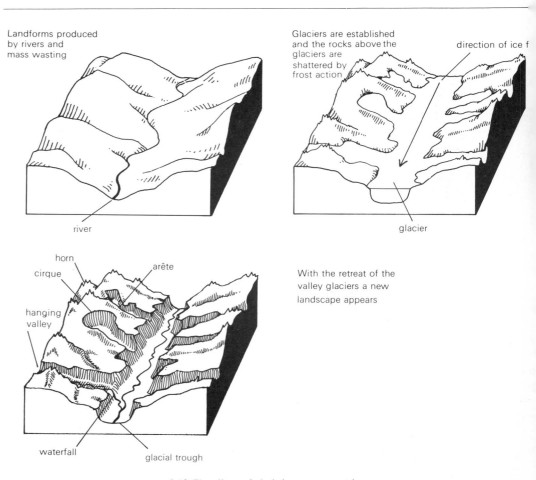

3.18 The effects of glaciation on a mountain area.

The edge of the Greenland ice sheet. Can you see a fiord, corries and arêtes? What is the direction of the ice flow?

reaches the sea a **fiord** or sea loch results. Waterfalls are common along the sides of glacial troughs because rivers have had their valleys cut off by the ice. Valleys like these are called **hanging valleys**. Small, nearly round lakes called **tarns** are often left in cirques.

Ice sheets

Like valley glaciers, moving ice sheets both erode and deposit material, but on a larger scale. The general effect of erosion is to wear down and round off the buried landscape. Where a mass of hard rock such as a sill or volcanic plug projects, the ice may not be able to erode it away completely and a feature called a **crag and tail** may result. The ice digs out a hollow in front of the crag but leaves a tail on the sheltered side (figure 3.19).

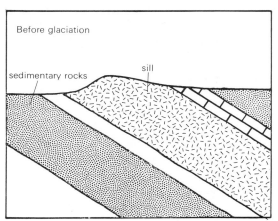

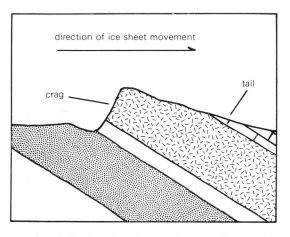

3.19 The formation of a crag and tail landform.

ou can see how valley glaciers transport erial by making a model glacier with water s and sand. Build the sand into a mound and e a valley which branches at the top. Pour the er glass into the valley tops and carefully erve how the sand is moved along. What do see where the two model glaciers join in the n valley? The material transported by glaciers is ed **moraine**. **Subglacial moraine** is carried g at the base of the glacier while **lateral raines** are carried at the sides. Where glaciers together as they did in your model their lateral aines join to form **medial moraines**.

As the glacier moves downhill it comes into a region of higher temperature and begins to melt. Some of the transported material is carried away in the meltwater stream running from the glacier and the rest of the material is deposited as **end moraine**. You should note that the word 'moraine' is used to denote material both transported and deposited by glaciers.

If the climate warms up again and the glaciers disappear, the landscape shows features in addition to those already mentioned. The valley left by the glacier may be occupied by a long, narrow lake called a **ribbon lake**. If the valley

Ice-deposited material is laid down as moraines and **drumlins**. Drumlins are oval mounds of **till** or **boulder clay** which is a deposit made up of large boulders called **erratics** mixed up with rock flour or clay.

Many of the depositional features associated with ice sheets are the result of the action of meltwater. Rivers running under the ice lay down long narrow mounds called **eskers** (figure 3.20). **Kames** are mounds of sand and gravel which seem to have been deposited in large hollows in the ice. Material washed out of the glacier is deposited over a large flat area called an **outwash plain**. Among glacial deposits, round lakes called **kettleholes** may be found. These are formed in hollows left by the melting of huge ice blocks which have been buried in the drift.

Wind

Put some wet sand into a tray and blow air over it with a hair drier. Does the sand move? Repeat the experiment using dry sand. What happens this time? Can you explain why the dry sand moves but the wet sand does not move? It seems that the water has acted like a weak glue to hold the sand grains together. In **desert** areas of the Earth rainfall is very low. There is no permanent covering of plants to protect the surface and the lack of moisture prevents the rock and mineral fragments from being held together. This means that the wind can easily blow away any loose surface material. Most deserts, such as the Sahara and Australian deserts, are found in areas of hot climate but a few occur in cooler climates, such as the Gobi desert of Mongolia.

Transport, erosion and deposition by wind

Blow the dry sand with the hair drier once more and look carefully to see if you can find out how the sand grains move along. How many different types of movement can you see? Wind can move particles in three ways. Firstly, the finest particles can be lifted high in the air to form dust clouds. Secondly, sand grains move by bouncing along the ground. When they do this they do not rise above a height of about 2 metres. Thirdly, small pebbles may roll or slide along.

Glacial erratics of sandstone perched on limestone at Settle in Yorkshire.

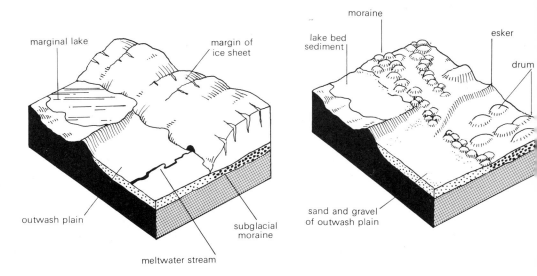

3.20 Deposition under and around an ice sheet.

Drumlins in Strangford Lough, County Down, Ireland.

pieces of frosted glass. Only the hardest minerals can stand up to the battering they receive in desert conditions. Most sand grains are quartz; weak minerals such as mica are not found in desert sands because they are quickly broken up and blown away as dust.

The finest wind-blown material may travel for many miles through the air before being deposited as **loess**. The thickest deposits of loess in the world have been formed in China from dust blown out from the deserts of central Asia. Desert sand does not lie in flat layers. Instead, it is heaped up into features called **dunes**. The most common type of dune is called a **barchan dune**; these dunes are shaped like boomerangs with their arms pointing away from the wind. Barchan dunes move continuously in the direction of the wind at speeds of up to 15 metres a year. How do you think this movement is brought about? The dunes move in a manner which is similar to the movement of ripples under flowing water; sand is continuously moved up the shallow slope from the back of the dune and tipped over the steep front slope (figure 3.21). At the seaside you may have seen dunes next to the beach. Can you explain how these dunes may have formed? How do these dunes differ from the desert dunes? Is there any difference in the type of sand in seaside and desert dunes? You should realize that although deserts are commonly thought of as being covered in sand this is often not the case. Deserts consist mostly of stones and bare rock left behind when the sand and other small fragments have been blown away. In the Sahara the stony desert is known as **reg** and the sandy desert is called **erg**.

Desert landforms

Surprising though it may seem, many of the landforms in deserts are the result of water action. Deserts are not necessarily completely dry and occasional rain storms can produce rivers which run for a short time then dry up. These rivers can erode most effectively because the lack of vegetation allows the water to run quickly downhill over unprotected surfaces. The valleys carved by temporary rivers are flat-bottomed, steep-sided trenches called **wadis**. Where the

Although some erosion takes place by the action the wind itself, it is mostly the result of the sting effect of moving sand grains. Since these ticles do not rise very high erosion is centrated on surfaces near ground level. This ses rock faces to be undercut. Will dercutting result in the development of steep or llow slopes? It is interesting to note that graph poles in arid regions are quickly cut ough at the base if they are not protected in e way.

The effectiveness of sand blasting in deserts is also shown by the presence of stones called **ventifacts**. These stones, which may have shapes like pyramids or Brazil nuts, are produced by the cutting away of the rounded faces of pebbles. Wind-blown sand grains are continually bumping into each other or being driven into rock faces. The repeated collisions cause any corners to be quickly worn away and the grains become nearly spherical in shape. The collisions cause the grains to be chipped so that they come to look like

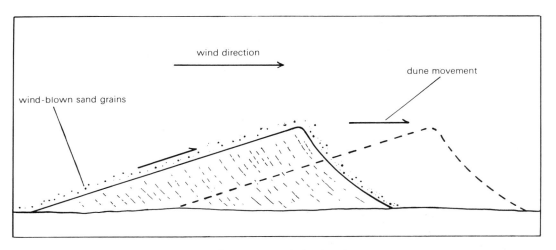

wind direction

dune movement

wind-blown sand grains

3.21 The movement of a barchan dune.

rivers run onto flat land the coarser transported material is deposited in alluvial fans. The finer material is carried further out to be deposited in flat areas called **playas** which have temporary lakes called **playa lakes**. Because playa lakes have no outlets they are often salty and when they dry up deposits of salts such as gypsum and halite may be formed.

Permanent rivers which cross deserts do not have the wide, V-shaped valleys of rivers in wet areas. Instead, they run in steep-walled **canyons**. This means that there is much less mass wasting in dry climates than in wet climates. Can you give any reasons for this? Can chemical weathering proceed to any great extent where there is no water? In deserts, weathering is so slow that rivers can cut down much faster than the valley sides can recede.

In areas where the rock beds are horizontal, resistant beds form protective covers over underlying strata so that desert plateaus may be cut to form flat-topped mountains called **mesas**. Mesas may be worn away to smaller features called **buttes**. **Inselbergs** ('island mountains') are isolated, dome-shaped hills of resistant rock such as granite which are most commonly found in semi-arid regions which have distinct wet and dry seasons. Inselbergs rise sharply from the surrounding gentle slopes or **pediments** which have been eroded down by seasonal flood water faster than the rocks of the inselbergs.

Structures of desert-laid rocks

How could you tell if a sandstone had been deposited by wind or water? You could begin by looking at the sand grains. Water-laid grains are usually shiny because they have been polish during transport. Are wind-blown sand gra shiny or dull? Also, a collision between grains water is cushioned by the water so they are often knocked into the nearly round shapes many wind-blown grains. You could also look the minerals present. Minerals with good cleav planes are not often found in desert sandsto but they may occur in water-deposited sandsto because transport in water does not break them to the same extent.

Cross bedding is found in both types sandstone but in desert sandstone the cr bedding is formed in dunes, and as a result cross bedded units may be on a very large sc

Put some soil into a basin and cover it w water. Stir the mixture well and leave the ba aside for a few days to let the water evapor. What do you see in the bottom of the basin? In same way, the drying of mud in desert la produces **mud cracks** which form in patte something like honeycombs. These cracks

A canyon formed by a river in an arid region – Canyonlands National Park, Colorado.

plain'), has meandering rivers on flat land interrupted by a few hills of resistant rock. In desert climates the young landscapes are mountains with little sediment between them. In maturity, the mountains are partly worn down and the low areas become filled with sediment brought in by wind and temporary rivers. In old age the mountains are reduced to a few hills and sediment covers large areas of low-lying ground.

If a human being was described to you as something made up mostly of carbon, hydrogen and oxygen you would think that this definition was too simple to describe something which is in fact very complicated. In the same way, you should be aware of the fact that landscapes may be too complex and varied simply to be described as young, mature and old. The idea of a cycle of erosion is a **theory** and not a fact. Find out what theories are and how they are used in science.

Many geologists now believe that the theory of the cycle of erosion is wrong. They would say, for instance, that there is no definite sequence of landscape development and that there can be no

Large-scale cross bedding in desert-laid sandstone at Mauchline in Ayrshire.

...etimes preserved in desert-laid rocks.

...ince desert sediments are laid on land, they are ...ontact with oxygen in the atmosphere. This ...etimes results in the grains of the rock being ...ted with iron oxide, and desert-laid rocks are ...n red in colour. Also, plants and animals are ...common in deserts so their preserved remains ...sils) are not common in wind-deposited rocks.

...anging landscapes

...ur study of the Earth's surface has shown it to ...nade up of a great variety of landforms such as ..., valleys, plains and deltas, all of which have ...n shaped by the processes of weathering, ...sport, erosion and deposition. These ...cesses act continuously, causing landscapes to ...nge very slowly or to evolve over long periods ...ime. The way in which a landscape changes ...ends on the kinds of processes acting on it, the ...e of rock and the length of time for which the ...cesses have been acting.

One method of describing changing landscapes is to liken them to the stages of youth, maturity and old age experienced by a person during his lifetime. In this scheme of description a newly raised area would be a **young landscape**. Through time, this landscape would be partially denuded to form a **mature landscape** which, in its turn, would be worn down to a nearly flat **old landscape**. This flat area could be uplifted to form a young landscape once again. This possible series of changes from young to mature to old, then back to young is called a **cycle of erosion** (figure 3.22).

The sequence of landscapes developed during a cycle of erosion is different in different climates. In wet climates, where rivers are mainly responsible for erosion, the young landscape consists of jagged mountains and deep valleys with rivers flowing down steep slopes. The mature landscape shows rounded hills and wide valleys and the old landscape, which is called a **peneplain** ('nearly a

A desert landscape—Jebel Ram, Jordan. What landforms can you see? How have the processes of erosion and deposition acted to produce this landscape?

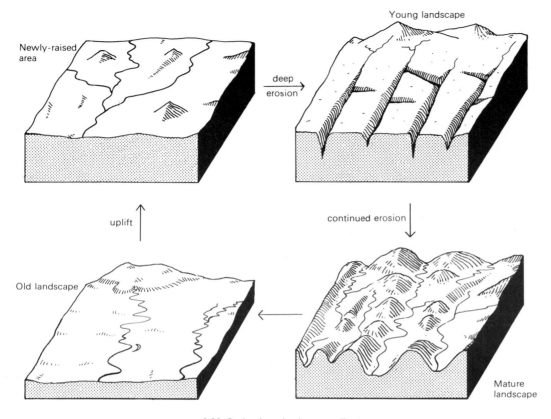

Newly-raised area

deep erosion

Young landscape

uplift

continued erosion

Old landscape

Mature landscape

3.22 Cycle of erosion in a wet climate.

end forms of landscape evolution such as the peneplain. In this alternative theory it is suggested that landscapes can have relatively unchanging forms. This means that landscapes do not go through continuous stages of historical development; instead, they evolve only as far as is necessary to attain a state of balance between rock resistance on the one hand and erosion on the other. Any alteration in conditions such as a change in climate or uplift will cause a landscape to adjust until it acquires a new form at balance with the new conditions.

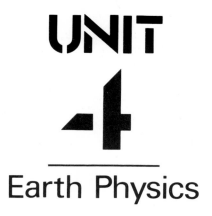

UNIT 4

Earth Physics

What is inside the Earth?

We can look in great detail at the rocks on the surface of the Earth. We can also go some distance below the surface by digging mines and drilling boreholes. But the deepest mine is only about 3.5 kilometres deep and the deepest bore hole only goes about 10 kilometres into the Earth. How do these figures compare with the radius of the Earth? Since the radius is nearly 6400 kilometres, even the deepest borehole does not tell us very much about the Earth's interior. Because we cannot look inside the Earth we have to rely largely on indirect evidence in our efforts to find out what the inside of the Earth is like. The problem is rather like trying to find out what is inside a box that you cannot open. Let us now look at the evidence available and see what it tells us about the structure and composition of the interior of the Earth.

The density of the Earth

You will recall from table 1.1 in Unit 1 that the average density of the Earth is about 5.5 g/cm³. However, most surface rocks have densities between 2.5 and 3.0 g/cm³. Does this indicate anything about the Earth's interior? Since the densities of surface rocks are below the average value for the Earth, this can only mean that somewhere inside the Earth there must be material with a density much greater than average. But where is this high density material and how is it situated inside the Earth? Is there a large internal mass whose density is slightly above average, or is there a small mass of very high density material? To answer questions like these we need more evidence. The study of earthquakes can help us–this is called **seismology**.

What are earthquakes?

What happens if you bang a table which has some cups and saucers on it? You can easily make the cups and saucers rattle. But why do the cups rattle when you don't touch them? You can probably guess that banging the table makes it shake, and the movement passes through the table to the cups and saucers. In fact, this is just like an earthquake. Earthquakes are produced by sudden breaks in the rocks, usually near the surface of the Earth. From the point of the break, energy travels out as earthquake waves which shake the surrounding rocks as they move through them.

Before we can understand how earthquakes happen we must look at the way materials behave when they are subjected to forces which might cause them to break. Take some plasticine, a piece of rubber and a piece of blackboard chalk and see how they behave when you pull, squeeze and twist them. You will see that plasticine and rubber change their shape when they are subjected to forces. This change of shape is called **deformation** or **strain**. When the force is removed from the rubber it goes back to its original shape; rubber is therefore an **elastic** substance. Substances such as plasticine remain deformed when the force is removed—such substances are **plastic**. What happens when you pull the blackboard chalk? This breaking is called **fracture** or **rupture**. Materials which break easily like this are **brittle**. Take two bars of toffee; warm one and put the other in a freezer for a short time. What happens to the toffee bars when you try to bend them? What you have found is that material which is brittle at low temperatures may be plastic at high temperatures. In the Earth, since temperature increases with depth this could mean that rocks which are brittle at the Earth's surface may be plastic when they are deeply buried. Most earthquakes occur at depths of less than 30 kilometres, and there are no earthquakes below 700 kilometres. Can you suggest why this is so? If the rock below 700 kilometres does not fracture what does this tell you about its properties?

The point at which fracture occurs within the Earth is called the **focus** of the earthquake and the point on the Earth's surface directly above the focus is the **epicentre**. The **magnitude** of an earthquake is a measure of the amount of energy given out by it. The more energy released, the greater the magnitude. A high magnitude earthquake could be compared to the explosion produced by a large bomb, while a low magnitude earthquake would be like the explosion of a firework. The energy from an earthquake travels out as waves in all directions through the Earth. There are three kinds of earthquake wave: **P** or **primary waves**, **S** or **secondary waves** and **L** or **long waves**.

P waves are just like sound waves—they are produced by pushing and pulling forces. In fact, P waves are often called push-and-pull waves. You can see how P waves travel by giving a stretched 'Slinky' a sharp pull or push (figure 4.1(a)). When a P wave moves through a rock, the rock particles shake backwards and forwards in the direction in

which the wave travels (figure 4.1(b)). Like sound waves, P waves can travel through solids and liquids so if any part of the Earth's interior is liquid, then they are able to pass through it.

S waves are often called shear or shake waves. What happens to a stretched 'Slinky' when you shake it (figure 4.1(c))? You can produce a wave which moves at right angles to the shaking direction. In a similar way, when S waves travel through rock the rock particles vibrate (shake) at right angles to the direction in which the waves move. Unlike P waves, S waves cannot travel through liquids. This means that if any part of the Earth's interior is liquid, S waves will stop at the liquid boundary. In general, S waves travel about half as quickly as P waves.

L waves are surface waves. They are restricted the upper layers of the Earth in much the same that waves on the sea are restricted to the wa near the surface. In this respect, L waves di from P and S waves. P and S waves can tra through the interior of the Earth, and for reason they are sometimes called body waves

The **intensity** of an earthquake is a measure how strongly the earthquake shakes the grou Intensity is measured on a 12-point scale; a sc III earthquake (slight) produces vibrations those of a passing lorry, a scale VI earthqu (strong) causes chimneys to fall and furniture move, and a scale XII earthquake (catastroph causes total destruction of buildings and bridg A measure of how disastrous earthquakes can b

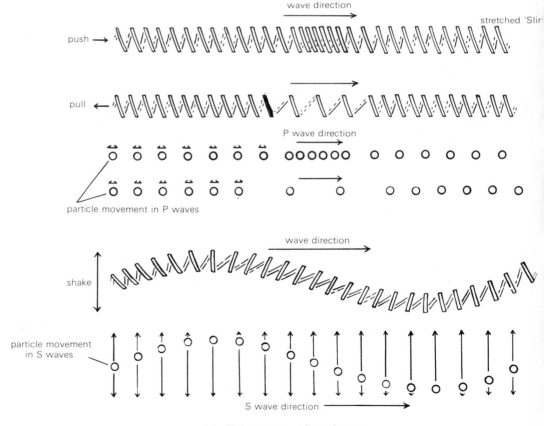

4.1 The movement of P and S waves.

cated by the fact that in July, 1976, 655 000
ple are reported to have died in an earthquake
angshan in China. The photographs show the
d of damage which an earthquake can do. Just
sounds become fainter with distance, the
nsity of an earthquake decreases outwards
n the focus. The greatest intensity is felt at the
entre. Lines on the Earth's surface joining
nts of equal intensity are called **isoseismal**
es (figure 4.2).

v are earthquakes recorded?

ne vibrations produced by earthquakes are re-
ded using instruments called **seismometers**

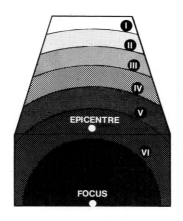

4.2   *Earthquake intensity decreases away
from the focus.*

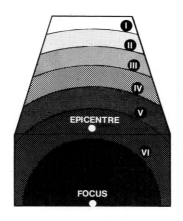

(figure 4.3). When earthquake vibrations arrive at
the seismometer the base of the instrument and the
recording drum are shaken. The heavy suspended
weight does not move, so the pen attached to it
marks the recording drum with a zig-zag trace. The
record of the earthquake produced in this manner
is called a **seismogram** (figure 4.4).

You will see that although the P, S and L waves
are produced at the same time they arrive at the
seismometer at different times. This is simply
because they travel at different velocities. The time
interval between the arrival of the P and S waves
allows us to work out how far the focus of the
earthquake is from the recording station. (You can
find out how far away a lightning flash is by

*Some examples of earthquake damage:
(a) Napier, New Zealand (1931)*

*(b) Niigata, Japan (1964). The thick smoke in the distance
comes from burning petrol storage tanks.*

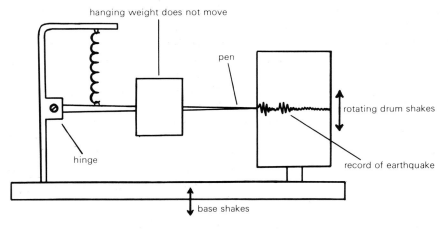

4.3 *A seismometer.*

counting the number of seconds between the flash and the arrival of the sound of the thunder–this is a similar situation. If you are not familiar with this your teacher will explain it to you.) In the case of earthquakes, the greater the time interval between the arrival of the P and S waves, the further away the earthquake focus. (Roughly speaking, every 1000 kilometres between the focus and the recording station produces a time lag of about one minute.) Although this method tells us how far away the focus is, it does not tell us the direction in which the focus lies. To find the position of the focus, or more correctly the epicentre, the distances from at least three recording centres must be known. With the recording stations as centres, circles are drawn whose radii are equal to the distances of the stations from the focus. The three circles meet at the position of the epicentre (figure 4.5).

Where do earthquakes occur?

Earthquakes do not occur in every part of the Earth. Those areas in which earthquakes are common are called **seismic zones**. You can see from figure 4.6 that the seismic zones are narrow

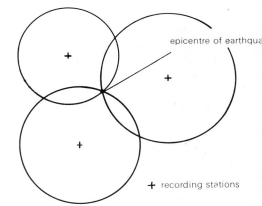

4.5 *Finding the position of an epicentre.*

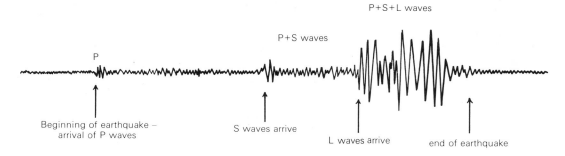

4.4 *A seismogram (earthquake record)*

trips which are most strongly marked around the Pacific and along the Alpine-Himalayan mountain chain. Seismic zones also occur along the oceanic ridges.

Study of earthquake foci has shown that the great majority of earthquakes occur within 30 kilometres of the Earth's surface. Earthquakes are in fact classified by depth of focus into shallow (down to 60 km), intermediate (60–300 km) and deep (300–700 km) focus earthquakes.

What do earthquakes tell us about the Earth's interior?

When a doctor wants to 'look inside' a patient he can take X-ray photographs. The X-rays pass through the person's body and show up the bones and other structures inside. In a somewhat similar way we can use earthquake waves to allow us to 'look inside' the Earth. To understand how this is done, consider what happens when a stone is thrown into water.

When a stone is dropped vertically into water what happens to its velocity? Does the direction of movement change? In a similar way, when earthquake waves pass vertically from one type of rock into another their velocities change.

What happens to a stone which strikes the water at an angle? This time the stone changes direction as well as velocity. Earthquake waves passing at an angle from one rock type into another behave in the same way. The change of direction is called **refraction**.

If a stone strikes the water at a very low angle it may bounce. Similarly, when earthquake waves meet a different rock layer at a very low angle they may not be able to pass into it. When this happens the waves are **reflected**.

The seismologist (a scientist who studies earthquakes) uses evidence from changes in wave velocity, refractions and reflections in his efforts to find out about the inside of the Earth. Let us look at some of the things seismologists have been able to find out about the Earth's interior.

It was found that earthquake waves come to the surface sooner than would be expected if they travelled in straight lines. The waves must follow curved paths. What does this change in direction of the waves tell you about the properties of the rocks through which the waves are passing? For refraction to take place the wave must pass through rocks with changing properties. If the wave path curves smoothly, the change in the rock properties must be gradual. The main change with increasing depth is that the rocks become more dense.

Seismologists have also discovered two well-marked surfaces within the Earth where earthquake waves change direction suddenly. This means that at these surfaces there has been a sudden change in rock properties. The surface dividing two markedly different rock layers is called a **discontinuity**.

The upper discontinuity lies near the surface; it is called the **Mohorovicic Discontinuity** or **Moho** for short. On average, the Moho is about 33 kilometres below the Earth's surface. The layer of the Earth above the Moho is called the **crust**; the layer below the Moho is the **mantle**. When an earthquake wave passes from the crust into the mantle the wave speeds up and is bent towards the horizontal.

The lower discontinuity is deep within the Earth and it has two marked effects on earthquake waves. Imagine an earthquake taking place at the North Pole. From this imaginary earthquake P and S waves would be received all over the northern hemisphere, but in the southern hemisphere the effect of the lower discontinuity would be that only P waves would reach Antarctica. In a wide band in the latitudes of Australia and New Zealand no P or S waves would be received at all (figure 4.7).

How can we account for this pattern? Can we produce a similar pattern with a light beam? Fill a beaker with water. Stand it in the middle of a circle with a diameter about twice that of the beaker. Place a 12 volt light bulb on the circumference of the circle and draw the pattern of light within the circle (figure 4.8(a)). Which parts of the circumference receive light? Are there any parts which receive no light from the bulb? In this experiment we cannot accurately reproduce the situation found in the Earth. Nevertheless, the agreement is close enough to allow you to understand what happens. The beaker of water

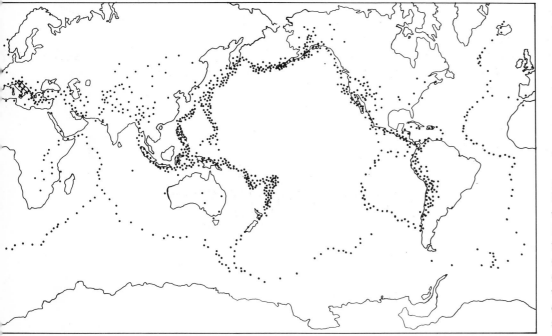

4.6   Earthquake distribution.

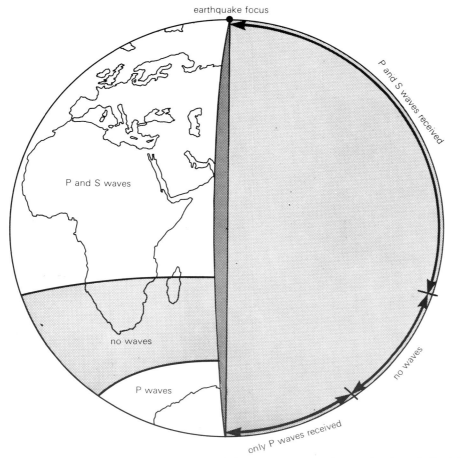

4.7 *The wave types received at different places around the world from an imaginary earthquake at the North Pole.*

the way in which earthquake waves behave a
they pass through the Earth we can see that th
Earth is made up of three different layers (figur
4.9). The outer layer is the crust with an averag
thickness of 33 kilometres. The middle layer, dow
to 2900 kilometres, is the mantle. The centra
sphere, which has a radius of about 350(
kilometres, is the core. We will now look at th
crust, mantle and core in more detail.

The crust

Earthquake data tells us that the level of th
Moho is different in different places. Under th
oceans the crust is very thin (about 5 kilometre
thick on average) but under the continents it i
much thicker. Under the non-mountainous part
of the continents the crust averages about 3(
kilometres but under major mountain chains it ma
reach thicknesses of more than 70 kilometres. Th
large difference in thickness between the oceani
and continental crust immediately suggests tha
these two parts of the crust are different in type a
well as thickness. In fact, there are two mai
differences between oceanic and continenta
crust.

The first difference is one of composition. Th
rocks of the continents are very variable in typ∈
but on the whole they seem to be roughly lik
granite in chemical composition. Besides oxyger
the main elements in granite are silicon an

acts like a lens. Light which falls on it is focused to
a point, leaving a shadow zone on each side. The
experiment suggests that the Earth contains a
spherical nucleus which focuses earthquake
waves in the same way that the beaker focuses
light rays (figure 4.8(b)). This central portion of
the Earth is called the **core**. The **core-mantle
boundary** (sometimes called the Gutenberg or
Oldham Discontinuity) is 2900 kilometres below
the Earth's surface.

If an imaginary earthquake took place at the
North Pole, only P waves would be received in
Antarctica. This must mean that S waves are not
able to pass through the core. Since S waves
cannot pass through liquids this tells us that the
core, on the outside at least, is liquid.

So what have we found so far? From a study of

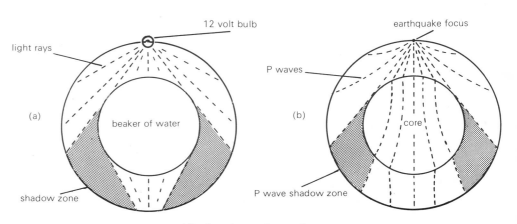

4.8 *How the core focuses P waves.*

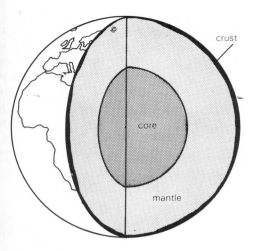

4.9 The structure of the Earth

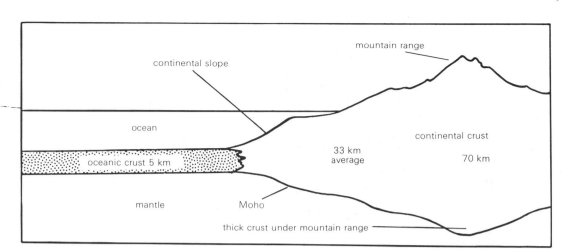

4.10 The structure of the crust. The figures give the thickness of various parts of the crust (not drawn to scale).

uminium. For this reason, continental crust is ometimes called **sial** (a word made up of the first vo letters of silicon and aluminium). Oceanic rust is of basaltic composition. Besides the ominant elements oxygen, silicon and uminium, basalts contain quite a lot of agnesium and because of this oceanic crust is ometimes called **sima**.

The second difference between oceanic and ontinental crust is one of age. Oceanic crust is latively young—nowhere is it more than about 00 million years old. Continental crust is often uch older than this; the oldest continental rocks e about 3800 million years old.

You should note that the continental crust does ot cease to exist at the seashore. The continental helf areas, for example the North Sea, are made p of continental crust which has been covered by e sea. Figure 4.10 shows how oceanic and ontinental crusts are related.

he mantle

Since the mantle lies beneath the crust we bviously cannot see directly what the mantle is ade of. Some years ago an attempt was made by nited States scientists to drill through the ceanic crust of the Pacific into the mantle. This rilling project was called the Mohole Project but was abandoned in 1966 without its aim of

reaching the mantle being realized. Despite this we can identify parts of the mantle, or at least, parts of the upper mantle. Mantle rocks come to the surface in two ways. Firstly, deforming processes responsible for mountain building sometimes squeeze a wedge of mantle material to the surface. For example, the Troodos Massif of western Cyprus seems to be partly composed of rocks derived from the mantle. The second way in which pieces of the mantle reach the surface is by being carried up in the lava from volcanoes. The mantle rocks at the surface are nearly always of a type of rock called **peridotite**, which is made up almost entirely of olivine and pyroxene.

The core

The core, beginning as it does at a depth of 2900 kilometres, is completely inaccessible and no parts of it have made their way to the Earth's surface. This means that we can do little more than guess at its composition. One suggestion is that the core is made up of material similar to that found in iron meteorites—they consist of about 91 per cent iron and 9 per cent nickel. But if the core has a pure nickel-iron composition, it is thought that its density should be greater than it actually is. It may be that a low density element, perhaps silicon, is also present.

In table 4.1 you will find a summary of the structure of the Earth.

Isostasy or the floating crust

Float wooden blocks of different sizes in water. Look carefully at how much of each block is submerged and how much sticks out of the water. Can you see any relationship between the portions in and out of the water?

Now compare figures 4.10 and 4.11. Figure 4.10 shows a section through the crust and figure 4.11 shows a series of wooden blocks floating in water. The similarity between the two diagrams suggests that the two situations are similar; it looks

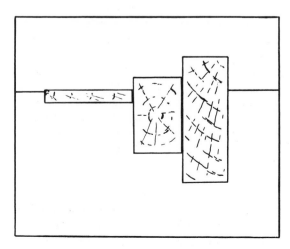

4.11 Wooden blocks floating in water.

Earth layer	Depth to base (km)	Percentage volume of Earth	Density (g/cm³)	Elemental composition (percentage weight)	Other details
crust	1.5		2.9	oxygen 47 silicon 27 aluminium 8 iron 5 calcium 4 sodium 3 potassium 3 magnesium 2 other elements 1	Thickness variable. Oceanic crust (sima), 5km average depth. Continental crust (sial), 33km average depth. Oceanic crust basaltic. Continental crust granitic.
Moho ——— 33			3.3		
mantle		82.5		oxygen 44 magnesium 23 silicon 21 iron 6 calcium 2 aluminium 2 other elements 2	Upper mantle composed of peridotite. Composition of lower mantle not known (see text)
core-mantle boundary	2900		5.5 10.0		
core		16		iron 73 silicon 20 nickel 7	Outer core liquid. Inner core solid. S waves stop at core-mantle boundary. Composition not known (see text)
centre of Earth	—6400—		13.6		

The chemical composition of the whole Earth is roughly as follows (elements given as percentages by weight: iron 38, oxygen 29, silicon 15, magnesium 8, nickel 3, calcium 3, aluminium 3, other elements 1.

Table 4.1 Summary of Earth structure.

as if the crust floats on the mantle. However, the apparent similarity might be deceptive–you might say that because the crust and mantle are both solid, one can hardly be said to be floating on the other. Does the crust have any other similarities to a floating object?

If you push down a floating block and then release it what happens? The block bobs up and returns to its original position. Similarly, if you pull a block partly out of the water it sinks back to its original position when you let it go. With blocks of wood in water the movement takes place very quickly. In places, the Earth's crust shows slow up or down movements similar to those shown by the wooden blocks when they are displaced. Let us look at a few examples.

At times during the last two million years northern Europe has been covered by thick ice sheets. The weight of the ice pushed the crust down. About 10 000 years ago the ice melted, and removal of the ice allowed the crust to rise. It is still rising–in parts of Scandinavia it has been calculated that the crust has been rising at a rate of about 1 centimetre per year for the last 10 000 years. The northern parts of the British Isles were also heavily glaciated and around our shores we commonly find evidence of recent uplift in the form of **raised beaches**. These are beaches which have risen as much as 30 metres above the present sea level.

In tropical oceans there are many ring-shaped coral islands called **atolls**. The atolls sit on volcanic islands which have sunk slowly enough for the coral growth to keep pace with the rate of sinking. Sinking may result from the piling up of lava to form an island. The weight of the lava may cause the crust to subside (figure 4.12). Sometimes the islands sink completely to form flat-topped mounds on the sea floor. The mounds are called **guyots** and they have flat tops because as the islands sink, the sea erodes their tops.

High mountains such as the Himalayas continue to rise even though they lose a great deal of material by erosion. If you look at a map of India and Tibet you will see that rivers such as the Indus and Brahmaputra cut through high mountain ranges. This can only mean that the rivers were there before the mountains. As the mountains rose the rivers were able to cut through them quickly enough to prevent the river paths from being diverted.

In all these cases we have evidence that the crust can move up or down. These movements are called **isostatic movements**. If the crust is loaded it sinks, and if it is unloaded it rises. A wooden block in its normal floating position has no tendency to move up or down and it is said to be in hydrostatic equilibrium (balance). In the

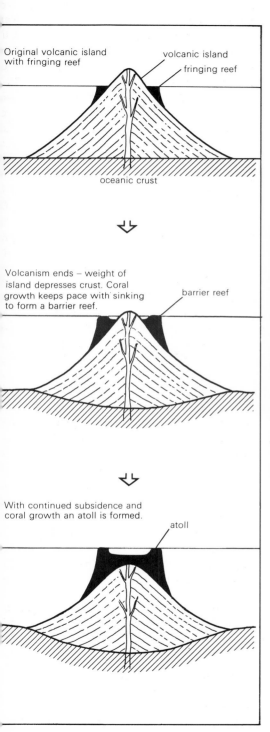

Original volcanic island with fringing reef
volcanic island
fringing reef
oceanic crust

Volcanism ends – weight of island depresses crust. Coral growth keeps pace with sinking to form a barrier reef.
barrier reef

With continued subsidence and coral growth an atoll is formed.
atoll

4.12 Possible methods of atoll formation.

A raised beach on the Isle of Arran. The old sea-cliffs are now some distance from the shore; the features projecting from the shore are dykes.

same way, if the crust shows no tendency to move up or down it is said to be in **isostatic equilibrium**.

The Earth's magnetic field

Take a compass and push the needle gently to one side. Release the needle and watch what happens. If you repeat this process a few times you will find that the compass needle always returns to the same position. Bring a bar magnet up to the needle. What happens? The needle takes up a new position. As before, push the needle to one side and release it. You will find that the compass needle always returns to the same position relative to the bar magnet. The Earth and the bar magnet both cause the compass needle to lie in a fixed position; the Earth therefore behaves as if it were a bar magnet.

A compass needle has two poles—a north pole at one end and a south pole at the other. The north pole of the compass needle always points north; what does this tell us? Bring the north pole of a bar magnet up to a compass needle. Which pole of the compass needle points to the north pole of the magnet? Repeat, bringing up the south pole of the magnet. Which pole of the compass needle points to the south pole of the magnet? You will find that the north pole of the compass needle always points towards the south pole of the magnet, and that the south pole of the compass needle always points to the north pole of the magnet. We have already said that the Earth behaves like a bar magnet. The fact that the north pole of a compass needle always points north therefore tells us that the Earth's internal magnet has its south pole pointing north, and its north pole pointing south (figure 4.13(a)).

But what effects does the Earth's magnetism produce over the surface of the Earth? On a sheet of paper draw a circle with a radius about equal to the length of a bar magnet. Place the sheet of paper over the magnet, taking care that the circle is

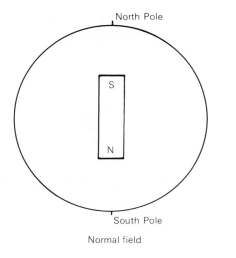

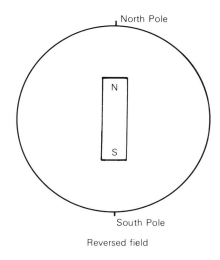

4.14 Normal and reversed magnetic fields.

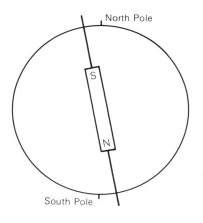

4.13 (a) The Earth's internal magnet.

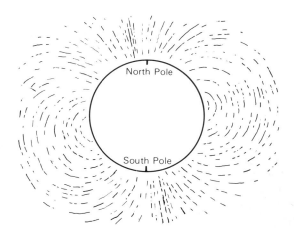

(b) The Earth's magnetic field.

centered on the magnet. Sprinkle iron filings on the paper and tap the paper gently. Make a drawing of what you see. You will find that for a certain distance away from the magnet the filings line themselves up. The zone of magnetic influence around a magnet is called its **magnetic field** and the Earth's magnetic field is very like the one around a bar magnet (figure 4.13(b)). Of course, the Earth does not have a bar magnet inside it, but it does look as if the magnetism is produced deep within the Earth, perhaps by electric currents flowing in the metallic core.

Palaeomagnetism

You saw in the last section that the Earth's magnetic field caused a compass needle to line itself up in a fixed position with its north pole pointing north. But there are many materials besides steel which can be magnetic. Iron-containing minerals in the Earth's crust a[re] magnetized by the Earth's field when the ro[ck] containing them is formed. These iron minera[ls] tend to become lined up like tiny compass needle[s] and we can use their weak magnetism to tell u[s] certain things about the Earth's magnetic field [at] the time when this rock was formed.

Study of how the Earth's magnetic field ha[s] changed during past ages is calle[d] **palaeomagnetism**. One thing that palaeo[-] magnetism has told us is that the Earth's fie[ld] frequently switches itself around. For example, i[n] the last 4 million years the Earth's field ha[s] changed round at least twenty times. When th[e] field is in its present condition, with the south po[le] of the Earth's internal magnet pointing north, it [is] said to be **normal**. When the internal magnet [is] turned around the field is said to be **reversed**. Figure 4.14 shows the difference between norm[al] and reversed fields.

UNIT 5

The Moving Earth

rike and dip

The photograph on this page shows some dimentary rocks which were laid down in the . What must have happened to these rocks after y were deposited? It looks as if they have been sed up and bent by forces acting within the rth. In fact, rocks are so often tilted, broken and nt that the Earth has frequently been described being 'restless' or 'mobile'. When sediments are posited they are usually laid down in horizontal ers, but when they are affected by Earth vements the bedding may not remain rizontal.

How can we describe the positions of tilted rock ers? Take a set square with three unequal sides prop it up with its shortest edge on the bench. at angle does this edge make with the rizontal? Find the direction of this edge in grees as accurately as possible using a compass.

Sedimentary rocks raised from the sea and folded.

62

Now measure the angles that the other two edges make with the bench. Are they equal? Which edge makes the greater angle? You should have found that the edge at right angles to the short edge makes the greater angle. Note this angle and the general direction (that is, to the west or south-east, etc.) in which the set square slopes down. Now take the set square to another bench and try to lay it down in exactly the same position as before. Do the measurements you have made allow you to do this? We can use these same measurements to define the position of a rock layer. The direction of any horizontal line on a tilted rock surface is called the **strike**. The position of a horizontal line can be found with a spirit level and its direction taken with a compass. The angle which the layer makes with the horizontal is called the **dip**; it is measured **at right angles** to the strike using a **clinometer** (figure 5.1). Your teacher will show you how to use these instruments. To record your measurements write the strike followed by the dip and dip direction. For example, readings from a bed striking exactly north east and dipping towards the south east would be written as strike 45°, dip 25° S.E.

Besides tilting rocks. Earth movements also break and bend rocks. We will now look at some of the structures produced by these movements.

Joints

Joints are cracks in rocks. Joints often run through rocks in what seems to be an irregular manner, but some may have quite regular patterns. For example, **columnar jointing**, seen in some fine-grained igneous rocks, results from shrinkage during cooling. **Sheet joints** form parallel to the ground surface in granites which expand as the weight of overlying rock is removed by erosion. Most joints, however, are produced not by shrinkage or expansion but by movements which cause the rock to split. Such joints are often found parallel and at right angles to the bedding of sedimentary rocks. An important feature of joints is that they can make a rock much more pervious than it would otherwise be.

Columnar jointing in basalt – the Giant's Causeway in Northern Ireland.

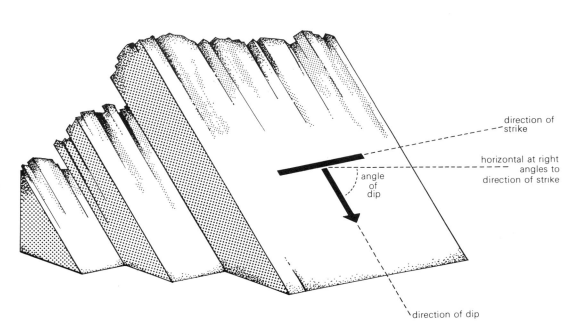

direction of strike

horizontal at right angles to direction of strike

angle of dip

direction of dip

5.1 Strike and dip.

Sheet joints in granite – Goat Fell, on the Isle of Arran. These joints form parallel to the ground surface as the overlying rock is removed by erosion.

...ults

When rocks are faulted they are first of all broken
...d then the rocks slide past each other along the
...rface of fracture. Faults can be divided into three
...ain groups depending on the type of móvement
...hich has occurred:

...ormal faults

These are produced by pulling forces or tension.
...ter fracture the rocks move apart (figure 5.2).
...is results in the rocks on one side of the fault
...ane being lowered relative to the rocks on the
...her side. The amount of vertical displacement or
...ovement on a fault plane is called the **throw**.
...cks which have been **downthrown** have
...oved down relative to the **upthrown** rocks on
...e other side of the fault plane. Sometimes very
...ge, parallel normal faults may form and a large
...ock may be lowered between them to form a **rift
...lley** (figure 5.3). The Midland Valley of
...otland is a rift valley bounded by the Southern
...lands Fault to the south and by the Highland
...undary Fault to the north. Other well-known rift
...leys are the Rhine Valley of Germany and the
...ican Rift Valleys which run from the Zambesi to
... Red Sea.

...verse faults

...his type of fault results from squeezing or
...mpression. After fracture the rocks are pushed
...ether and one block moves up over the other
...gure 5.4). In mountainous areas, low-angle

A normal fault at Kilve in Somerset. The beds above the
fault plane have moved down relative to those beneath.

reverse faults called **thrust faults** or **thrusts** are
sometimes found. The large rock mass which has
been pushed over the rocks underneath is called a
nappe. In north-west Scotland there are many
well-known thrusts which have carried nappes
from the mountain belt out towards the west. In
places the movement has been at least 10
kilometres.

Tear faults

These faults are caused by forces which make
the fault blocks slide past each other horizontally
(figure 5.5). A well-known tear fault is the Great
Glen Fault of northern Scotland which is thought
to have produced movement of about 100
kilometres (figure 5.6). Tear faults are sometimes
called wrench or transcurrent faults.

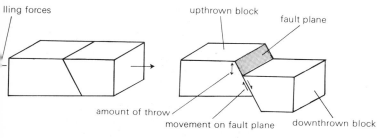

...lling forces

upthrown block

fault plane

amount of throw

movement on fault plane

downthrown block

rift valley

fault block downthrown between two normal faults

5.2   The formation of a normal fault.

5.3   A rift valley.

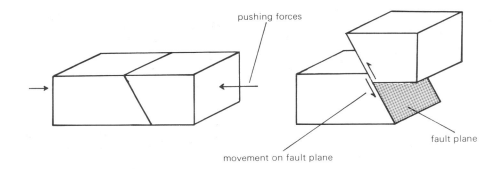

5.4 *Formation of a reverse fault.*

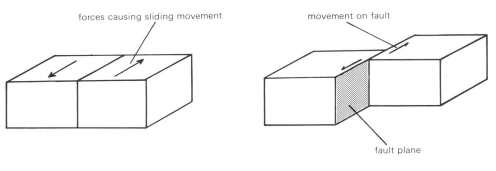

5.5 *Formation of a tear fault.*

A reverse fault – the beds above the fault plane have been pushed about 2 metres over the beds beneath.

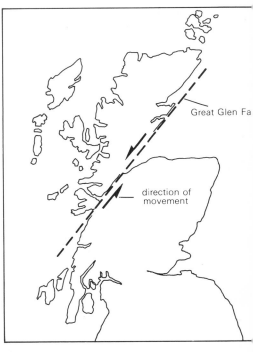

5.6 *The geography of Scotland as it might have been had there been no movement on the Great Glen Fault.*

Folds

Make some layered sheets of plasticine of different colours and bend them in as many ways as you can. In a similar way, when rocks are deformed deep in the Earth they may bend into **folds**. In your experiment with the plasticine you should have been able to make folds with many different shapes. To describe folds we have to look at the parts which make them up. In figure 5.7 you will see some of the terms used. Just as a book opens and closes by rotation of the pages around its spine, so a fold is formed by movement of rock layers around the **hinge line** or **axis** of the fold. At the hinge line there is a change in dip direction. Can you see why? The **axial surface** of a fold is the surface which contains the hinge lines of all the folded layers. The **limbs** of a fold are the parts between the hinges, and the **core** is the central area of a fold.

There are two main types of fold. The first of these is an upfold or **anticline** (figure 5.8(a)). In an anticline the fold limbs dip away from each other and the oldest rocks are in the core. The second main type is a downfold or **syncline** (figure 5.8(b)). In a syncline the limbs dip towards

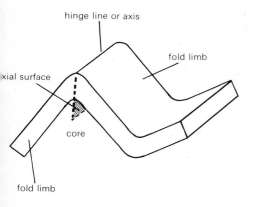

5.7 Parts of a fold.

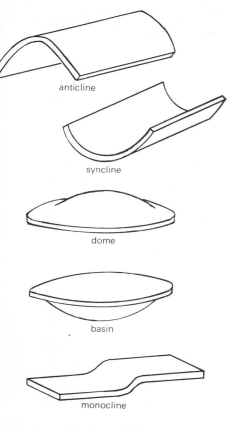

anticline

syncline

dome

basin

monocline

5.8 Types of fold.

each other and the youngest rocks are in the fold core. Other fold types include the **dome** which is an anticline shaped like a skull-cap, the **basin** or saucer-shaped syncline and the **monocline** which is a fold shaped like a step. There are many other terms used to describe folds; you will find some of these illustrated in figure 5.9.

Most folds are formed by squeezing or compression of the rock layers. If you squeeze a paper-back book between your hands you will find that it soon buckles to form a fold. It is possible, however, for folds to form without compression along the layers. Mark a line on a pack of cards as shown in figure 5.10. Now push your finger into the bottom of the pack. What happens to the line? The line has been folded because the cards have slid over each other. Put small quantities of two oil paints of different colours in a tin lid then gently tilt the lid. What do you see? How have these folds formed? When rocks are buried deep in the Earth they may behave like thick liquids and folds may form in them by a process of slow flow.

Unconformity

In places such as deserts and beaches loose sediment may be laid down on bare rock. If the sediment is buried and turns to hard rock then there is a sharp break in sequence between the old

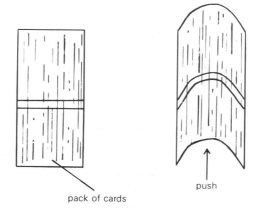

pack of cards

push

5.10 Making folds without compression along the layers.

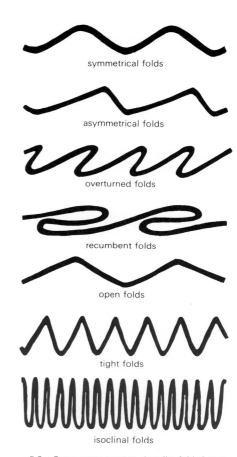

symmetrical folds

asymmetrical folds

overturned folds

recumbent folds

open folds

tight folds

isoclinal folds

5.9 Some terms used to describe fold shapes.

rock and the new rock above it. Such a discordant relationship between rock groups is described as **unconformity**. The old and new rocks are separated by a surface called a **plane of unconformity**.

Unconformity represents an interval when deposition ceased for a long or short period of time. After the early rocks have been formed they suffer uplift and erosion. They are then buried under newer sedimentary rocks (figure 5.11). Some types of unconformable relationships are shown in figure 5.12.

Build a sloping pile of soil against the side of a tank. Now add sand and chalk in horizontal layers. What do you see? The upper layers cover a larger area than the lower layers. In the same way, as sediments are deposited above a plane of unconformity it sometimes happens that the

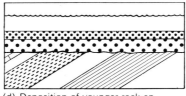

(a) Formation of early rock

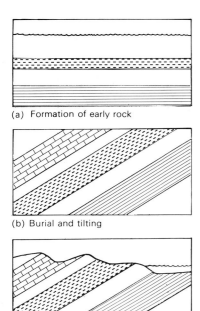

(b) Burial and tilting

(c) Uplift and erosion

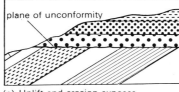

(d) Deposition of younger rock on older rock

plane of unconformity

(e) Uplift and erosion exposes unconformity

5.11 Stages in the formation of an unconformity.

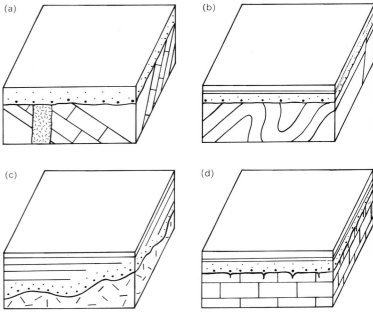

(a) (b) (c) (d)

5.12 Types of unconformity. In (a), (b) and (c) there is a sharp break between rocks of different type or orientation. In (d) the beds above and below the plane of unconformity are parallel.

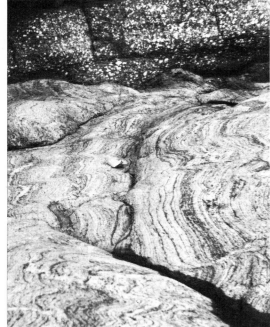

Unconformity – strongly folded gneiss overlain by conglomerate.

upper, younger beds spread over a wider area than the lower, older beds. When this happens the upper beds are said to **overlap** the lower beds.

Geological maps

An **outcrop** is the area over which a rock type comes to the Earth's surface even though the ro[ck] may be covered by soil, peat or some oth[er] material. If the rock can actually be seen it is said [to] be **exposed**. Figure 5.13 will show you t[he] difference between an outcrop and an exposu[re.] In the same way that we can make maps of roa[ds] and fields we can make maps of rock outcrops[.]

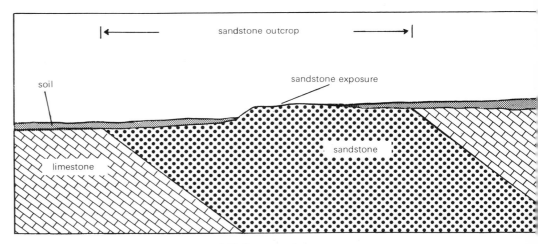

5.13 Outcrop and exposure.

o begin with let us see what outcrops look like
ere the ground surface is perfectly flat. To see
at happens to the rock layers under the surface
ck diagrams can be drawn. You can make
sticine models similar to the diagrams or you
paint the rock layers on upturned shoe boxes.
Where the bedding is horizontal only one rock
e is seen at the surface (figure 5.14(a)). With
ping beds the outcrops run parallel to the strike
gure 5.14(b)). Can you see why? What happens
he widths of the outcrops as the dip becomes
eper? As the dip increases the outcrops become
rower until, when the beds are vertical, the
dths of the outcrops are equal to the thicknesses
the beds (figure 5.14(c)). To estimate the
ckness of a bed dipping at a low angle first
ide the angle of dip by 60. If you multiply the
dth of the outcrop by this fraction you will have
approximate value for the thickness of the bed.
example, find the thickness of a bed with
tcrop width 120 metres which dips at 10°.
viding 10 by 60 gives 1/6, and multiplying 120
tres by 1/6 gives 20 metres as the thickness of
bed. Note that this rule does not work for beds

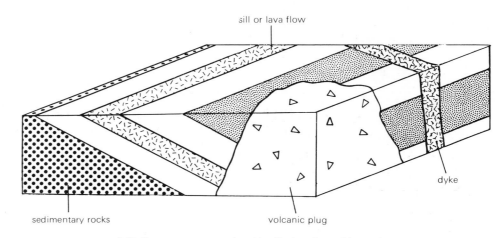

5.15 Outcrop patterns produced by sills, lava flows, dykes and
volcanic plugs.

dipping at angles of more than 45°. In areas
containing igneous rock, sills and lava flows
have the same orientations as beds but other
intrusions such as dykes and volcanic plugs cut
across the bedding (figure 5.15). Rocks such as
igneous rocks which have no distinct layering are
often described as **massive**. Can dip and strike be

measured in massive rocks?

Faults act to displace beds. The displacement
depends on the type of fault, on how the fault is
oriented and on the dip of the beds. When
horizontal beds are moved up or down by normal
or reverse faults older and younger beds are
brought into contact across the fault (figure 5.18).
A tear fault acting on horizontal beds does not
change the outcrop pattern; the beds are simply
shifted to one side.

Normal and reverse faults which run parallel to
the strike of inclined beds may cause beds to have
repeated outcrops, or they may prevent beds from
reaching the surface (figures 5.16 and 5.17).

Normal and reverse faults which run perpendicular
to the strike of inclined beds cause a sideways
displacement of the outcrops (figure 5.19(a) and
(b)). A tear fault parallel to the strike of inclined
beds does not affect the outcrop pattern, but a tear
fault running perpendicular to the strike moves the
beds to the side (figure 5.19(c)). If you look at
figure 5.19 you will see that different types of fault
running parallel to the direction of dip (i.e.
perpendicular to the strike) produce similar
displacements of the outcrops.

Use plasticine models to find the outcrop
patterns produced by faults running at angles to
the strike and dip. If vertical beds are moved
straight up or down the outcrop pattern is not
changed. Where an inclined fault plane runs
parallel to the direction of the strike, vertical beds

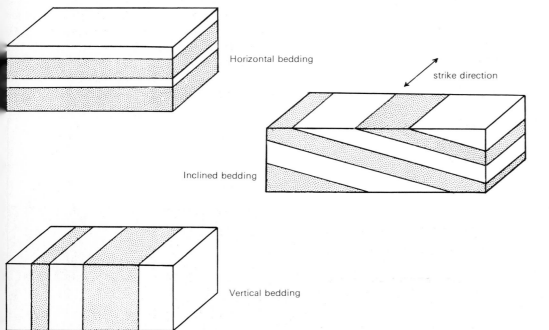

5.14 Outcrop patterns on horizontal ground.

68

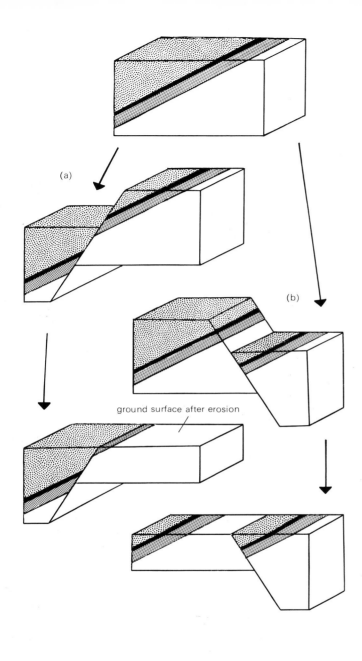

(a)

(b)

ground surface after erosion

5.16 *Normal faulting of inclined beds (fault running parallel to the strike). In (a) the fault plane dips in the same direction as the beds but at a higher angle. When this happens some beds may not appear at the surface. In (b) the fault plane dips in the opposite direction to the beds, causing some beds to outcrop twice.*

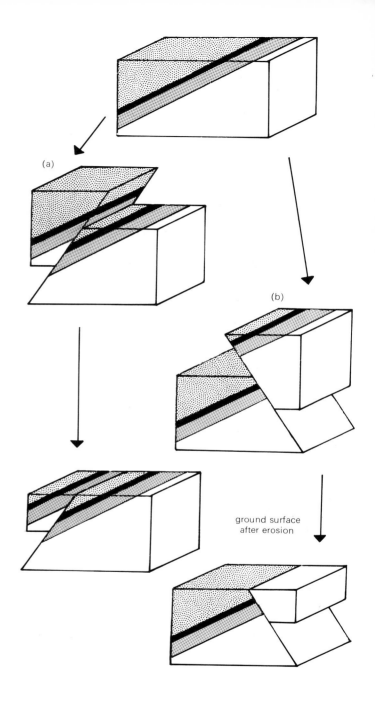

(a)

(b)

ground surface after erosion

5.17 *Reverse faulting of inclined beds (fault running parallel to the strike). In (a) the fault plane dips in the same direction as the beds but more steeply. This causes some beds to outcrop twice. In (b) the fault plane dips in the opposite direction to the beds, causing some beds to be concealed.*

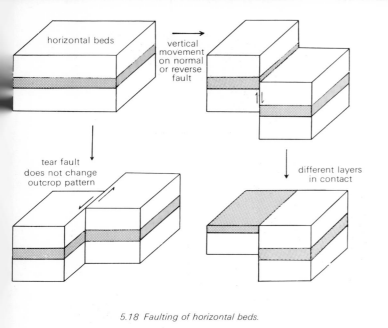

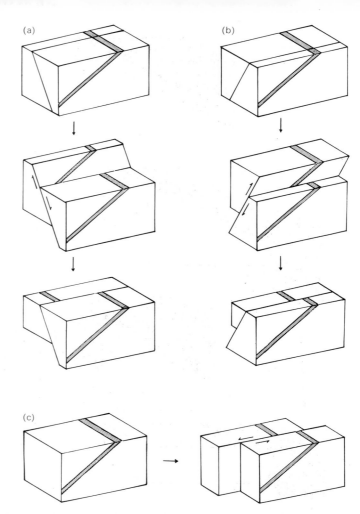

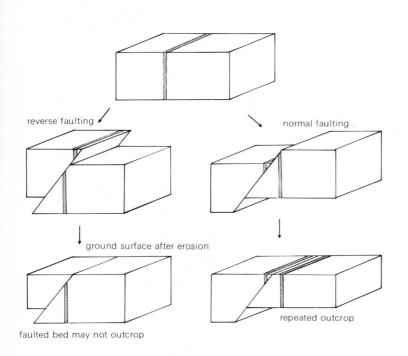

5.18 Faulting of horizontal beds.

5.19 Faulting of inclined beds (fault running at right angles to the strike). Note that normal faulting (a), reverse faulting (b), and tear faulting (c) produce similar outcrop patterns even though the displacements of the beds have been quite different.

5.20 Normal and reverse faulting of a vertical bed (fault running parallel to the strike).

may be repeated if the fault is normal or concealed if the fault is reversed (figure 5.20). Inclined normal and reverse faults running at right angles to the strike do not change the outcrop patterns of vertical beds. Tear faults do not alter the outcrops of vertical beds when the faults run parallel to the strike, but they displace the outcrops when the faults run perpendicular to the strike.

On flat ground, all folds except monoclines cause outcrops to be repeated. Some of the outcrop patterns produced by folds are shown in figure 5.21. When the axis of a fold is inclined to

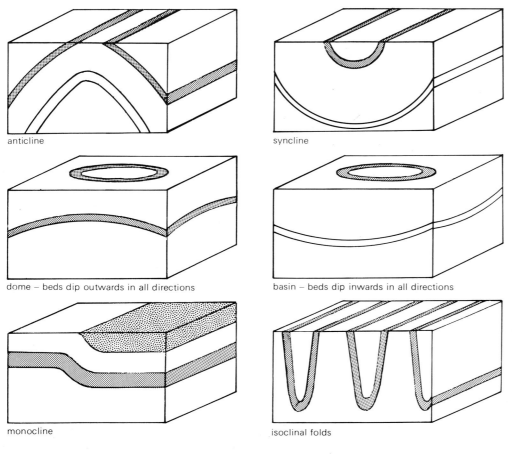

anticline

syncline

dome – beds dip outwards in all directions

basin – beds dip inwards in all directions

monocline

isoclinal folds

5.21 Outcrop patterns produced by folding.

the horizontal the fold is said to **plunge**. The outcrops of the beds in the limbs of a plunging fold do not remain parallel. Instead, the outcrops converge to produce a V-shaped pattern (figure 5.22(a) and (b)). A series of plunging anticlines and synclines gives rise to a wavy outcrop pattern (figure 5.22(c)). Look at a geological map of Britain—you should be able to see many outcrop patterns suggestive of folds. For example, the south of England shows some huge open folds such as the Wealden anticline (figure 5.25), the London basin and the Isle of Wight monocline. From this you will see that folds can be enormous structures. On the other hand, some folds are so small that they can only be seen under a microscope.

Folded rocks are often faulted. Some of the outcrop patterns produced by the faulting of rocks which are already folded are shown in figure 5.23.

So far we have only considered outcrops as they would appear on level ground. In practice the ground surface is rarely flat. How will hills and valleys affect outcrop patterns? You can use plasticine models to help you understand how the patterns are produced.

Outcrop patterns depend on the dip of the beds and on the shape of the ground surface. Vertical beds have the simplest outcrops because they run straight across hills and valleys without changing direction (figure 5.26). On the other hand, horizontal beds have very wavy outcrops which follow contours without ever cutting across them

(figure 5.26). Can you see why this should be The outcrops of dipping beds are curved, unlike those of horizontal beds, they cut acr contours. Steeply dipping beds have outcr which do not curve very much as they cross I and valleys, while shallow beds have stror curved outcrops. In valleys the outcrop of inclined bed takes on a V-shape which points the valley if the bed dips up the valley, a down the valley if the bed dips down the va (figure 5.24). The outcrop curves in the oppo direction across the spurs between valleys. straight slopes the outcrop is also straight. Fig 5.28 shows how outcrop width is determined dip and ground form.

The outcrops of planar structures such as fau and surfaces of unconformity behave in the sa way as the bottom surface of a bed. A vertical fa has a straight outcrop whereas an inclined fa has a curved outcrop. Since thrusts are low-an faults their outcrops are very wavy. How do y think unconformities will appear on ma Usually, the discordance between the youn beds above the plane of unconformity and older beds below the plane can be detected differences in strike and dip between the two rc groups. Also, the older rocks may have be folded, faulted or intruded by igneous rocks befc the newer rocks were deposited on top of the (figure 5.27).

Weathering and erosion sometimes act to lea isolated outcrops surrounded by older or young rocks. Where a rock type is surrounded by olc rocks it is said to form an **outlier** and where it surrounded by younger rocks it forms an **inli** (figure 5.29).

Making geological maps

Mapping is an important part of geologic fieldwork. To help you to understand geologic maps you would find it very useful to make simple map of an area near your home. Beside being properly dressed for the field you will nee the following equipment; a geological hammer, chisel, safety spectacles, a compass, a clinomete a hand lens, a small notebook with strong cover.

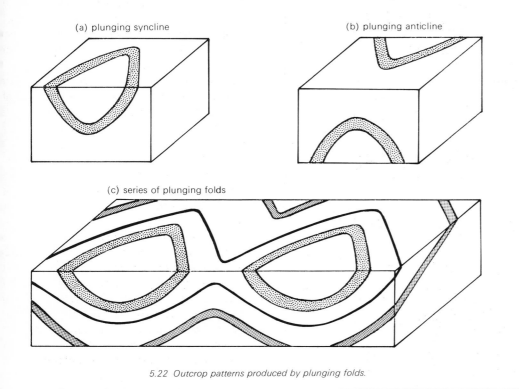

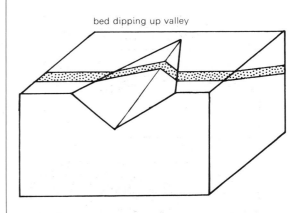

(a) plunging syncline

(b) plunging anticline

(c) series of plunging folds

5.22 Outcrop patterns produced by plunging folds.

bed dipping up valley

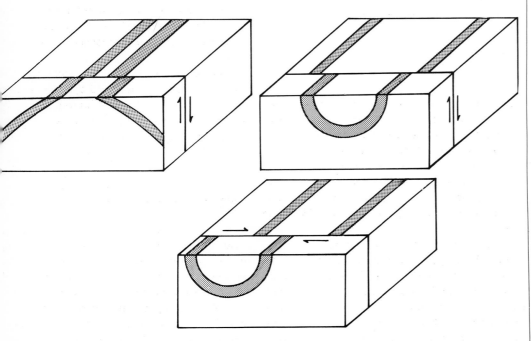

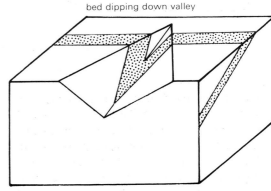

5.23 Some outcrop patterns produced by folds which have been faulted.

bed dipping down valley

5.24 The outcrop patterns of inclined beds in valleys. The outcrop forms a V-shape which points in the direction of dip.

72

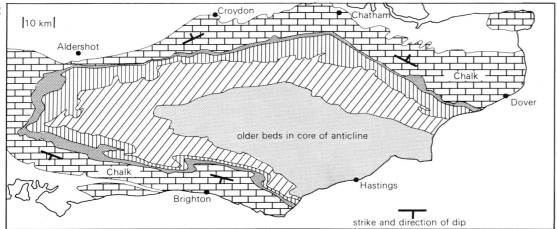

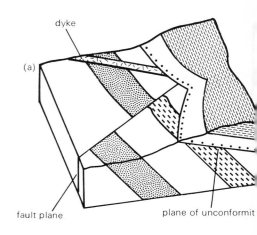

dyke

(a)

fault plane — plane of unconformit

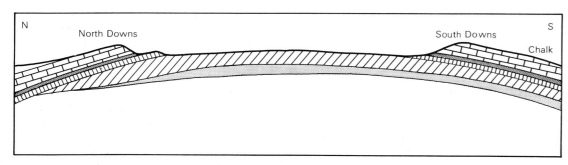

N   North Downs   South Downs   S

Chalk

5.25 (a) The Wealden Anticline.

(b) Section through the Wealden Anticline from north to south.

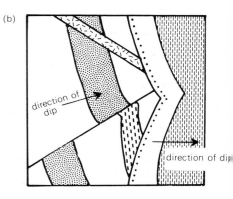

(b)

direction of dip

direction of dip

5.27 Showing the relationship between rocks above and be a plane of unconformity (a) as they appear in solid form as they would appear on a map.

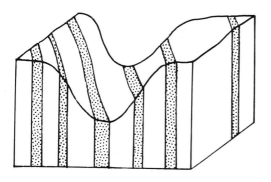

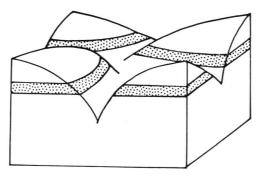

5.26 Outcrops on uneven ground. (a) Vertical beds run across hills and valleys without changing direction. (b) Horizontal beds run around hills and along valley sides.

some pens and pencils and a map on a scale about 1 in 10 000. You should also be familiar w the contents of the pamphlet *A Code Geological Field Work* which is issued by Geologists' Association. This code requests t 'Geologists must be seen to use the countrys with responsibility'. Among other things means that you should not cause trouble landowners, you should not disturb livestock wildlife, and you should not take any risks w your own or anyone else's safety.

To construct your map you should find draw in the exposures in the area you are study Every exposure should be examined in detail all observations on such things as strike and

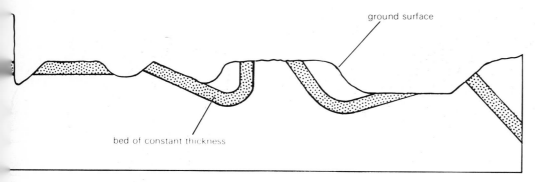

5.28 The width of an outcrop depends on dip and ground form.

k type and the directions of rock boundaries ould be noted carefully. Do not waste exposures hammering too much and do not collect any re rock specimens than are absolutely essary. On your map you can draw in visible undaries between rock types and you can enter details of strike and dip. You can show different k types in different colours. In the field you ould also make observations on such things as ges, which might indicate the presence of derlying hard rock; depressions, which could icate the presence of soft rock or a fault line; Is, which often contain fragments of the underlying rock; sudden changes in vegetation, which may indicate changes of rock type; springs, which often appear where an impervious bed is overlain by a pervious bed, or along the line of a fault; and stream bed material, which may give clues about the rock types upstream.

Your field map may end up looking something like figure 5.30(a). The next step is to complete the drawing of the rock boundaries between exposures. This is done with dashed lines because you cannot be absolutely certain of their positions. The result is a map like figure 5.30(b) Note that a fault has been inserted. The fault line was indicated in the field by a river valley and a depression. The final step is to copy the boundaries onto a new map as shown in figure 5.30(c). An explanatory key should be given with the map so that other people know what the various symbols and colours represent.

When the map has been completed you can write the geological history of the area. Can you identify the four main events in the history of the area shown in figure 5.30(c)? Firstly, a sequence of sedimentary rocks has been laid down; secondly, these beds have been folded; thirdly, faulting has occurred; and finally, a dyke has been intruded. Field notes can be used to make the history much more detailed.

A useful addition to a geological history is a geological section drawn through the area. A section is the view which would be seen if the area could be cut vertically downwards. The sides and ends of the models which you have made previously were sections. To construct a section you first draw a section showing the ground surface along a line on the map. On this, you mark the positions of the geological boundaries with their dips. Then you simply draw the boundaries underground. A section from A to B on figure 5.30(c) is shown in figure 5.31.

It is important that you are familiar with geological maps. Besides working on the problem maps supplied by your teacher you should look at maps published by the Institute of Geological Sciences. These maps, drawn to various scales, cover the geology of the whole of Britain.

Structure and scenery

You will remember that landscapes are shaped by processes such as weathering, erosion and deposition. However, some rocks are more resistant to erosion than others. Which rocks do you think will be more resistant–crystalline or fragmental; massive or bedded; and jointed or unjointed? In landscapes, the more resistant rocks tend to stand out as hills whereas the less resistant rocks may be eroded away to form depressions. We have already seen an example of this in the crag and tail landform. Can you remember how this landform was produced?

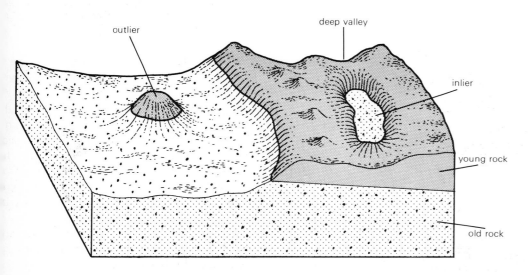

5.29 An outlier and an inlier.

74

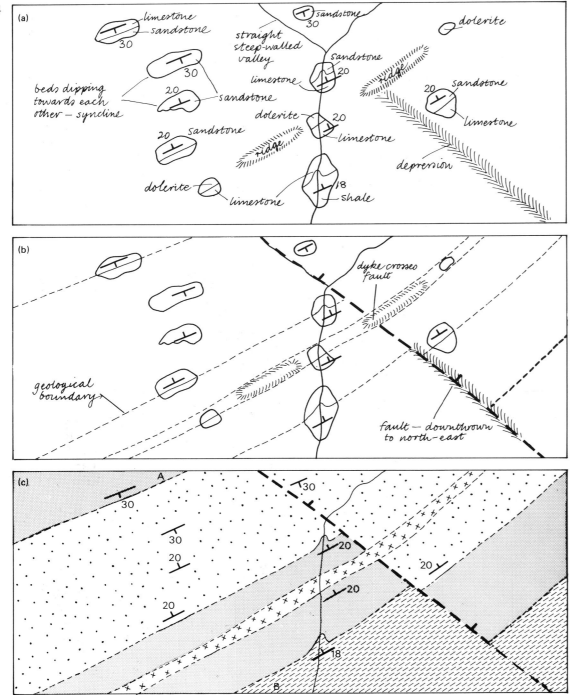

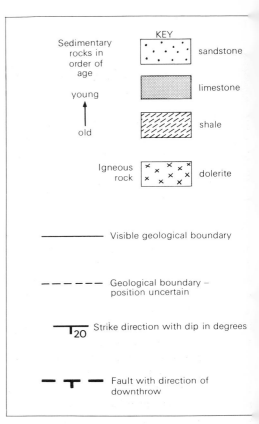

KEY

Sedimentary rocks in order of age

young ↑ old

	sandstone
	limestone
	shale

Igneous rock

| | dolerite |

———— Visible geological boundary

– – – – Geological boundary – position uncertain

⊤20 Strike direction with dip in degrees

▬ ▬ ⊥ ▬ ▬ Fault with direction of downthrow

5.30 Making a geological map (for simplicity this represents nearly level ground).
(a) Field map showing exposures outlined with field c
(b) Field map with probable positions of hid geological boundaries and with a fault inserted.
(c) Completed geological map with key explaining symbols used.

In addition to the resistance of the rocks erosion, the landscape is influenced by the dip the rock layering and by the presence of faults a folds. Where gently-dipping beds form an ou crop, the less resistant beds may be removed, lea ing the more resistant beds projecting to form steep **scarp** and a less steep **dip slope**. A vertic or steeply-dipping resistant bed may project a ridge or **hog's back**. In coastal areas the shapes cliffs may partly be determined by the dip of t beds. Beds dipping into the sea tend to form lo

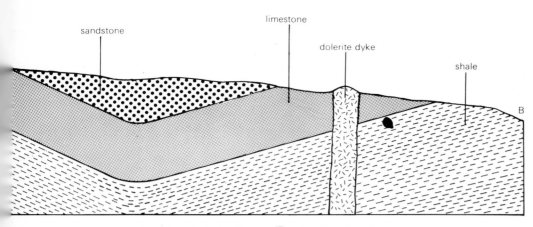

5.31 A geological section from A to B in figure 5.30 (c).

to erosion (figure 5.32(a) and (b)). When drainage patterns are established on rocks above a plane of unconformity, the rivers cut down into the rocks below the unconformity and they keep their form despite the change in rock structure. A drainage pattern such as this which is not controlled by the underlying rock structure is called a **superimposed** pattern (figure 5.32(d).

The forms of coastlines may be strongly influenced by the strike of the coastal rocks. In south-west Ireland the strike is at a high angle to the coast so that the rocks stick out into the sea like long fingers. A coastline such as this is said to be of **transverse** type. In Yugoslavia the rocks strike parallel to the shore giving a **longitudinal** type of coastline.

's because weathered blocks can easily slip n the rock face into the water. Beds dipping ay from the sea may form cliffs with a stepped earance, and vertical cliffs may develop in stant beds lying horizontally.

n a fault zone, the rocks may be broken up to m a rock called **fault breccia**. Fault breccia is ily eroded so the outcrop of the fault may be rked by a depression. On the shore, wave sion may pick out caves and narrow inlets ng faults. A significant effect of faulting is that it y bring resistant and less resistant rocks ether. Erosion may then remove the less istant rock more quickly, leaving the line of the lt marked by a scarp.

Although anticlines are upfolds and synclines downfolds, you should not be misled into nking that anticlines always form hills and nclines always form valleys. In fact, the action of sion on folded strata very often leaves the nclinally folded rocks higher than the anticlines. lding causes repetition of beds at the surface. sion may leave the resistant beds protruding as eries of ridges. On a landscape such as this the th followed by rivers is often dictated by the ections of the ridges. The drainage pattern oduced is called a **trellis** pattern (figure 32(c)). Other drainage patterns may also give an dication of the rock structure. For example, dial patterns tend to develop on cone-shaped ountains and **dendritic** ('tree-like') patterns rm on areas of rock which have equal resistance

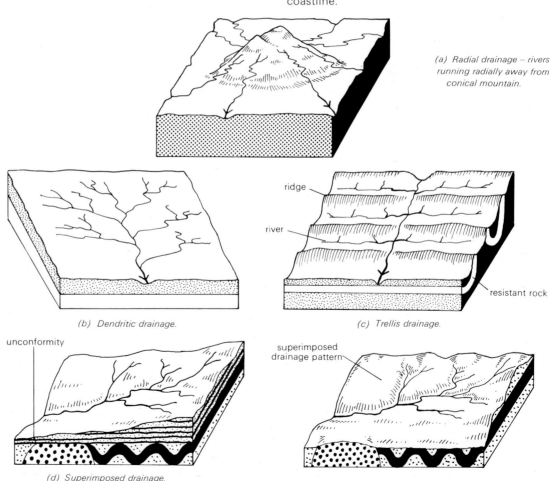

(a) Radial drainage – rivers running radially away from conical mountain.

(b) Dendritic drainage.

(c) Trellis drainage.

(d) Superimposed drainage.

5.32 Drainage patterns.

76   In this section we have looked at a few examples of how the structures of rocks and their differing resistances to weathering and erosion can influence the landforms developed. Careful observation of landforms in the field may tell you quite a lot about the underlying rock structure.

Large-scale Earth movements

Carefully examine the shapes of South America and Africa on a globe. Do the two shapes suggest anything to you? Make tracings of the shapes and cut them out. Now see if you can fit them together. You should find that the two continents fit together reasonably well along their coastlines (figure 5.33(a)). But do coastlines represent the edges of continents? What would happen if you considered the true edge of the continent to be part of the way down the continental slope? Figures 5.33(b) and (c) show the continents with their surrounding shelves and the continental slope down to a depth of about 1000 metres. Make tracings of these and fit them together. What do you find this time? You should find that a much better fit is obtained (figure 5.33(d)). Does the fact that South America and Africa fit together so well suggest anything to you? You might say that it seems reasonable to suggest that South America and Africa were once part of the same land mass and that this huge continent has split apart at some time in the Earth's history. This idea has given rise to suggestions that South America, Africa and the other continents have moved over the surface of the Earth. The suggested movement is called **continental drift**.

Besides the apparent fit of their shapes, is there any other evidence which suggests that South America and Africa were once joined? Can you think of any other types of evidence which could be looked for? You could begin by comparing the rock types on the two continents to see if they are similar. Look at figure 5.34(a); shield areas in South America and Africa seem to match both in terms of position and age. Between the shield areas old worn-down mountain or **orogenic** belts appear to run in similar directions.

Over parts of South America and Africa there are thick layers of ancient glacial deposits. There are

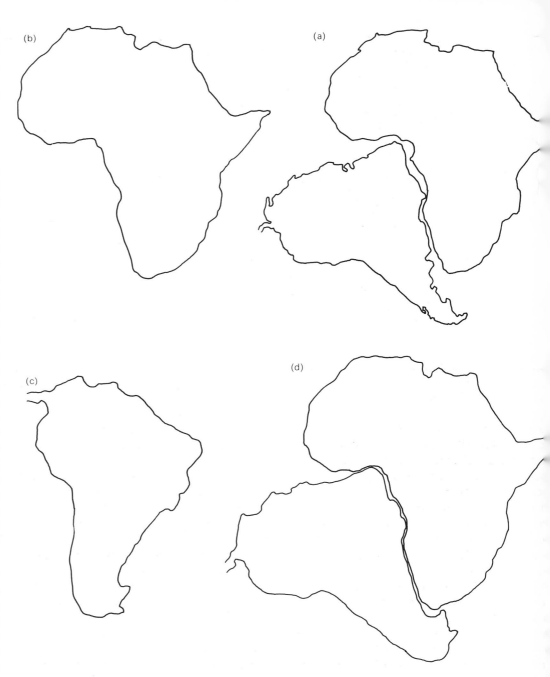

5.33 *Fitting Africa and South America together.*
(a) Coastline fit.
(b) and (c) – Africa and South America shown with their continental slopes down to 1000m.
(d) Improved fit obtained by placing (b) and (c) together.

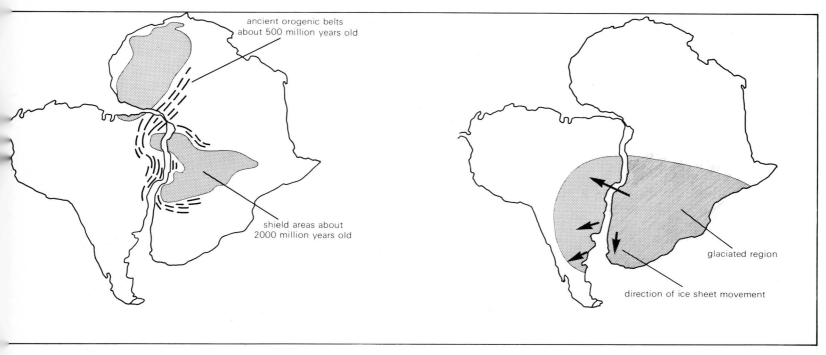

5.34 (a) Geological matching of Africa and South America.

(b) Matching indicated by glaciation of 250 million years ago. At this time the continents seem to have been near the South Pole.

areas of glacial erosion. This glaciation took place about 250 million years ago–some directions of ice flow are shown in figure 5.34(b). These directions indicate that some of the South American deposits may have come from Africa, and indeed some of the erratics found in Brazil are of rock types otherwise found only in Africa. The glaciation suggests that both continents were near the South Pole 250 million years ago, and that they have drifted north and separated since then. Another line of evidence which suggests that South America and Africa were once joined lies in the similarity of ancient plants and animals now preserved as fossils. An example of this is the small, lake-living reptile called *Mesosaurus*. Remains of this reptile are only found in rocks about 300 million years old, in both South America and Africa. Since this reptile could not have crossed a wide sea it seems reasonable to suggest that the continents were joined or were very close 300 million years ago.

More evidence comes from the study of ancient magnetism. It is possible to work out the positions of South America and Africa with respect to the South Pole. This sort of data indicates that the continents were close together until about 125 million years ago. After this time the continents had different positions relative to the pole.

The final piece of evidence comes from the study of sedimentary rock sequences laid down on the edges of Brazil and West Africa between 140 and 100 million years ago. The sequences are so similar that the rocks appear to have been deposited in the same area. This may have been in shallow seas between the continents as they began to move apart.

So far we have considered continental drift only in terms of South America and Africa. Although the evidence collected applies mostly to these continents, similar (but not as good) evidence for drift also comes from the other continents. For example, glacial deposits of the same age as those of South America and Africa are found in Australia and India. Also, the rocks of Antarctica, Australia and India show many similarities.

It is possible to fit together the southern continents along with India, Sri Lanka, New Zealand and Madagascar to make one single land mass. This huge continent called **Gondwanaland** (figure 5.35) is thought to have existed until about 200 million years ago before it began to break up. The northern continents also fit together quite well to make a continent called **Laurasia** (figure 5.36) which seems to have been breaking up for about the last 130 million years. Before the separate existence of Gondwanaland and Laurasia it is thought that they together formed a single continent called **Pangaea** (figure 5.37). Pangaea seems to have been formed by the drifting together of separate land masses about 300 million years ago, and it existed for about 100 million years.

But how do continents move? To see if you can answer this question look at the following facts:

(i) Oceanic ridges are areas where earthquakes and basaltic volcanism are common.
(ii) The ridges have rift valleys running up their centres.

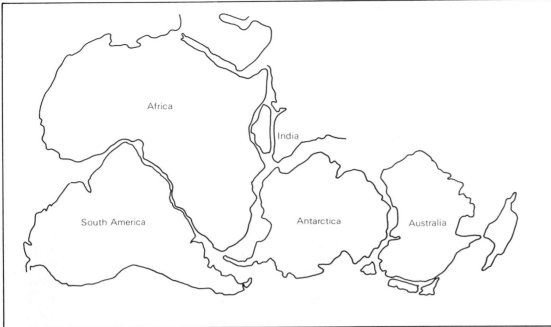

5.35 *The huge continent of Gondwanaland made by fitting together the southern continents.*

Considerations like these led to the sugges[tion] in 1960 that the oceans form by growing from [the] oceanic ridges. As the oceans widen [the] continents are pushed apart (figure 5.38). [This] process of ocean growth was called **sea-fl[oor] spreading**. The suggested mechanism of s[ea] floor spreading was shown to be correct by st[udy] of the magnetism of the basaltic rock beside [the] ridges. As the basalts are extruded they cool [and] become weakly magnetized in a way which sh[ows] the direction and strength of the Earth's magn[etic] field at the time of solidification. It was found [that] the basalts showed normal and rever[se] magnetization in opposite patterns of strips [on] each side of the oceanic ridge (figure 5.39). W[hat] does this mean? It seems that the basalts on e[ach] side of the ridge were intruded into the ridge, t[hat] they were magnetized before being broken in t[wo] and moved apart (figure 5.40). In the Atla[ntic] about 2 centimetres of material is being added [to] each side of the Mid-Atlantic Ridge every y[ear].

(iii) Sediments on the oceanic ridges are very thin. Towards the continents the oceanic sediments become thicker and older.

(iv) Oceanic crust is made up of relatively young rocks—nowhere are they more than about 200 million years old.

Do these facts suggest anything to you? The volcanic activity means that new material is being added to the oceanic crust along the ridges. The large number of earthquakes indicates that the ridges are zones of crustal weakness where frequent movements are taking place. These movements may be related to the presence of the rift valleys which run along the ridges. Since rift valleys are formed by forces pulling the rocks apart, the rifts may indicate that the sides of the ridges are moving away from each other. The absence of sediment on the ridges suggests that the ridges have not been in existence long enough for them to be covered. Since oceanic sediments accumulate slowly, the thicker deposits away from the ridges may indicate that the ocean floor near the continents is older than the ocean floor near the ridges.

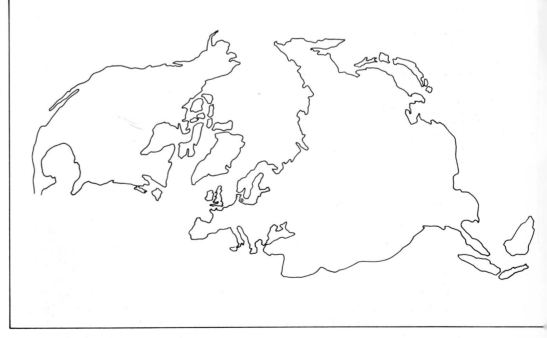

5.36 *The giant continent of Laurasia.*

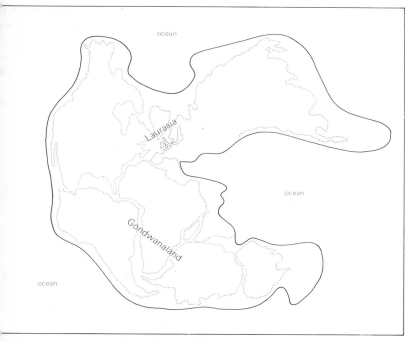

5.37 *The giant continent of Pangaea formed by the coming together of all the land masses about 300 million years ago.*

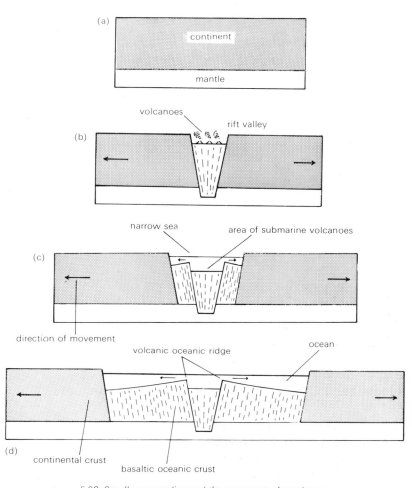

5.38 *Sea-floor spreading and the movement of continents.*

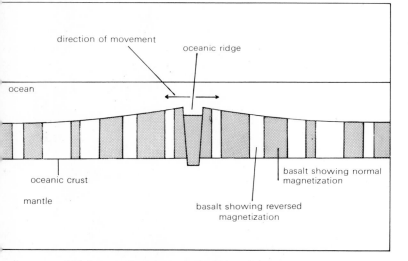

5.39 *Patterns of rock magnetization in the sea floor on each side of an oceanic ridge.*

his means that the Atlantic is growing wider by 4 centimetres a year. Spreading rates do, however, ary quite a lot. The fastest spreading rates are ound in the Pacific, which in places is growing vider at a rate of 18 centimetres a year.

It has also been found that the crests of oceanic ridges are frequently offset by large faults which look like tear faults (figure 5.41). Copy part of figure 5.42 and, using arrows, draw in what you think are the movement directions on the faults.

However, study of these faults has shown that, as a result of the spreading movements from the oceanic ridges, the rocks on each side of the faults are actually moving in the opposite direction to that expected (figure 5.43). Because of this these faults could not be called tear faults; they have been named **transform faults**.

Since the oceans are growing wider, this either means that the Earth is getting larger quite quickly, or that the added material is somewhere sinking back into the mantle. It seems reasonable to

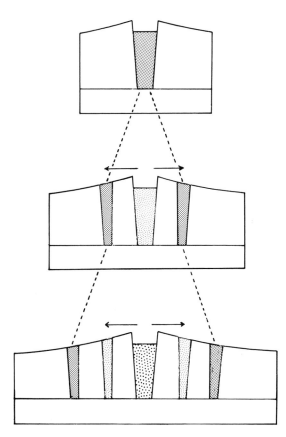

5.40 *Movement of material away from the oceanic ridge has been proved by study of ancient rock magnetism.*

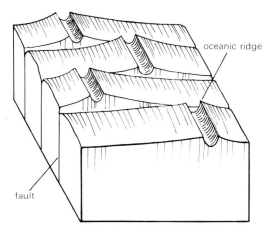

5.41 *Oceanic ridges are frequently offset along large faults.*

suggest that the sinking of large rock masses would be accompanied by the sort of movements indicated by earthquakes and volcanoes. There is a great deal of earthquake and volcanic activity associated with oceanic trenches and it seems that oceanic material is swallowed or **subducted** down sloping zones called **Benioff Zones** which descend under oceanic trenches (figure 5.44). As the oceanic material sinks, part of it melts to give andesitic magma which rises and is extruded through volcanoes in the island arcs and mountain chains above the Benioff Zones.

So far, then, we have seen that the continents are moving over the surface of the Earth, that the oceans grow by the addition of material along their oceanic ridges, and that oceanic material is consumed beneath oceanic trenches. Could it b that all of these different processes are really jus parts of a single large-scale process? If you look a figure 5.45 you will see that the Earth can b divided up like a jigsaw into six large sections (an a few smaller ones) separated by areas c earthquake and volcanic activity (compare thi diagram with figures 2.12 and 4.6). Thes sections, which may include both continental an oceanic crust, are called **plates** and the study c the movements taking place between them i called **plate tectonics**.

There are three ways in which plates can mov with respect to each other—they can move awa from each other, towards each other or past eac other. Where plates move away from each othe

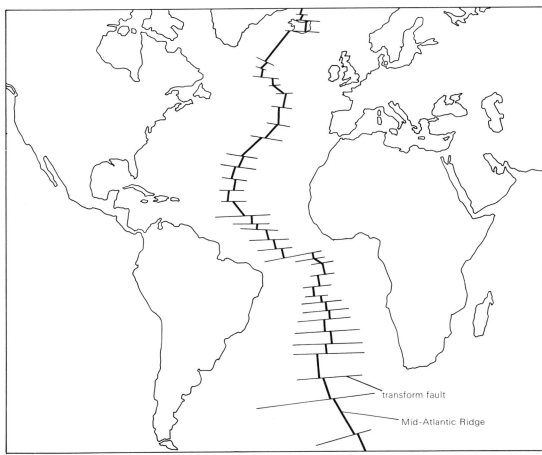

5.42 *The Atlantic Ocean showing how the Mid-Atlantic Ridge is offset by large transform faults.*

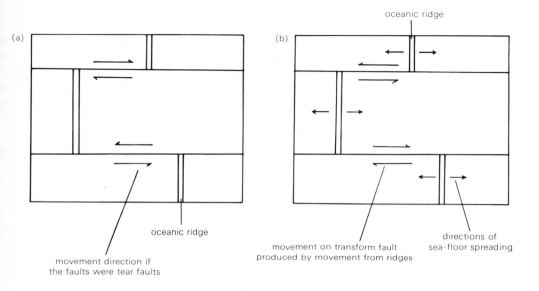

(a)

oceanic ridge

movement direction if
the faults were tear faults

5.43 The faults which offset the ridges are transform faults
whose movement is opposite to that of tear faults.

(b)

oceanic ridge

movement on transform fault
produced by movement from ridges

directions of
sea-floor spreading

Mountains are thought to have been formed in this way by the movement of the Pacific Plate under the American Plate. Besides crumpling the rocks, this type of plate collision gives rise to andesitic volcanism, regional metamorphism deep in the mountain roots, and the formation of granites which rise as batholiths (figure 5.46(b)). Thirdly, continental crust may meet continental crust. This again leads to the formation of mountains; for example, the Himalayas may have been formed by the collision of the Asian and Indian Plates in the way shown in figure 5.46(c).

When plates slide past each other the edges of the plates are neither built up nor destroyed. Because of this, the plate boundaries are described as being **conservative**. Conservative boundaries are formed by the transform faults which are mostly found associated with oceanic ridges. A well-known transform fault which appears on land is the San Andreas fault of western North America. This fault is carrying the Pacific Plate north-west past the American Plate at a rate of about 5 centimetres a year. The fault system ends in Alaska

e space between them is filled by new material ought up by volcanic activity. In this way the dges of the plates are built up. Plate building kes place in oceanic ridges, and such areas are lled **sources** or **constructive plate oundaries**.

When plates move towards each other one plate des below the other at an angle of about 45° wn a **subduction** or **Benioff Zone**. The nking plate melts as it moves down and it is ventually taken back into the mantle.

Areas in which plates collide are called **sinks** or estructive plate boundaries. Since plates ay contain both oceanic and continental crust, ate collision may take place in three ways. Firstly, ceanic crust may meet oceanic crust. When this appens an island arc built up of andesitic lavas ke that of the Philippines) forms above the bduction zone (figure 5.46(a)). Secondly, ceanic crust may meet continental crust. In this se, the margin of the continental plate is umpled up by the force of the collision into a ountain or **orogenic belt**. The Andes

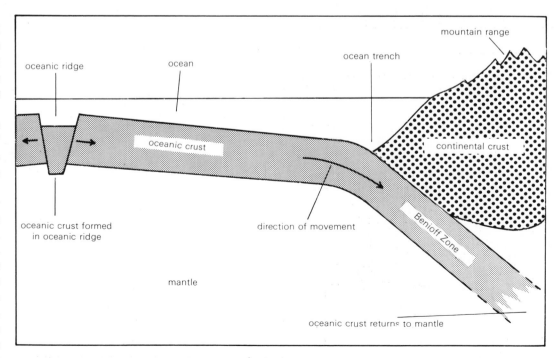

5.44 The oceanic crust is swallowed down Benioff Zones
which descend under oceanic trenches.

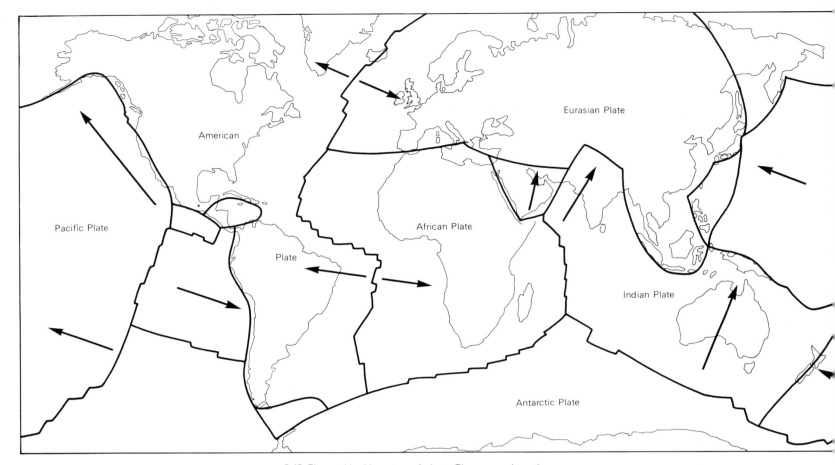

5.45 *The world-wide system of plates. The arrows show the directions of plate movement.*

where the Pacific Plate slides under the Aleutian Island Arc. In 1906, movement on a fault close to the San Andreas fault produced an earthquake which destroyed San Francisco.

The idea of plate tectonics tells us a great deal about the Earth. It tells us, for example, why the ocean floor is much younger than many parts of the continents. Oceanic crust is continuously being produced at the oceanic ridges and destroyed under the oceanic trenches. This means that it does not exist for very long. On the other hand, continental crust is not dense enough to sink into the mantle so it can exist for very long periods of time. Plate tectonics also tells us why earthquakes and volcanoes are mostly found in narrow strips on the Earth's surface. These narrow zones are where the moving edges of the plates meet. The movements give rise to earthquakes, and magma can easily rise up through the weak crustal areas at the plate edges. When plates collide mountain ranges are built up by the buckling of plate margins. Under the mountains the rocks are heated and squeezed so that they undergo regional metamorphism; this heating also produces andesitic and granitic magma. Plate tectonics also tells us that when continents drift they do not move about by themselves like rafts on water. Instead, they are simply carried along on the backs of moving plates. We shall see later (Unit 7) that plate tectonics can also give us an idea of where to look for such things as oil and ore minerals. Overall, the concept of plate tectonics is a very important idea because it shows us that such things as continental drift, sea-floor spreading and mountain building are all just part of a single large-scale process.

As yet no one is quite sure where the enormous forces come from which cause the plates to move. One suggestion is that the plates are driven by **convection currents** in the mantle. Earthquake evidence has shown that the mantle is partly molten at a depth of between about 70 and 150 kilometres. The plates may be driven by underlying convection currents running through the whole mantle, or it may be that the currents flow only in the partly molten upper layer. Other suggestions to account for plate movement have also been made. One is that as a plate sinks down a subduction zone it pulls the rest of the plate with it. Another is that the plates just slide off the oceanic ridges and down into the sinks under the action of gravity.

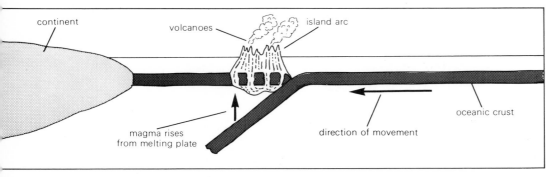

a) When oceanic plate meets oceanic plate an island arc is formed.

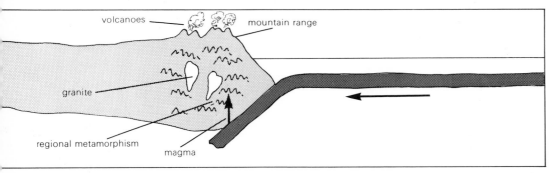

b) When oceanic plate meets continental plate the edge of the continent is crumpled to form a mountain range.

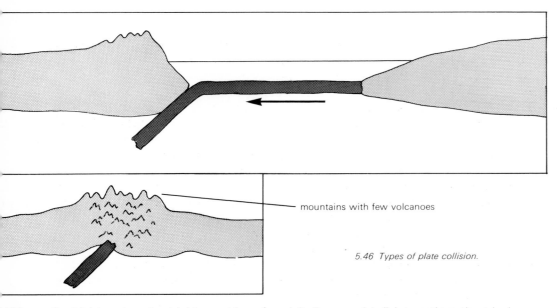

5.46 Types of plate collision.

c) When continental plate meets continental plate mountains are formed after the ocean originally between the continents has been destroyed.

UNIT 6

Earth History

Geological time

Since its formation about 4600 million years ago, the Earth has gone through a great many changes. Continents have formed and grown (and are still growing); plate movements have opened and closed oceans and driven the continents around the surface of the Earth; mountains have been pushed up by colliding plates and worn down by weathering and erosion; and life forms have appeared and changed through the ages. Many of the events which have taken place in ancient times have left their marks on the Earth, and just as we can place the reigns of kings and queens in order in human history, so we can place geological events in order by studying **historical geology** or **stratigraphy**. One way of doing this is to look at the relationships between rocks. If you find a limestone lying on top of a sandstone, you can say that the limestone is younger than the

sandstone because it has been laid down on top of it. (This is assuming that the rocks have not been turned over by folding.) Continuing upwards, you would find younger and younger rocks laid in layers; such a sequence of sedimentary rocks is called a succession. Suppose you find a dyke intruded into the succession. What can you say about the age of the igneous rock? Intrusions are always younger than the rocks through which they cut, and faults are always younger than the rocks which they break apart.

By studying the successions which have formed through geological time we can place sedimentary rocks in order of deposition into a sequence called the **geological** or **stratigraphical column**. This is shown in table 6.1. You will see that the sedimentary rocks have been separated into large groups called **systems**; for example, all Cambrian rocks are part of the Cambrian system and all Jurassic rocks are part of the Jurassic system.

We can also divide up geological time. Lo[ng] intervals of time are called **eras**. The longest era [is] the Precambrian which lasted for about 400[0] million years, from the formation of the Earth un[til] about 570 million years ago. Following t[he] Precambrian came the Palaeozoic era which last[ed] for about 350 million years and then the Mesozo[ic] era which lasted for about 160 million years. W[e] are at present in the Cainozoic era which has last[ed] for the past 65 million years. Eras are divided in[to] shorter time intervals called **periods**. For exampl[e] the Mesozoic era is divided into the Triass[ic] Jurassic and Cretaceous periods (table 6.1). Y[ou] will see that the systems and periods are describ[ed] by the same names this is because all the rocks [of] the Cambrian system were laid down during t[he] 70 million years of the Cambrian period, and t[he] rocks of the Jurassic system were laid dow[n] during the 55 million years of the Jurassic perio[d] and so on. We can estimate how long eras a[nd]

ERAS	SYSTEMS OR PERIODS	MILLIONS OF YEARS BEFORE PRESENT
Cainozoic	Quaternary	
	Tertiary	— 2.5 —
		— 65 —
Mesozoic	Cretaceous	
		— 136 —
	Jurassic	
		— 190 —
	Triassic	
		— 225 —
Palaeozoic	Permian	
		— 280 —
	Carboniferous	
		— 345 —
	Devonian	
		— 395 —
	Silurian	
		— 430 —
	Ordovician	
		— 500 —
	Cambrian	
		— 570 —
Precambrian		
		— 4600 —

Table 6.1 The Stratigraphical Column.

iods have lasted because we can determine the
e of rocks by measuring the changes of cer-
n elements contained in them. Some ele-
nts are radioactive—this means that as time
es past they slowly alter into other elements. By
culating how much of the original element has
nged, the age of the rock in which the new
ment is found can be worked out. In this way
can estimate the ages of rocks which are
ions of years old.

he stratigraphical column has been put
ether using the evidence of successions from
ny areas—you will never find rocks of all ages in
particular place. Rocks are continuously being
ken down under the action of weathering and
sion, therefore rocks may have been deposited
one time and completely removed later. This
ans that the successions which we are left with

today may only represent small parts of what once
existed. Also, the further back we go in time the
more fragmentary the rock record becomes. Can
you see why this should be so?

Besides looking at rocks, we can obtain a great
deal of very useful information which can help us
to interpret the geological past by studying the
remains of past life forms. Let us now look at
ancient plants and animals.

Fossils

The preserved traces of animals and plants
found in rocks are called **fossils**. What happens to
an animal when it dies? The soft parts may rot
away or be eaten by other animals but the hard
parts such as shells or bones may be left behind.
Because of this most fossils are the remains of the

hard parts of organisms; soft parts are only rarely
preserved. Also, for an organism to be preserved it
must be covered by sediment soon after it dies,
therefore preservation is much more likely in areas
of deposition than in areas of erosion. Since land
areas usually suffer erosion while deposition takes
place in most parts of the sea, this means that
fossils of land organisms are much less common
than fossils of marine organisms. But all marine
animals do not have the same chance of being
preserved. For example, animals such as limpets
which live attached to rocks on the shore will only
be preserved if their shells are washed into areas of
deposition. On the other hand, cockles live buried
in beach sand so many of them may be preserved
in their living positions after they die. Also, floating
and swimming organisms are less likely to be
preserved than organisms which live on the
bottom of the sea. Can you suggest why this
should be so? Because some organisms may have
quite a good chance of being preserved, while
others are never or hardly ever preserved, the
fossils found at any time in the geological past
represent only a small proportion of the plants and
animals which lived at the time. Different types of
organism are not equally represented in the fossil
record. Most fossils are those of marine animals
with hard parts. Land animals and animals with
soft parts only are not often found as fossils.

The process by which organic remains are
turned into fossils is called **fossilization**; it can
take place in a number of ways. Sometimes hard
parts such as shells and teeth are preserved
without being changed. More often, however, the
hard parts are altered by being **replaced** by some
other material. For example, fossilized bones are
not often found as bone. Instead, the bone is
slowly replaced by minerals such as calcite or
quartz which are deposited from water in the
surrounding sediment. Replacement often
preserves the original structure of the organic
material in near-perfect detail. Fossils are also
found as **impressions** which are marks in rocks
left by organic remains which have been removed,
perhaps by being dissolved away by ground water.
Press a shell into some plasticine. When you
remove the shell what you see in the plasticine is
an impression of the shell. If you pour some plaster

of Paris into the impression you should be able to make a good copy of the shell. **Trace fossils** are marks left behind by organisms; they include footprints and burrows.

Plants and animals

Here are a few common plants and animals: daisy, dog, seaweed, trout, locust, frog, crab, moss, sea-urchin, snake, mushroom, sparrow, worm, fern, mussel, pine tree, spider, jellyfish, amoeba, snail and octopus. Examine as many of these organisms as possible and try to make up a key which divides them into sets and sub-sets. For example, you could begin by dividing the plants into those which produce seeds and those which do not produce seeds, and you could divide the animals into those with backbones and those with no backbones. To divide the organisms into further groups look for the presence of such things as green colour and roots in plants, and shells and jointed outer skeletons in animals. Your key might end up looking like table 6.2, which contains the names of the main plant and animal groups along with a few examples of the organisms in the groups.

Plants and animals are divided into large groups called **phyla** (singular phylum) which are then divided into smaller groups called **classes**. For example, the molluscs form a phylum which is made up of three main classes; these are the **gastropods** (snail, whelk, limpet, winkle), the **lamellibranchs** or **bivalves** (mussel, cockle, oyster) and the **cephalopods** (octopus, squid, cuttlefish). The name of any type of organism is written in two parts which are both in Latin; for example, the cockle is *Cardium edule*, the mussel is *Mytilus edulis* and the oyster is *Ostrea edulis*. The first name (which always begins with a capital letter) is that of the **genus** to which the organism belongs. A genus is a small group used to classify organisms. The organisms in a genus are all fairly similar—for example, there are different kinds of cockle but they all belong to the same genus. The second name (which always begins with a small letter) is the name of the **species** to which the organism belongs. A species is a group whose

members are all of the same type; human beings all belong to the same species. A genus may be made up of many species; for example, *Littorina neritoides* (the small winkle), *Littorina saxatilis* (the rough winkle), *Littorina littoralis* (the flat winkle) and *Littorina littorea* (the common winkle) are the different species making up the genus *Littorina*.

The plants and animals mentioned so far are all living today and they should be quite familiar to you. But when we look back through the many millions of years covered by the fossil record we find some very interesting things. Plants and animals which are living today have not always been in existence—life forms have been changing gradually through time by a process called **evolution**. An example of the kinds of changes which can take place is shown by the evolution of the horse during the last 60 million years. The first horses were small animals about the size of terrier dogs. They had spreading toes and they did not have the jagged teeth found in modern horses. As time passed horses became bigger, the feet became hoofed and the teeth took on a saw-like shape (figure. 6.1).

Another thing the fossil record shows us is that groups of plants and animals often die out completely. When this happens the organism is said to have become **extinct**. This means that organisms commonly found as fossils may not exist today. Examples of extinct organisms are ammonoids, belemnites, trilobites and graptolites. Ammonoids and belemnites are both classed as cephalopods, that is, they are related to the octopus and squid. Ammonoids were marine animals which had coiled, chambered shells. They were quite like the present-day organism *Nautilus*. Belemnites were like cuttlefish and their fossilized remains are their bullet-shaped internal shells. The trilobites were marine arthropods which looked something like enormous woodlice, and graptolites were floating marine animals whose fossil remains often look like pencil drawings on the rock. Graptolites were colonial animals, that is, they were made up of numerous small, individual, but connected, animals housed in separate cup-shaped depressions along the sides of the organism.

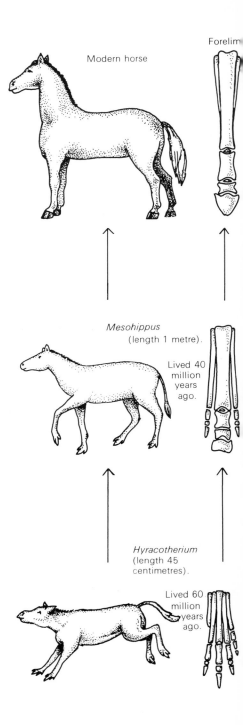

Modern horse

Forelim

Mesohippus (length 1 metre).

Lived 40 million years ago.

Hyracotherium (length 45 centimetres).

Lived 60 million years ago.

6.1 *The evolution of the horse from its primitive anc* Hyracotherium.

87

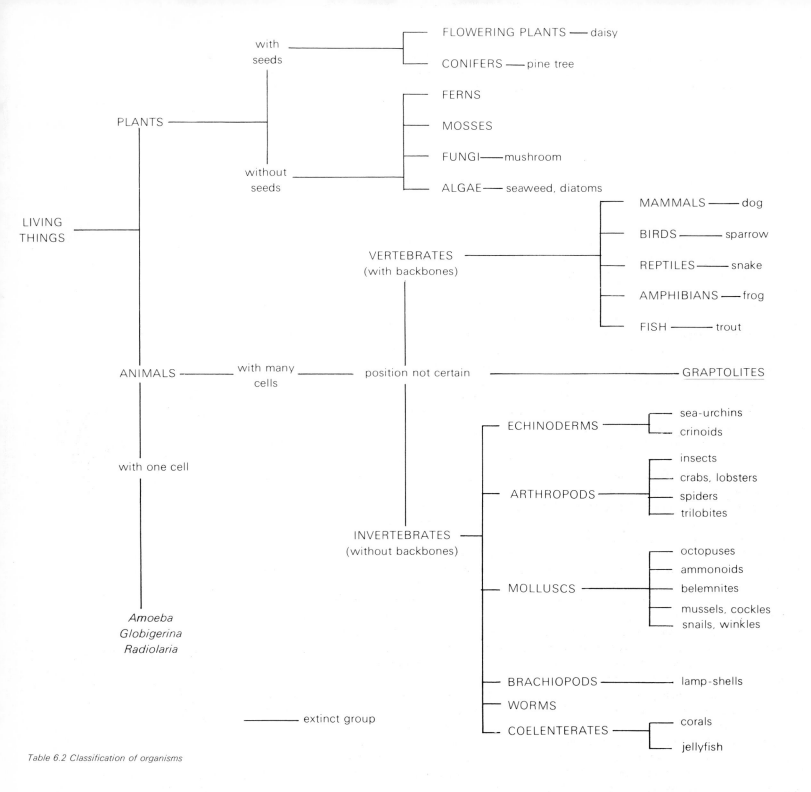

Table 6.2 Classification of organisms

In some cases groups of organisms did not die out completely, so that plants and animals which were once common are today represented by only a few living forms. Good examples of this are the horse-tail plant, the coelacanth fish, lamp-shells and sea-lilies. The horse-tail is a small garden weed whose ancestors about 300 million years ago were huge plants growing in thick forests. See if you can find some horse-tails and examine them to see how they differ from flowering plants. The coelacanth (figure 6.2) belongs to a group of fish which was thought to have been extinct for 65 million years until a coelacanth was discovered in the Indian Ocean in 1938. Lamp-shells or brachiopods are often found as fossils but they are not very common today. Brachiopods are marine animals with two shells which are usually attached to the sea floor by a stalk coming from a round hole in one of the shells. Sea-lilies or crinoids are now rare but they were once very common. Crinoids are related to sea-urchins, that is, they are echinoderms.

Before we look at individual fossils in more detail let us first of all see how life forms have changed through the ages.

The history of life

Life began, probably in the sea, about 3500 million years ago. The first organisms were very simple, perhaps similar to the bacteria of the

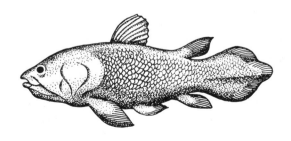

6.2   The coelacanth fish (length 1.5 metres)

present day. About 2500 million years ago simple green plants called **algae** appeared. At this time the Earth's atmosphere contained hardly any oxygen. By the process of photosynthesis green plants take in carbon dioxide and give out oxygen, so as the number of green plants increased so did the amount of oxygen in the air. (At present about 20% of the atmosphere is oxygen.) About 600 million years ago the oxygen had risen to the level of about 2% of the atmosphere which was high enough to allow fairly large, many-celled animals to breathe. In the late Precambrian era trace fossils start to become common and these show that fairly large marine invertebrates were active at that time. Fossil remains are not common because the animals had no hard parts which could be easily preserved. The few fossils which have been found show that the organisms resembled jellyfish and worms.

During the Cambrian period (570–500 million years ago) there was a very rapid increase in the number and variety of large invertebrates. Since many of these animals had hard parts, fossils are fairly common and about one thousand species including molluscs, brachiopods, trilobites and echinoderms have been found in the Lower Cambrian period. The Ordovician period, which began about 500 million years ago, saw a widespread increase in the number of corals and graptolites. In the Devonian period (400–350 million years ago) insects and ammonoids appeared, graptolites became extinct and trilobites declined in number. During the Carboniferous period (350–280 million years ago) corals and crinoids became abundant. Insects were common on land and spiders, millipedes and centipedes appeared. The Permian period (280–225 million years ago) marks the end of the Palaeozoic era and at this time extinctions and near-extinctions were common. Trilobites disappeared along with many corals, brachiopods, and crinoids.

In general, the life forms of the Mesozoic era were very different from those of the Palaeozoic era. The Mesozoic plants and animals became established during the Triassic period (225–190 million years ago). Among the changes which occurred were the increase in the number of bivalves and the rise of belemnites and

ammonoids, while corals developed in for different from those of the Palaeozoic era. T Jurassic period (190–135 million years ago) s the continuation of patterns already set in Triassic period. Ammonoids became very comm and coral reefs developed. At the end of Cretaceous period (135–65 million years ago, a the end of the Mesozoic era), the ammono became extinct and the belemnites almost d out.

In the Tertiary period few changes occur among the marine invertebrates except t squids, octopuses and floating unicellular anim such as *Globigerina* became more common. land, insects increased greatly in number.

The first vertebrates, which were simple t with sucking mouths and no jaws (similar to modern lamprey) appeared in the Mid Ordovician period. These fish (figure 6.3(a which were covered by a thick armour of bt plates, became widespread in the Silurian per but they declined in number at the start Devonian times. **Placoderms** (figure 6.3(t which were armoured fish with jaws, evolved f

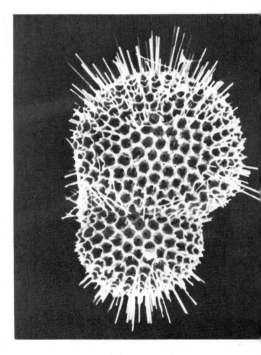

The shell of Globigerina *(× 314)*

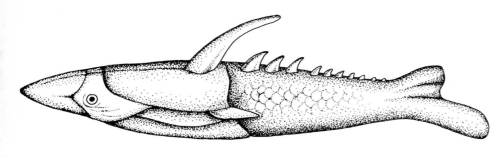

6.3 (a) Pteraspis – a primitive, jawless armour-plated fish (length 15 centimetres).

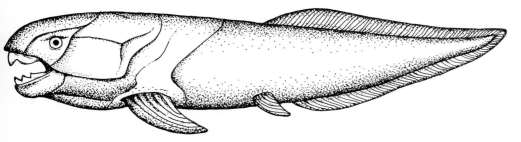

(b) Dinichthys – a gigantic armoured fish with jaws (length 10 metres).

jawless fish in the late Silurian period and were [ex]nct by the end of the Palaeozoic era. Modern [speci]es of fish evolved from the placoderms during [the] Devonian period. There are now two main [typ]es: fish with skeletons of bone (cod, herring, [had]dock, trout, etc.) and fish with skeletons of [cart]ilage (shark, dogfish, skate and ray). Cartilage [is n]ot a material which can easily be fossilized so [cart]ilaginous fish are identified mainly from their [fos]sil teeth. An important group of bony fish are [tho]se with their fins attached to small armlike [lob]es. These fish are represented at present by the [lun]gfish and the coelacanth.

[It] was from the lobe-fin fish that the first [amp]hibians (called **labyrinthodonts**) evolved in [the] late Devonian period. Labyrinthodonts looked [som]ething like large newts (figure 6.4) and they [bec]ame extinct by the end of the Triassic period. [The] first reptiles evolved from the labyrinthodonts [tow]ards the end of the Carboniferous period, and [they] increased greatly in number and type during [the] Permian period as they evolved along three [mai]n branches. The first branch produced the [mam]mal-like reptiles which, although they did not

look like mammals, had skulls, teeth and limbs like those of mammals; they may also have been warm-blooded and hairy like mammals. (Mammals evolved from these reptiles in the Triassic period.) The second evolutionary branch gave rise to modern reptiles such as turtles, snakes

6.4 A primitive amphibian – the labyrinthodont (length 1 metre).

and lizards while the third branch produced **dinosaurs**, flying reptiles called **pterosaurs** (figure 6.5) and the modern crocodiles and alligators. The gigantic dinosaurs ruled the land throughout the Jurassic and Cretaceous periods, while large **plesiosaurs** and **ichthyosaurs** swam in the seas (figure 6.6). Plant-eating dinosaurs included the duck-billed dinosaurs, the long-necked dinosaurs and the horned and armoured dinosaurs. The flesh-eating dinosaurs included the well-known *Tyrannosaurus rex* which was about 6 metres tall (figure 6.8).

The first bird was *Archaeopteryx* (figure 6.7), which evolved during the Jurassic period from small two-legged dinosaurs. *Archaeopteryx* could not fly and the main function of its feathers was probably to keep it warm. It is thought that the first flying birds appeared during the Cretaceous period.

Mesozoic mammals were small animals shaped something like shrews which at their largest were about the size of cats. With the extinction of the giant reptiles at the end of the Cretaceous period, mammals increased and evolved through the Tertiary period to give the great variety of forms which we have today. Human-like features began to appear in our ape ancestors about 14 million years ago. Development remained slow for about 10 million years, but over the last 4 million years more rapid changes brought about the appearance of modern man within the last 500 000 years.

The earliest land plants were ferns and related plants which appeared in the late Silurian period. These seedless plants spread during the Devonian period to form the first forests, and they remained common until the end of the Palaeozoic era. During the Carboniferous period the first **gymnosperms** (primitive seed-bearing plants) evolved from the ferns. They are called seed-ferns because although they had seeds, they looked very like ferns. Seedless plants grew to the size of trees during this period, and along with the seed-ferns they formed thick forests. During the Permian period primitive conifers partly replaced the ferns and other seedless plants, and by the end of the Triassic period gymnosperms had become the dominant land plants. In the Jurassic period palm-like gymnosperms and conifers expanded

6.5   A pterosaur, Pteranodon (wing span 8 metres).

6.7   Archaeopteryx – the first bird (length 30 centimetres).

6.6   Marine reptiles-(a) The skeleton of an ichthyosaur

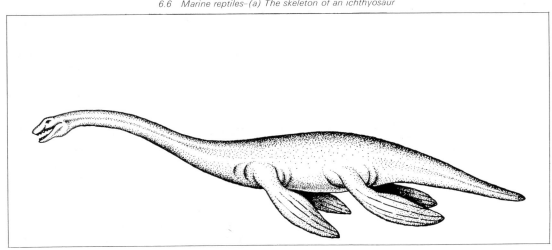

(b) A plesiosaur (length 12 metres).

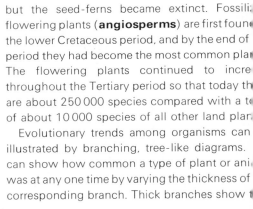

The skeleton of a plesiosaur.

but the seed-ferns became extinct. Fossil flowering plants (**angiosperms**) are first found the lower Cretaceous period, and by the end of period they had become the most common plan The flowering plants continued to incre throughout the Tertiary period so that today th are about 250 000 species compared with a t of about 10 000 species of all other land plan

Evolutionary trends among organisms can illustrated by branching, tree-like diagrams. can show how common a type of plant or ani was at any one time by varying the thickness of corresponding branch. Thick branches show t

A long-necked dinosaur – *Diplodocus*
(length 30 metres)

An armoured dinosaur –
Stegasaurus
(length 6 metres)

Tyrannosaurus rex – a
flesh-eating dinosaur
(height 6 metres)

Triceratops – a horned
dinosaur
(length 10 metres)

Duck-billed dinosaur
Anatosaurus
(length 12 metres)

6.8   Dinosaurs.

the organism was abundant, while thin branches show that the organism was uncommon. Where a branch ends the plant or animal has become extinct. Figures 6.9 and 6.10 show the evolutionary paths of invertebrates, vertebrates and plants.

Now let us look at some examples of common fossils. You will find that the great majority of fossils are those of marine invertebrates which possessed hard parts. Can you say why this is so?

Common fossil types

Coelenterates

Among the coelenterates **corals** are by far the most commonly preserved. Corals are made up of soft parts called **polyps** which are like sea-anemones, and skeletons which have tube-shaped walls divided by horizontal partitions called **tabulae** (singular tabula) and by vertical partitions called **septa** (singular septum). Small oblique partitions called **dissepiments** and a **central column** may be present (figure 6.11(a)). Corals live either as separate individuals (solitary corals) or as compact masses (colonial corals) made up of many separate **corallites** (figure 6.11(b)).

Corals are divided into three groups depending on the structure of the skeleton. Figure 6.11 shows the different types of coral.

(i) **Tabulate corals** have tabulae but septa are either absent or very small. They have no dissepiments or central columns. The tabulate corals are colonial and they are found mostly in Palaeozoic rocks. Examples are *Halysites* (Ordovician-Silurian) and *Favosites* (Ordovician-Carboniferous).

(ii) **Rugose corals** usually have well-developed septa, tabulae and dissepiments, and central columns are often present. Rugose corals are only found in Palaeozoic rocks where they occur as both solitary and colonial forms. Examples are *Zaphrentis* and *Lithostrotion* (both Carboniferous).

(iii) **Scleractinian corals** have well-developed septa but dissepiments, tabulae and central columns are usually not strongly

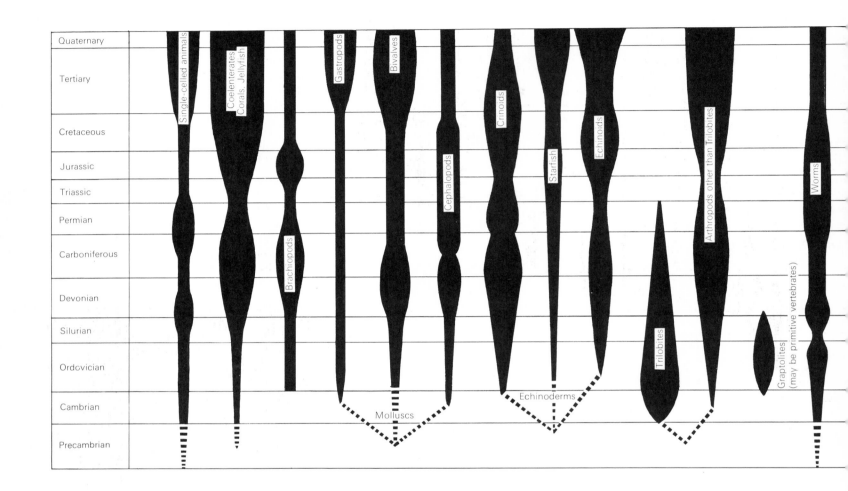

6.9 (a) Geological record of the main invertebrate groups. The column width indicates the abundance of the group.

developed. They occur as colonial and solitary forms from the Triassic period onwards. The reef-building corals of the present day are scleractinian corals. Examples are *Parasmilia* (Cretaceous-present) and *Isastrea* (Jurassic-Cretaceous).

Corals live attached to the sea bed. Present day reef-building corals live to depths of about 50 metres in clear, oxygen-rich seas where the temperature does not fall below 20°C. Because of this coral reefs are mostly restricted to a zone within a latitude of 30° from the equator.

Molluscs

These are commonly known as 'shellfish'. The main groups found as fossils are the **gastropods** (snails, whelks, etc.), the **bivalves** or **lamellibranchs** (cockles, oysters, etc.) and the **cephalopods** (ammonoids and belemnites).

6.9 (b) The main evolutionary trends among the vertebrates.

Present-day scleractinian coral.

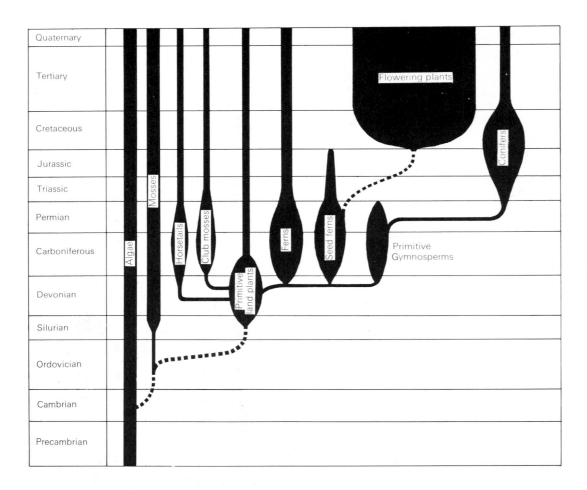

6.10 The main evolutionary trends among plants.

(i) **Gastropods** are mostly marine ani
living on the bottom of the sea, but some
in fresh water and on land. The soft boc
the animal is housed within a shell whi
usually twisted round a central column
a shape like a spire. Each twist of the sh
called a **whorl**, and the whorls ar
contact along lines called **sutures**.
opening of the shell is called the **apert**
If the tip or **apex** of the shell is
upwards, most gastropods have
apertures on the right-hand side. Exam
of gastropods (figure 6.12) are *Bellerop*
(Silurian-Permian). *Turritella*, the tc
shell (Cretaceous-present) and *Buccic*
the common whelk (Tertiary-present).

(ii) **Bivalves**—the soft parts of the anima
enclosed between two **valves** which
along the **hinge**. Each valve usually h
pointed beak or **umbo** (plural umbo
lying just above the hinge. In the hinge t
is an elastic **ligament** which acts to c
the shell. There may also be project
called **hinge teeth** which fit into **soc**
in the opposite valve. The shell is close
muscles which leave rounded marks c
muscle scars on the insides of the va
The inside margin of each valve also h
mark called a **pallial line** where the edg
the soft part of the animal has been attac
to the shell. Bivalves are mostly ma
many of them live attached to the sea
(e.g. the mussel and the oyster), s
burrow in sand (e.g. the cockle and
razor-shell) and a few can swim by clap
their valves together (e.g. the scal
Examples of bivalves are *Ostrea*, the o
(Triassic-present), *Trigonia* (Jura
present), *Glycimeris*, the dog cc
(Cretaceous-present), *Gryph*
(Jurassic), *Cardium*, the cockle (Tria
present) and *Carbonicola* (Carbonifero

Carbonicola lived in fresh water; the ot
are all marine species (figure 6.13).

(iii) **Cephalopods**—the main fossil gro
among the cephalopods are the ex

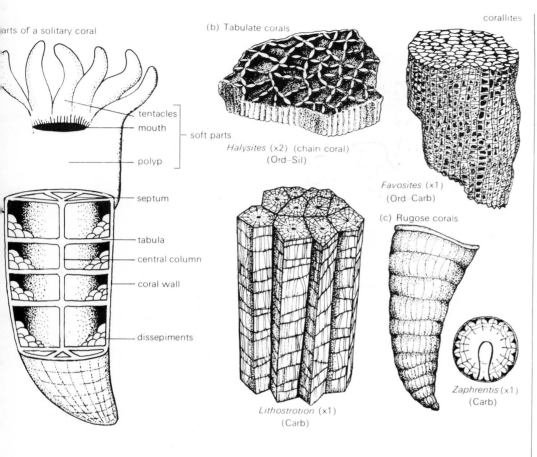

parts of a solitary coral

tentacles
mouth — soft parts
polyp

septum

tabula

central column

coral wall

dissepiments

(b) Tabulate corals

corallites

Halysites (x2) (chain coral)
(Ord–Sil)

Favosites (x1)
(Ord–Carb)

(c) Rugose corals

Lithostrotion (x1)
(Carb)

Zaphrentis (x1)
(Carb)

6.11 Corals.

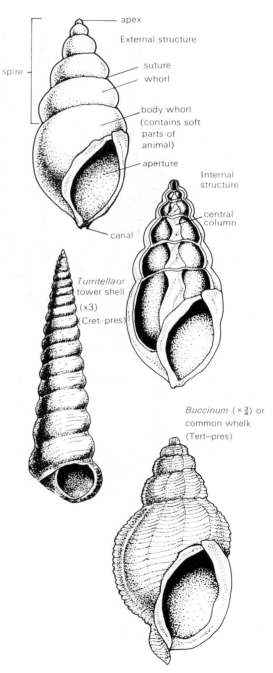

apex

External structure

spire

suture

whorl

body whorl
(contains soft
parts of
animal)

aperture

Internal
structure

central
column

canal

Turritella or
tower shell
(x3)
(Cret–pres)

Buccinum (× ¾) or
common whelk
(Tert–pres)

6.12 Gastropods.

---

ammonoids and **belemnites** (figures 6.14 and 6.15). The ammonoids have flat, coiled shells which are separated into gas-filled chambers by partitions called **septa**. The chambers are connected by a tube called a **siphuncle** which runs through the septa. Where a septum meets the wall of the shell a line called a **suture** is formed. Suture lines often follow very twisted paths. The last and largest chamber of the shell held the soft parts of the animal, which probably looked quite like a cuttlefish or squid. The ammonoids were free-swimming marine animals so their fossils are found in rocks deposited in both shallow and deep water. The ammonoids may be divided into **goniatites** and **ammonites**. The

goniatites are found in late Palaeozoic rocks and they have relatively simple suture lines. *Goniatites* (Carboniferous) is an example. Ammonites all belong to the Mesozoic era and they have very wavy suture lines. Examples are *Phylloceras* (Jurassic-Cretaceous), *Ceratites* (Triassic), *Amaltheus* (Jurassic), *Androgynoceras* (Jurassic) and *Dactylioceras* (Jurassic).

Belemnites are the internal shells of free-swimming animals which resembled cuttlefish. They were entirely marine. The shell is made up of three parts; the solid, bullet-shaped **guard**, the hollow, chambered **phragmocone** which fits into the guard and the elongated **pro-ostracum** which is a forward extension of

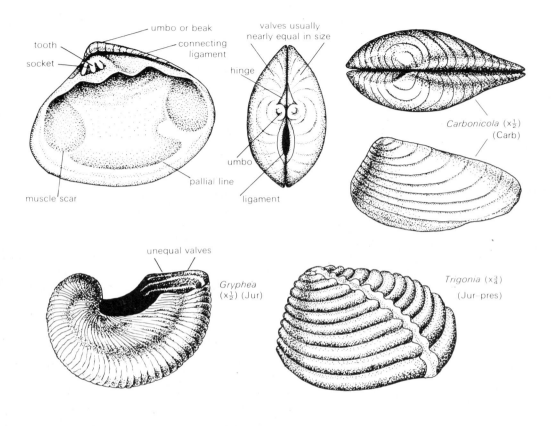

6.13 Bivalves.

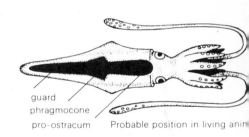

Probable position in living ani[m]

is represented by small plates called **cru**[...]
Examples of articulate brachiopods [...]
Productus (Carboniferous-Permia[n]), *Spirifer* (Silurian-Permian), *Rhyncor*[...]
(Jurasic) and *Terebratula* (Juras[...]
present).

Echinoderms

The skeletons of echinoderms are made u[p]
small plates fitting closely together. The m[...]
common fossil echinoderms are the **crinoids** [...]
the **echinoids**. Crinoids or sea-lilies are attac[...]
to the sea bed by stems made up of small pl[...]
which often look very like 'Polo' mints. At the [...]
of the stem is a rounded **calyx** surrounded by [...]
feather-like arms (figure 6.17). Crinoids v[...]

the phragmocone. Belemnites are found mostly in Jurassic and Cretaceous rocks; guards are found much more often than the other parts.

Brachiopods

Brachiopods are marine animals which live on the bottom of the sea and have two valves which are usually of different sizes. Brachiopod valves are 'equal-sided', that is, a line drawn at right angles to the middle of the hinge divides the valve into two equal parts. How does this property distinguish brachiopods from bivalves?

Brachiopods are usually attached to the sea floor by a string-like structure called a **pedicle**. Marks inside the shells are the scars of pedicle and

muscle attachment. Brachiopods can be divided into two groups (figure 6.16)

(i) The **inarticulate** brachiopods have no hinge structures, teeth or sockets between the valves. An example of this type is *Lingula* (Ordovician-present). In *Lingula* the pedicle passes out between the umbones of the two nearly equal valves.

(ii) The **articulate** brachiopods are hinged between teeth and sockets on the two shells. The pedicle comes out through an opening in the larger valve. The smaller valves of articulate brachiopods have internal **brachial skeletons** supporting **brachia** or arms. The brachia are used by the animal to extract food particles from the sea water. In some brachiopods the skeleton

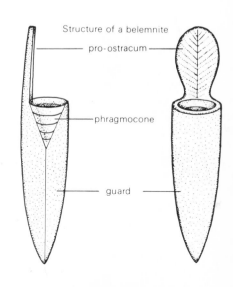

6.15 Belemnites.

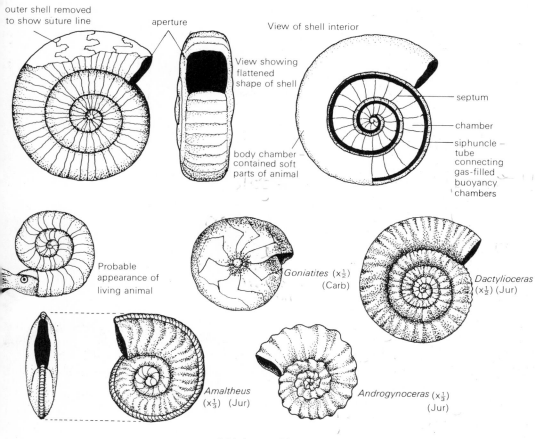

outer shell removed to show suture line

aperture

View of shell interior

View showing flattened shape of shell

septum

chamber

siphuncle – tube connecting gas-filled buoyancy chambers

body chamber contained soft parts of animal

Probable appearance of living animal

Goniatites (x½) (Carb)

Dactylioceras (x½) (Jur)

Amaltheus (x⅓) (Jur)

Androgynoceras (x⅓) (Jur)

6.14 Ammonoids.

round knobs to which spines are attached. The topmost point of the skeleton is made of a double circle of plates surrounding a small anal opening, and the lowest point of the skeleton has a larger opening for the mouth.

(ii) **Irregular** echinoids are heart-shaped rather than round. The anus is not central as in the regular echinoids but is displaced towards the back of the animal, and the mouth on the lower surface is usually forward of centre. Irregular echinoids are burrowing forms like the present day sea potato (*Echinocardium*) and heart-urchin (*Spatangus*), whereas regular echinoids are surface-living forms.

Echinus (Tertiary-present) and *Cidaris* (Jurassic-present) are examples of regular echinoids. *Conulus* (Cretaceous), *Micraster* (Cretaceous) and *Clypeus* (Jurassic) are irregular (see figure 6.18).

Trilobites

The trilobites were marine arthropods which lived in shallow water. They are found only in Palaeozoic rocks. Trilobites have flattened bodies made up of three parts—the head or **cephalon**, the **thorax** and the tail or **pygidium**. They have jointed legs and antennae which are not often seen in fossils. The central part of the cephalon is swollen to form the **glabella** and beside the

mmon in the Palaeozoic and early Mesozoic s where their remains often form crinoidal estone.

chinoids or sea-urchins have spiny, rounded letons made up of ten rows of paired plates. inoids may be divided into **regular** and egular** forms:

) **Regular** echinoids such as *Echinus*, the present day sea-urchin, have round skeletons with five rows of perforated plates called **ambulacral plates**. From the pores emerge **tube-feet** which are used by the animal for movement and attachment. Between the rows of ambulacral plates there are another five rows of larger **inter-ambulacral plates** which are covered in

The sea-urchin Echinus, shown with and without its spines

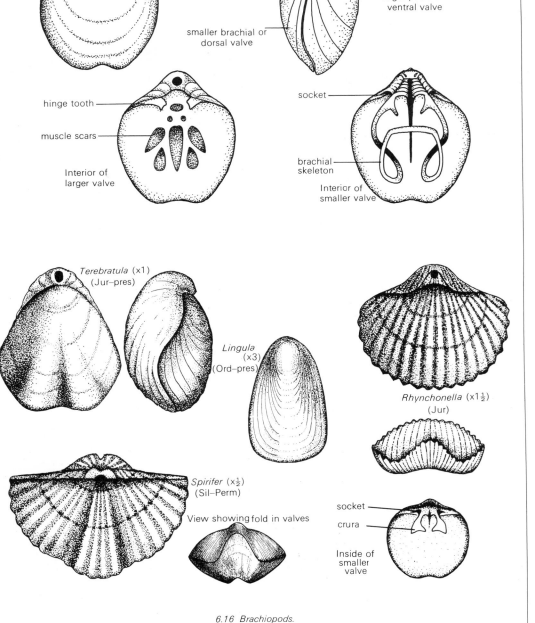

Parts of a brachiopod

pedicle opening

pedicle

umbo

larger pedicle or ventral valve

smaller brachial or dorsal valve

hinge tooth

muscle scars

Interior of larger valve

socket

brachial skeleton

Interior of smaller valve

Terebratula (x1) (Jur–pres)

Lingula (x3) (Ord–pres)

Rhynchonella (x1½) (Jur)

Spirifer (x½) (Sil–Perm)

View showing fold in valves

socket

crura

Inside of smaller valve

6.16 Brachiopods.

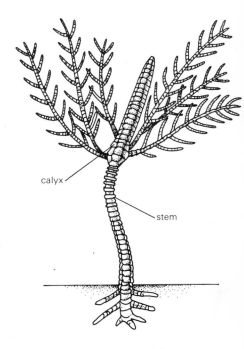

calyx

stem

6.17 A crinoid.

glabella are the eyes. The thorax and pygidium
made up of segments (figure 6.19). So
examples of trilobites are Paradox
(Cambrian), Olenus (Cambrian), Trinuc
(Ordovician), Calymene (Ordovician-Silur
and Dalmanites (Silurian).

The trilobite Calymene.

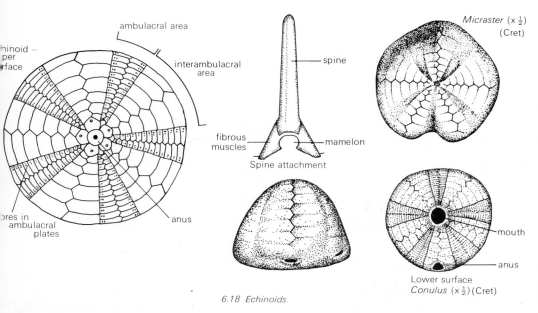

6.18 Echinoids.

Labels for the echinoid diagram: echinoid – upper surface, ambulacral area, interambulacral area, pores in ambulacral plates, anus, spine, fibrous muscles, mamelon, Spine attachment, Micraster (x ½) (Cret), mouth, anus, Lower surface Conulus (x ½) (Cret)

Monograptus (Silurian). Graptolites were almost extinct by the end of the Silurian period.

Evolutionary trends in the graptolites include reduction in the number of stipes, change in stipe position in the forms with two stipes, from hanging through horizontal to bent back, and changes in the shapes and reduction in the number of thecae (figure 6.21).

Plants

The best known fossil plants are found in Carboniferous rocks. Among the common fossils are stem fragments of *Lepidodendron* and *Sigillaria* which were tree-like plants called club-mosses, and *Calamites* which was like a gigantic horse-tail. The commonest fossil is *Stigmaria* which is the remains of the roots of *Lepidodendron* and *Sigillaria*. *Annularia*, the leaves of horse-tails, and *Sphenopteris*, the leaves of seed-ferns, are also found (figure 6.22).

Reconstructing the past

We have already said that in its long history the Earth has gone through many changes. But how do we know what kinds of change have taken place? What methods can we use to allow us to look back through geological time to see how the geology and geography of the Earth have changed? We can do three things. Firstly, we can

otolites

raptolites may have been primitive vertebrates. y lived floating in the sea and were colonial anisms made up of branches called **stipes**. The es are lined by one or two rows of cups called **cae** which contained the individual animals of

the colony. The number of stipes in a colony ranges from about sixty in the early (late Cambrian) forms down to one in the late (Silurian) forms. Examples of graptolites (figure 6.20) are *Dictyonema* (late Cambrian-Silurian), *Tetragraptus, Didymograptus, Dicellograptus, Climacograptus* (all Ordovician) and

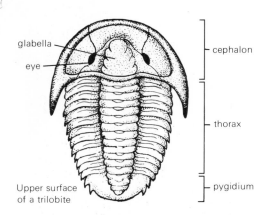

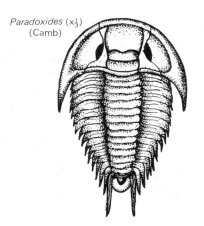

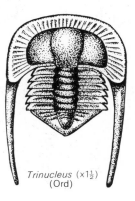

Labels for trilobite diagram: glabella, eye, cephalon, thorax, pygidium, Upper surface of a trilobite, *Paradoxides* (x ⅓) (Camb), *Trinucleus* (x 1½) (Ord)

6.19 Trilobites.

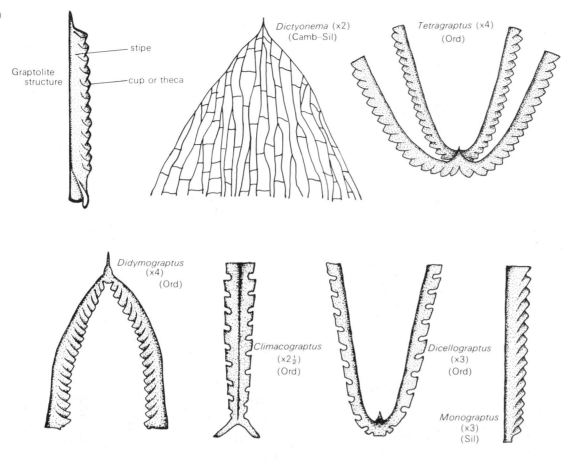

Graptolite structure
- stipe
- cup or theca

Dictyonema (x2)
(Camb–Sil)

Tetragraptus (x4)
(Ord)

Didymograptus
(x4)
(Ord)

Climacograptus
(x2½)
(Ord)

Dicellograptus
(x3)
(Ord)

Monograptus
(x3)
(Sil)

6.20 Graptolites.

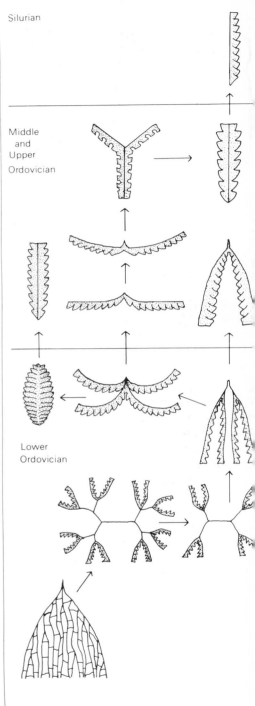

Silurian

Middle
and
Upper
Ordovician

Lower
Ordovician

6.21 Evolution of graptolites showing the main tren
reduction in stipe number and change in stipe po
from hanging to curved back.

look at the processes acting on the Earth today because these same processes may have acted in ancient times. Secondly, we can study the rocks which have formed at various times to see if we can work out the conditions which existed when they were produced. Thirdly, fossils can be used as indicators of ancient environments.

At present, the processes of weathering, transport, erosion and deposition act to change and reshape the surface of the Earth. These processes take place very slowly so the changes which they produce are very gradual. It is thought that these same processes have acted in similar ways throughout geological time. If this is the case, it means that we can interpret past changes in terms of present changes. For example, the sand at present laid in deserts forms dunes, so if we

found a sandstone with cross-bedding developed on a large scale it would be reasonable to suggest that these ancient features were produced under conditions similar to those which produced the present-day dunes.

The idea that we can use the present as a key to the past is called the **principle of uniformitarianism**. You might think that this idea is very obvious, but up to the start of the nineteenth century it was thought that mountains rose suddenly, that oceans rushed over the continents or dried up very rapidly, and that plants and animals appeared or became extinct all at once. The principle of uniformitarianism replaced these ideas by explaining that changes on the Earth had always been gradual rather than sudden. Of course, processes in the past have not

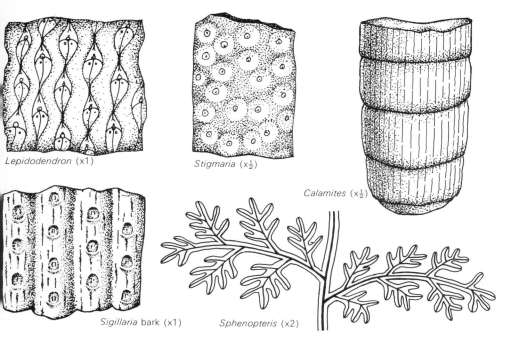

Lepidodendron (x1)

Stigmaria (x½)

Calamites (x½)

Sigillaria bark (x1)

Sphenopteris (x2)

6.22 Fossils of Carboniferous plants.

unpolished grains. We can also look at the variation in grain size in a sedimentary rock. A greywacke is made up of grains of many sizes mixed together. This wide range of grain size indicates that the rock was deposited fairly rapidly. On the other hand, a sandstone made up of grains of mostly the same size would appear to have been deposited by currents which sifted the sand about a lot and removed the smaller grains. The minerals present in a sedimentary rock can also give useful information. Some minerals are easily broken down by weathering and transport; for example, arkose contains a lot of feldspar whose presence indicates that the grains have not been subjected to long weathering and transport. On the other hand, a sandstone made up only of resistant quartz grains results from long transport and weathering processes.

Sedimentary structures are useful indicators of depositional environments. For example, graded bedding indicates rapid deposition, perhaps from a turbidity current; large-scale cross-bedding may

essarily always acted at exactly the same rate those of the present. For example, changing nates may have affected rates of denudation, the changes produced by volcanic eruptions, thquakes and floods may have been rapid.

We can apply the ideas of uniformitarianism to study of sedimentary rocks to see what they us about past environments. Different imentary rocks are formed under different ditions. Can you remember how ooliths are ned? If an oolitic limestone is found high up on d this indicates that the land was once under a llow, warm, turbulent sea because present-day iths only form in such seas. In this way we can what we know of modern environments to tell about ancient environments. What could you n about past conditions of deposition from ks such as conglomerates, sandstones, dstones and evaporites?

tudy of sedimentary grains may also give quite lot of information about conditions of osition. For example, desert sandstones tend ave well-rounded, frosted grains, while beach dstones often have rounded, polished grains glacial sand tends to be made up of angular,

Fossilized stumps of the giant club-moss Sigillaria – Victoria Park, Glasgow.

101

indicate deposition under desert conditions; mud cracks show that the sediment has been exposed to air during deposition; and ripple marks indicate deposition in windy conditions or under fairly shallow water. We can also use cross-bedding and ripple marks to determine the direction in which the depositing currents moved.

Study of igneous and metamorphic rocks can also help us to understand Earth history because igneous and metamorphic activity often take place near or at moving plate boundaries. For example, large amounts of lava in a sedimentary succession may indicate that a plate boundary was nearby at the time of deposition. Regionally metamorphosed rocks form in the roots of mountains pushed up by colliding plates, so if these rocks appear at the surface they indicate the previous existence of long-removed mountains. Where rocks have been greatly folded, sedimentary structures are useful along with such things as animal burrows and roots because they can tell us if beds have been turned upside down during folding. Figure 6.23 shows some structures in the positions in which they formed along with their appearance after they have been inverted.

Fossils can tell us a great deal about past environments. For example, the types of fossil present can tell us if the sediment was laid down in the sea, in fresh water or on land. This assumes, of course, that the plant or animal remains have not been transported from one place to the other. What would you say if you found a piece of fossilized wood in a rock along with brachiopods and echinoderms? Besides indicating the general conditions of deposition, fossils can give us much more exact ideas of environmental factors such as temperature and salinity. However, we must assume that the living conditions of plants and animals today are like those of similar organisms of the past. This assumption is quite a good one for the Tertiary and Cretaceous periods, when organisms were often like modern ones, but further back in time the assumption may not be so valid.

One thing that study of modern organisms tells us is that the shapes of shells and skeletons can differ according to the living conditions. Corals growing in uncrowded, sheltered reefs may have

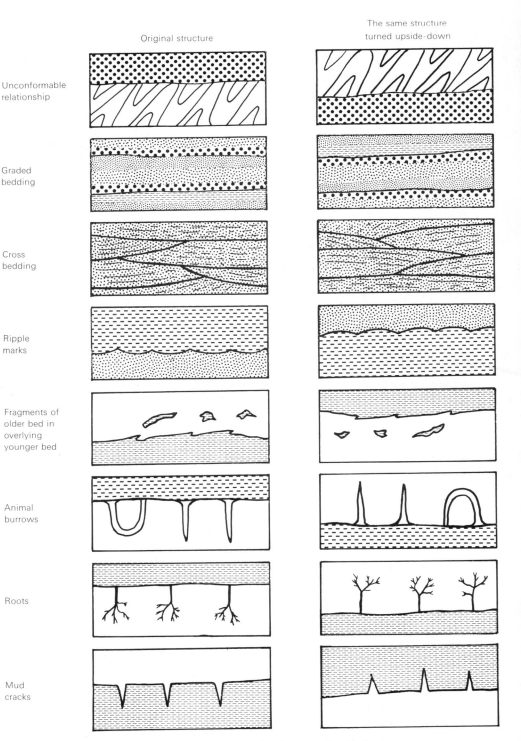

Original structure   The same structure turned upside-down

Unconformable relationship

Graded bedding

Cross bedding

Ripple marks

Fragments of older bed in overlying younger bed

Animal burrows

Roots

Mud cracks

6.23 Some ways of telling if beds have been turned upside down during folding.

are found in a thin mudstone this shows that deposition was very slow because it would take a long time for large numbers of skeletons to accumulate. Also, if graptolites are the only fossils this indicates that deposition took place in deep water because of the absence of fossils such as brachiopods and trilobites which are found mostly in shallow water sediments.

Some relationships between successions

We have already said that sedimentary rocks change in type upwards through successions. What kinds of sediment would you find on a modern shoreline? You might find pebble and boulder beaches, sandy beaches and mud deposits where tidal currents were weak. Suppose these sediments were suddenly turned to hard rock; there would then be a number of different rock types all of the same age which merged sideways into each other. Towards the mudstone of the mudflats the sandstone of the sandy beach would gradually become finer, and towards the conglomerate of the pebble beach the sandstone would gradually become coarser. Sideways changes like these are commonly found in rock successions where they are known as **lateral variations** (figure 6.24).

Suppose a new road were to be built from London to Edinburgh and that the road workers started laying the road in London and worked towards Edinburgh. The completed road would be a single structure, but would all parts of it be of the same age? In the same way, when a layer of sediment is laid down it often happens that different parts of the layer are deposited at different times. The rock unit which results is a single structure which gets older or younger in a sideways direction. This can happen, for example, when a delta is built up. The sediment on the outer fringe of a delta is younger than the sediment on the inner margins. But if the deltaic deposits are turned to hard rock they could form a large sandstone deposit which, at first glance, might be thought to be all of the same age, or to have its youngest beds at the bottom rather than to one side. Beds like this which are nearly horizontal but which vary in age sideways are called **diachronous** beds (figure 6.25).

Examine the shapes of these ripple marks. When they were formed, in which direction did the current flow?

pen, spreading branches while the same coral rowing in a crowded or exposed reef may have its ranches squashed closely together. Limpets in xposed places have high, pointed shells whereas mpets in sheltered places have low, flat shells; ysters growing in mud have cup-shaped shells vhile oysters growing on underwater rock have atter shells moulded to the rock surface. In other vords, a species can show variations in shape vhich may indicate the conditions under which it as grown.

Temperature is the major factor which controls he distribution of organisms. Because animals nd plants tend to be restricted to certain climatic ones, we can get an idea of past temperatures rom the fossils present in rocks. For example, the Carboniferous system of Britain contains coral eefs and a good deal of coal which formed from he remains of thick forests something like those at present growing in equatorial regions. This

indicates that during the Carboniferous period Britain lay on or near to the equator. Fossils can sometimes give fairly accurate estimates of temperature. For example, certain chemicals in belemnites have been used to show that in the early Cretaceous period the sea which covered Britain had an average temperature of about 15°C, while in the late Cretaceous period the temperature was just a little higher.

An interesting fact which has been discovered by counting the daily growth rings on coral is that the length of the day is slowly becoming greater. In the Cambrian period there were about 420 days in the year, by the Permian period the number had fallen to 390, and there are now 365 days in a year. This means that over the last 570 million years the Earth's rate of rotation has become slower and the day has lengthened from 21 hours to 24 hours.

Fossils can also indicate the rate at which sedimentation has taken place. If many graptolites

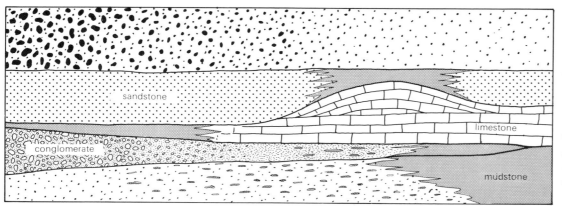

6.24 Lateral variation in rock type.

Because rock types can change sideways, successions of rocks of the same age in different areas may be completely different. So how can we tell if different successions are of the same age, and how can we match up or **correlate** these successions? One thing which it may be possible to do is to trace one succession into another in the field. For example, if exposures are good enough we might be able to trace a reef limestone sideways and see how it differs from rocks of the same age on the sides of the ancient reef. Correlation is sometimes made easy by the presence of a distinctive **marker** bed which is a thin layer deposited relatively quickly over a wide area. Such beds can result, for example, from volcanic eruptions which can spread layers of ash or dust quite rapidly across the different sediments which are being deposited over large areas. Finally, we can use fossils to correlate different successions. The best fossils to use are those which are changing rapidly through evolution so that any one fossil type is only found in a narrow band of rock. The fossil should also be widespread. In marine rocks the best fossils for use in correlation are those of floating or swimming animals because their remains are found in both deep and shallow water sediments. Fossils which fulfil these requirements are called **zone fossils**. A zone fossil is one which occurs in, and is restricted to, a narrow sequence of sedimentary rocks called

a **zone** which has been laid down over a relatively short period. The best-known zone fossils are graptolites from the Lower Palaeozoic era and ammonites from the Mesozoic era.

The geological history of Britain

If we look at the events which shaped the area of the British Isles as we know it today we will find that its geological history is long and varied. The oldest British rocks are about 3000 million years old and since these early times Britain has seen rocks formed under many different conditions.

Sediments have been deposited on land and in t[he] sea in hot and cold climates; igneous rocks ha[ve] been intruded and volcanoes have been active [at] various times; and metamorphic rocks have be[en] formed in the roots of growing mountains.

Britain only began to emerge from the sea for t[he] last time about 60 million years ago, so you w[ill] realize that its present geography was develop[ed] fairly recently. If you went further back in time t[he] shapes of Britain and Ireland would not [be] recognizable. It is possible from study of the ro[ck] types of different ages to work out the positions [of] land and sea in ancient times. Maps showing t[he] geography of past ages are called **palae[o] geographical maps**. These maps are much le[ss] accurate than modern maps—why should this [be] so?

To some extent we can interpret the geologic[al] history of Britain in terms of plate collisi[on] processes leading up to periods of mounta[in] building. After the mountains had been built the[y] were denuded and the material derived from the[m] was deposited in seas, lakes and deserts. T[he] changing climate of Britain through the age[s is] partly due to changing world climates and part[ly] due to the slow drift of Britain from the southe[rn] hemisphere through the tropics to its prese[nt] northerly position. The changing latitude of Brita[in] during the last 600 million years is shown in figu[re] 6.26.

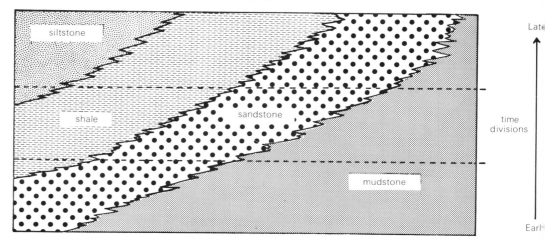

6.25 Diachronous beds – different parts of each rock unit have been deposited at different times.

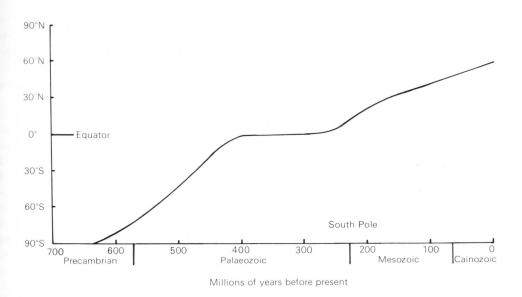

6.26 *Changing latitude of Britain through geological time.*
(Note that changing longitude cannot be worked out).

and appear to have been deposited fairly rapidly (remember that in these early times there were no land plants to protect the rocks from weathering and erosion). Most of the Torridonian series seems to have been deposited on land or in shallow lakes, although some of it may have been deposited by rivers on the continental shelf around the northern continent.

At the same time as the Torridonian Series was being deposited on the continent, the sediments of the **Moine Series** were being deposited in the sea. The Moinian rocks are mostly sandstones which seem to have been deposited in shallow water although some may have been deposited in deeper water by turbidity currents. The Moinian takes up a large part of the north-west Highlands of Scotland, and it is separated from the Lewisian and Torridonian rocks by the **Moine Thrust** which runs from the north coast of Sutherland to Islay.

The deposition of the Moine Series was succeeded by the deposition of the **Dalradian Series** which now occupies part of the area

The Precambrian era

Precambrian rocks are found over most of the Highlands of Scotland, in the north of Ireland and in a few scattered outcrops in England and Wales (figure 6.27). The oldest British rock is the Lewisian Gneiss of north-west Scotland. This rock was formed deep in the Earth by the metamorphism of pre-existing rocks. Two main periods of metamorphism can be recognized. The first of these gave rise to the **Scourian** gneisses which occupy the central area of the Lewisian outcrop on the Scottish mainland. The Scourian gneisses were formed by high temperature metamorphism between 3000 and 2600 million years ago. Some of the rocks which were metamorphosed to give the Scourian gneisses were igneous rocks, and some were sedimentary rocks which have been dated as being 2900 million years old. About 1500 million years ago the Scourian gneisses were in places metamorphosed again, at a lower temperature than before. This second metamorphism produced the **Laxfordian**

gneiss. It is probable that the Lewisian Gneiss was formed by metamorphic processes deep within developing mountain chains so the presence of two main periods of metamorphism may indicate that two episodes of mountain building took place. In England and Wales the gneisses of the Malvern Hills and Anglesey may have formed at the same time as the Lewisian Gneiss.

In this early stage of its history it seems that Britain was part of a continent which included the gneisses of the Canadian Shield, Greenland and Scandinavia. In the later Precambrian era, about 1000 million years ago, it seems that this continent broke apart along a constructive plate boundary. This resulted in the formation of a wide ocean separating a northern continent containing the Lewisian Gneiss and a southern continent containing the gneisses of England and Wales.

The Lewisian Gneiss is overlain with strong unconformity by an overall total of about 6000 metres of red conglomerates, arkoses, sandstones and shales called the **Torridonian Series**. These rocks are between 1000 and 850 million years old

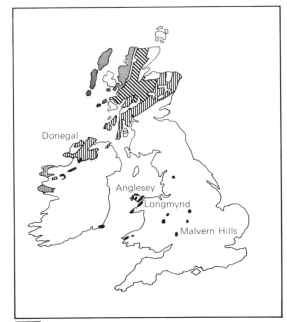

| Dalradian |
| Lewisian and Torridonian |
| Moinian |
| Other Precambrian rocks |

6.27 *Distribution of Precambrian rocks.*

between the Great Glen Fault and the Highland Boundary Fault. Dalradian rocks are also found in the north of Ireland. The lower part of the Dalradian Series is made up of shallow water deposits including sandstones, mudstones and limestones while the upper rocks contain many greywackes which seem to have been deposited by turbidity currents in deep water. Near the middle of the Dalradian Series is a rock called a **tillite** which is an ancient glacial deposit. Perhaps at this time the area which is now the Scottish Highlands lay near the South Pole. Dalradian sedimentation seems to have continued right through into the Cambrian period because Cambrian fossils are found in its topmost layers.

On the margins of the southern continent events roughly similar to those happening on the northern continent may have been taking place. In Shropshire there is a thick succession of conglomerates, sandstones and shales called the **Longmyndian Series**. These rocks may have been deposited on the edge of the southern continent at the same time as the Torridonian and Moinian were being formed in the north. In Anglesey, a very thick succession of sediments quite·like the Dalradian Series lies uncomformably on the older gneiss. These sediments seem to have been deposited far from land, perhaps in an oceanic trench. If this was the case they would have overlain a destructive plate boundary.

To summarize–during the early Precambrian era Britain was part of a continent which included the Canadian Shield, Greenland and the Baltic Shield. About 1000 million years ago this continent broke apart along a constructive plate boundary and formed a northern continent on which lay northern Scotland, and a southern continent which included the southern part of England. On the northern continent and in the seas around its shores Torridonian, Moinian and Dalradian sediments were deposited. On the southern continent and its marginal seas Longmyndian sediments were deposited. At this time Anglesey may have been on a destructive plate boundary.

The Lower Palaeozoic era.

The Lower Palaeozoic era is made up of the Cambrian, Ordovician and Silurian periods. It began about 570 million years ago and ended about 400 million years ago. At this time a sequence of events took place which saw the filling in of the ocean between the northern and southern continents, and the coming together of these continents so that the sediments between them were squeezed and raised to form a huge mountain range called the **Caledonian Mountains**. These mountains must have looked quite like the present-day Himalayas but now only the worn-down stumps of the mountain chain remain; these lie in a zone between the Baltic Shield on one side and the gneisses of Canada, Greenland and the north-west Highlands of Scotland on the other.

In the open ocean between the northern and southern continents deep-water Cambrian sediments were laid down on the Dalradian rocks without unconformity, but on the margins of the continents a shallow, spreading sea laid the Cambrian rocks on to the Precambrian basement with striking unconformity. Such an invasion of the sea is called a **marine transgression** and it lays sediments over a wide area. The first rock to be laid by the Cambrian transgression was a conglomerate which represents the remains of spreading shingle beaches. Above the conglomerate in the north-west Highlands there are quartzites and limestones which seem to have been deposited in shallow seas on the shelf of the northern continent. In the Midlands of England, Shropshire and the Malvern Hills, which all lay on the margins of the southern continent, quartzites again form the lowest part of the Cambrian system. Green sandstones and shales follow the quartzite. In north Wales there are 5 kilometres of Cambrian greywackes and mudstones which seem to have been deposited in deep water off the edge of the continental shelf (figure 6.28(a)). An interesting point is that the trilobites found in England and Wales are different from those of northern Scotland. This may have been because the two areas were separated by a wide ocean which the trilobites could not cross (figure 6.28(b)).

In essence, the Ordovician period shows a continuation of the pattern of sedimentation established in the Cambrian period; that is,

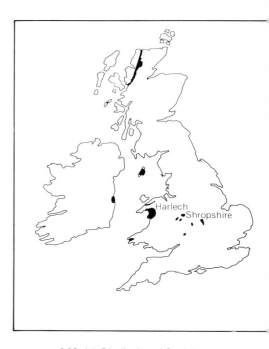

6.28 (a) Distribution of Cambrian rocks.

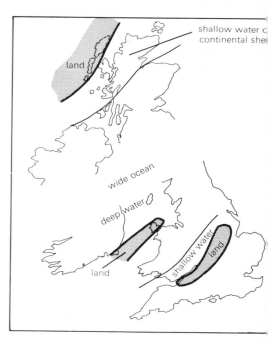

6.28 (b) Britain during the Cambrian period.

allow water deposition took place on the margins of the northern and southern continents th deep water sedimentation in the open ocean. ut the Ordovician period differs from the mbrian period in two major respects. Firstly, ring Ordovician times the continents began to ove together and destructive plate boundaries rmed along the continental margins. Secondly, a result of the onset of plate collision igneous tivity was triggered off, and the Ordovician stem is notable for its great abundance of lcanic rocks.

In Scotland, among the Moinian and Dalradian cks of the Highlands, the first signs of the **aledonian Orogeny** began to appear. These cks were deformed and pushed up so that the argin of the northern continent was moved to the uthern edge of the Highlands. In southern cotland the start of the Ordovician period saw lcanic rocks extruded in what is now south yrshire. These rocks, which include pillow lavas, dicate that a destructive plate boundary was rming across Scotland from north of the Solway south of the Forth. The Upper Ordovician rocks this area show some remarkable variations in ickness. At Girvan in south Ayrshire there are out 2500 metres of shallow-water onglomerates, mudstones, sandstones and mestones which thicken to the south-east into out 5000 metres of greywackes and shales eposited in deep water. Near Moffat in umfriesshire, which is about 90 kilometres east Girvan, there are 50 metres of black shales hich were deposited at the same time as the irvan rocks. But how do we know that the Girvan nd Moffat rocks are of the same age? At Moffat aptolites are extremely numerous. At Girvan the ssils are mainly shallow-water corals, trilobites, achiopods and molluscs but there are enough aptolites present to allow the two rock groups to e correlated. Can you explain the enormous fference in thickness between the Upper rdovician rocks of Girvan and Moffat? Girvan obably lay on the continental side of an oceanic ench which trapped sediment coming from the ighlands, while Moffat lay beyond the trench nd the accumulation of fine sediment was very ow (figure 6.29).

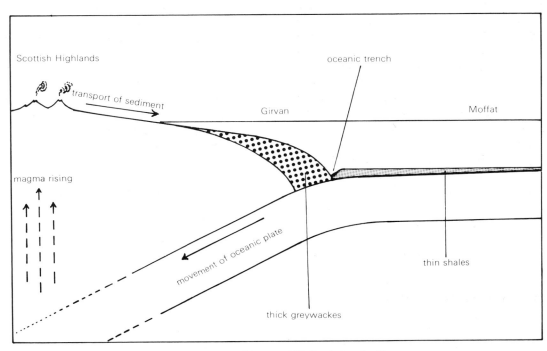

6.29 Sedimentation at Girvan and Moffat during the Upper Ordovician period.

In the south, part of the margin of the Ordovician ocean ran from Pembroke to Shropshire. In the Welsh border counties there are shallow-water limestones and sandstones deposited on the continental shelf while in central Wales the Ordovician sediments are greywackes and shales which were laid down in deep water over the edge of the shelf (figure 6.30(a)). Between the northern and southern continents, the Lake District may have lain on an island arc because part of it is made up of thick andesitic lavas. The mountains of north Wales also consist largely of volcanic rocks, some of which are pillow lavas. Can you remember how pillow lavas are formed? It seems that while the Lake District stood up as an island arc over a subduction zone, north Wales lay under deep water (figure 6.30(b)). The continued existence of a wide ocean during Ordovician times is again shown by differences in the fossils from the margins of the northern and southern continents.

The Silurian system which lies over the Ordovician system is notable for its absence of volcanic rocks. In Scotland, the early part of the Silurian period showed the same features as the

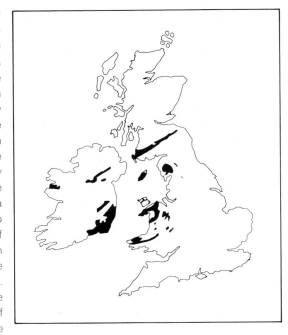

6.30 (a) Distribution of Ordovician rocks.

108

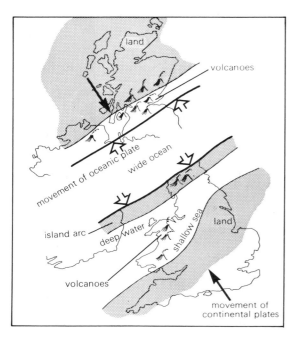

6.30 (b) Britain during the Ordovician period.

that the seas were warm. At this time, therefore, Britain may have lain quite close to the equator. Deep-water sedimentation continued off the continental shelf in central Wales; here there are thick deposits of greywackes and shales which thin away towards the north (figures 6.31(a) and (b)).

Towards the end of the Silurian period the ocean was becoming narrow and filled with thick sediments. The coming together of the Continents which had been going on throughout the Lower Palaeozoic era jostled and buckled the sediments between the continents so that sedimentation was interrupted from time to time and land areas were raised in different places. Can you explain why interruptions in sedimentation are more liable to occur in shelf seas rather than in the deeper water of the ocean basins? The process of plate collision reached its climax at the end of the Silurian period. It led to the building of the Caledonian Mountains with associated metamorphism, deformation and granite intrusion in many places. The regional metamorphism strongly affected the Moinian and

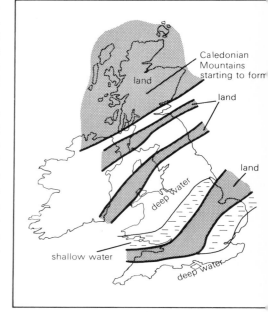

6.31 (b) Britain during the Silurian period.

Ordovician period. The Scottish Highlands still lay above water and the Midland Valley formed a sea with a shallow shelf which fell into deep water where the Southern Uplands now lie. Towards the middle of the Silurian period, however, thick greywackes were deposited over the thin black shales at Moffat. These greywackes may have reached Moffat by being transported north from the Lake District island arc, or perhaps by this time Moffat had moved north on its moving plate onto the edge of a subduction zone where sedimentation was more rapid.

Along the edge of the southern continent we again find the contrast between the deep-water sediments of central Wales and the shallow-water sediments of the Welsh Borders. The main difference compared with Ordovician times is that the sea spread over the Midlands and shallow-water deposits are found around Birmingham. In Shropshire many features including bays, inlets, stacks and beach gravels can be found around the Longmynd, which stood as an island in the Silurian sea. The fossils of this area are shallow-water forms and the presence of coral reefs shows

6.31 (a) Distribution of Silurian rocks.

Dalradian rocks and converted many of them schists. Metamorphism was weaker in the other areas affected by the mountain building, and places such as Wales and the Lake District resulted in many of the mudstones being converted to slates.

Major faults were also set moving by the squeezing of the moving continents. These include the Moine Thrust, the Great Glen Fault, the Highland Boundary Fault and the Church Stretton Fault. It is most important to realize that all the folding, faulting, metamorphism and granite intrusion did not take place all at once. The process of plate collision is long and varied; things such as metamorphism and folding can go on in different places at different times and they can be repeated again and again. For example, the Scottish Highlands rose to form land in the Ordovician period, and they supplied much of the Ordovician and Silurian sediment to the Southern Upland area. At the same time granites were intruded in the Highlands and metamorphism was taking place while sediments were being deposited in other areas.

You should note that the mountains of Scotland, the Lake District and Wales are not the mains of the Caledonian Mountains, which were completely levelled off a long time ago. The present mountains are the result of erosion over the last 60 million years which has removed surrounding younger rocks more quickly than the older, more resistant rocks.

The Upper Palaeozoic era

The Upper Palaeozoic era includes the Devonian, Carboniferous and Permian periods and it lasted from about 400 million years ago to about 225 million years ago. The history of the Upper Palaeozoic era is completely different from that of the Lower Palaeozoic era because by this time most of Britain lay on a stable continent far away from moving plate margins. The Caledonian Mountains which had been raised at the end of the Lower Palaeozoic era were levelled off during the Upper Palaeozoic era. At this time Britain seems to have been drifting through the tropics. In the Devonian period deposition took place mostly on land, in a climate perhaps like that of southern Africa today. During the Carboniferous period Britain seems to have been on the equator and coal was formed from the remains of thick forests. In the Permian period we see a return to desert conditions—Britain may then have been in a position similar to that of Arabia today.

By early Devonian times the ocean which had existed throughout the Lower Palaeozoic era had been closed up. The coming together of the northern and southern continents of the Lower Palaeozoic era had pushed up the Caledonian Mountains which ran from Norway through Britain to North America. Remember that this was long before the formation of the Atlantic Ocean, so Britain and eastern North America lay on the same continent. Britain lay on the southern edge of the continent and to the south there was a wide ocean whose shoreline ran through southern England. On this continent the Caledonian Mountains, as yet unprotected by land plants, were rapidly attacked by weathering and erosion and the material derived from them was swept down to be deposited in alluvial fans, deltas, lakes and flood plains around the base of the mountain ranges. The Devonian rocks deposited on land are known as the **Old Red Sandstone**. In most places the Old Red Sandstone, which consists largely of red and brown sandstones and mudstones, lies with strong unconformity on older rocks. Deposition took place in three main basins or **cuvettes** between the mountain ranges (figures 6.32(a) and (b)). In the extreme north-east of Scotland deposition occurred mostly in a large freshwater lake. A very thick succession of conglomerates, sandstones, mudstones and limestones was laid down which contains fish and some land plants as fossils. In central Scotland conglomerates, sandstones and mudstones were again deposited. In this basin volcanism accompanied sedimentation, and thick basaltic and andesitic lavas form some of the hills of east central Scotland. The third main basin of deposition was in south Wales. Here the rocks are mostly sandstones and mudstones which were laid down in deltas on coastal plains which stretched from the base of the mountains down to the ocean in

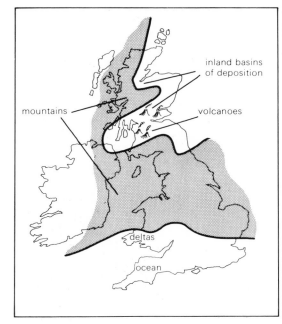

6.32 (b) Britain during the Devonian period.

the south. The presence of occasional marine deposits shows that the sea sometimes advanced into this area.

The Devonian rocks of south Devon and Cornwall were laid down in the sea. Here there are thick shales, greywackes, pillow lavas and tuffs, and typical marine organisms such as corals, brachiopods and goniatites are found as fossils. In north Devon and Somerset the Devonian system is partly marine and partly continental in origin. The inter-fingering of these two rock types shows that the shoreline changed its position at various times.

By the end of the Devonian period the high Caledonian Mountains had been reduced to deeply-eroded stumps jutting up from what was probably a semi-arid landscape. In Lower Carboniferous times the sea spread from the south and west until eventually it reached into the Midland Valley of Scotland. Deposition took place on the continental shelf in basins separated by islands and stretches of shallow water. The main islands which stood out from the Lower Carboniferous sea were part of Wales and the

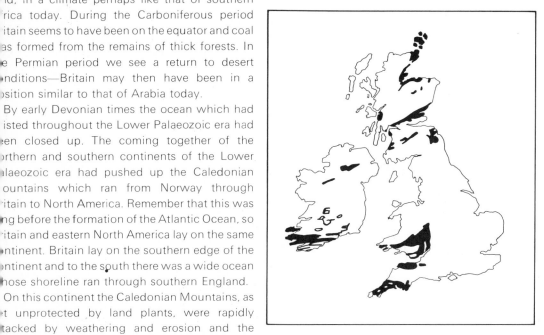

6.32 (a) Distribution of Devonian rocks.

Midlands (this island is sometimes called **St George's Land**), the Lake District and the Southern Uplands, while the Pennines were submerged about half-way through the Lower Carboniferous period. The Scottish Highlands formed the southern edge of a continent which lay to the north of Britain and the shelf sea extended as far south as Devon and Cornwall where the sea floor fell off into deep water. Although the Lower Carboniferous rocks are known as **Carboniferous Limestone**, this does not mean that the system only contains limestone. Other sedimentary rocks such as sandstones and shales are commonly found with the limestone, especially in the north of Britain.

During the lower Carboniferous period there were five main areas of deposition (figures 6.33(a) and (b)). In Devon and Cornwall there are greywackes and black shales with some lavas and tuffs. These rocks were deposited in deep water south of the continental shelf, and the fossils present include goniatites. Further north in south Wales and around Bristol the Lower

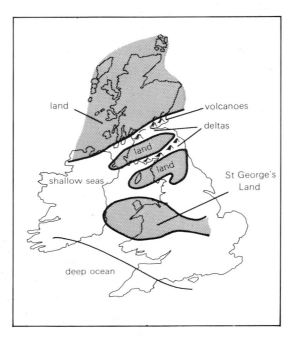

6.33 (b) Britain during the Lower Carboniferous period.

Carboniferous system is made up of shallow-water limestones, shales and sandstones deposited by the advancing sea. The limestones contain enormous numbers of fossilized corals, crinoids and productid brachiopods. Between St George's Land and the Lake District a thick sequence of limestones (often forming reefs), shales and sandstones was laid down in a deep trough. These rocks become thinner across the Pennines then thicken into another basin of sedimentation in Northumberland. The advancing Lower Carboniferous sea arrived late in Northumberland, so here the earliest Carboniferous rocks were laid down in fresh water. These fresh-water deposits are succeeded by sandstones laid down in the deltas of rivers which ran into the area. Thick forests grew on the deltas and the remains of these forests produced coal. The marine transgression was still later in reaching the Midland Valley of Scotland and, as in Northumberland, the first Carboniferous sediments were deposited in fresh water. Among these fresh-water deposits are the oil-shales of the Lothians; these used to be mined and heated to

give mineral oil. After the arrival of the sea Northumberland and Scotland both lay i shallow water regularly invaded by forested delta so that repeated sequences of marine limeston and shales, then non-marine sandstones follow by coal were often formed. In the Midland Vall many volcanoes were active and enormo quantities of lava are found among the Low Carboniferous sediments.

Towards the end of the Lower Carbonifero period the sea began to retreat as the land w uplifted. This led to the deposition of coar sandstones by rivers flowing into the sedimenta basins from the surrounding land. In Engla these deltaic deposits, which are at their thickest Yorkshire and Lancashire, are called **Millsto Grit** (grit is a coarse sandstone made up angular grains). Among the sandstones a occasional marine shales which show that the s advanced over the deltas from time to time. No of St George's Land the Millstone Grit w deposited in the deltas of huge rivers similar to t Mississippi which flowed south from the Scotti Highlands. In south Wales and around Bristol t sandstones were deposited by rivers runni south into the area from St George's Lar Because deltas are built nearly horizontally wi their youngest sediments on their margins, roc of Millstone Grit type are of different ages different areas; that is, they are diachronous.

Above the Millstone Grit deposits come t **Coal Measures**, the main coal-bearing rocks Britain. You should note that only about 3% these rocks are actually coal; the remaining roc are mostly sandstones and shales. The Co Measures were deposited in widespread coas swamps (perhaps like those of the present-d Everglades in Florida) which lay both south of George's Land and between St George's Land a the Scottish Highlands (figures 6.34(a) and (b The forests which grew in these swamps we made up of huge ferns, horse-tails, seed-ferns a club-mosses. When these plants died th remains formed thick layers of peat which we buried to produce coal. A common feature of Co Measure sedimentation was that deposition oft took place in repeated sequences call **cyclothems**. Cyclothems are made up

6.33 (a) Distribution of Lower Carboniferous rocks.

6.34 (a) Distribution of Upper Carboniferous rocks.

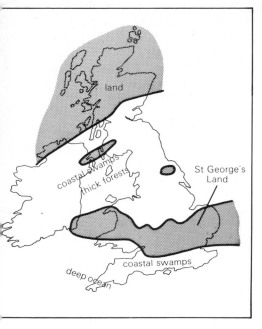

6.34 (b) Britain during the Upper Carboniferous period.

Reconstruction of a forest growing in a Coal Measure swamp, showing giant ferns, mosses and horsetails.

sequences of shale, sandstone and coal repeated again and again (figure 6.35). How could you account for such repetitions? Some cyclothems have marine rocks at the bottom, perhaps indicating sinking then gradual building up of the edge of the coal swamp delta. However, most cyclothems have no marine beds and they may have been formed by the infilling of lakes among the swamps. Occasionally, the coastal swamps were widely inundated by the sea and the marine bands deposited at those times are very useful in correlating the Coal Measures of different areas.

At the end of the Carboniferous period the climate was becoming drier and the top of the Carboniferous system is made up of red sandstones and shales deposited on land under arid conditions. The general uplift of Britain at this time was caused by mountain-building going on in the south. During the Upper Palaeozoic era an ocean had run across the middle of what is now Europe. Devon and Cornwall lay in deep water on the northern edge of this ocean. Towards the end of the Carboniferous period the plates north and south of this ocean came together to push up the **Variscan Mountains** in between (these mountains are also known as the Hercynian and Armorican Mountains). The northern edge of the Variscan chain ran across southern England, through the Bristol Channel and South Wales and across into the south of Ireland (figure 6.36). The mountain-building processes caused thrusting, folding on east-west axes and slight metamorphism in the Devonian and Carboniferous rocks of south-west England. At

112

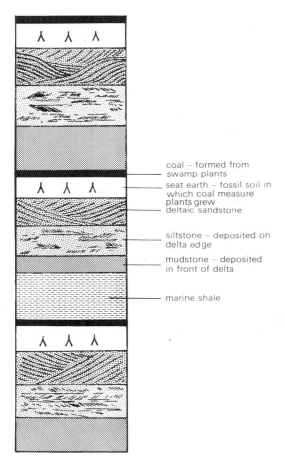

coal – formed from swamp plants
seat earth – fossil soil in which coal measure plants grew
deltaic sandstone

siltstone – deposited on delta edge

mudstone – deposited in front of delta

marine shale

6.35 Coal measure cyclothems.

this time the granites of Devon and Cornwall were intruded. Further north, the Variscan movements produced more open folds in the Devonian and Carboniferous rocks and caused general uplift of the land above sea-level. The Carboniferous igneous activity of northern England and Scotland may have been distantly related to the Variscan plate collision processes going on in the south.

The uplift which accompanied the Variscan movements raised Britain above the sea and the Permian rocks which follow the Carboniferous rocks were laid under desert conditions. Material was carried down from upland areas to be deposited in alluvial cones and scree slopes against the sides of the hills, while in low-lying areas, desert sand dunes were formed. The main basin of deposition formed a wide, irregular ring

around the Pennines and the Lake District while some deposition also took place in Devon and Cornwall (figures 6.37(a) and (b)). In late Permian times a sea called the Zechstein Sea spread from the east into north-east England. At times the sea also reached through the Vale of Eden so that marine deposits were laid down west of the Pennines (figure 6.37(c)). The main deposit formed in the Zechstein Sea was **Magnesian Limestone** which is found between Sunderland and Nottingham. The Magnesian Limestone has this name because it contains quite a lot of magnesium carbonate in the form of dolomite (calcium and magnesium carbonate). Towards the end of the Permian period the Zechstein Sea

began to retreat and dry up so that it became a la of very salty water. Continued evaporation caus the salts to be precipitated as evaporites made of calcium, sodium, magnesium and potassiu compounds. The end of the Permian period, whi is also the end of the Palaeozoic era, saw a retu to hot desert conditions. An interesting feature the Permian system is that the dune-bedding the sandstones can be used to work out the wi directions in Permian times. It has been found th the winds blew from an easterly direction just they do in the north African deserts at present. Th indicates that during the Permian period Britain in the track of the north-east trade winds, that it lay not far north of the equator.

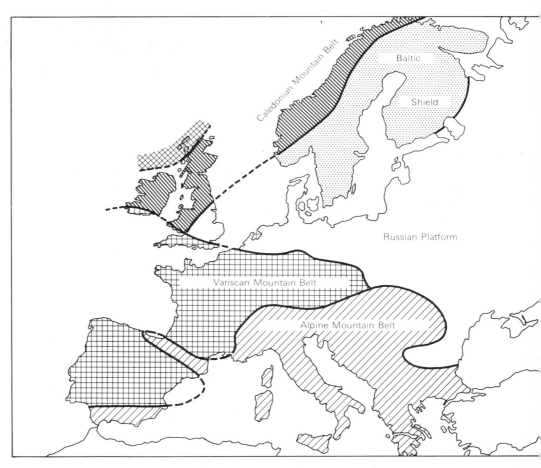

6.36 Present positions of zones of mountain building which have affected Europe at various times.

6.37 (a) Distribution of Permian rocks.

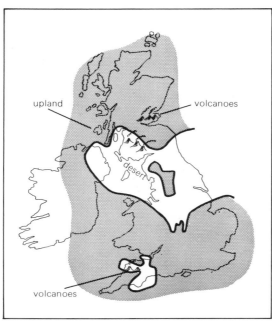

6.37 (b) Britain during the Lower Permian period.

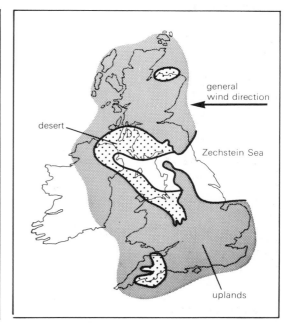

6.37 (c) Britain during the Upper Permian period.

The Mesozoic era

The Mesozoic era is made up of the Triassic, the Jurassic and the Cretaceous periods. It lasted from about 225 million years ago until about 65 million years ago. You will remember that after the Caledonian Orogeny Britain was part of a continent which also included the Canadian Shield, Greenland and the Baltic Shield. With the closing of the Variscan ocean near the end of the Palaeozoic era, this northern continent was joined to the rest of Europe and Asia to form the giant continent of Laurasia. The Triassic rocks were laid on land but during the succeeding Jurassic and Cretaceous periods deposition took place mostly under advancing and retreating seas.

The Triassic period saw the uninterrupted continuation of the desert conditions of Permian times, so in Britain there is no break in sedimentation between the Palaeozoic and the Mesozoic eras. The main difference between the Permian and Triassic systems is that deposition took place over a wider area during the Triassic period (figures 6.38(a) and (b)). In Lower Triassic times the south of England and part of the Midlands received thick deposits of pebbles carried by rivers from the Variscan Mountains of northern France. By the middle of the Triassic period the Variscan Mountains had probably been reduced to low hills, and during Upper Triassic times Britain was a low-lying area partly covered by fine, wind-blown dust (loess) which is now seen as a red mudstone. In the depressions there were salt lakes fringed with sandy deltas. Evaporation of salt lakes which may have been frequently recharged with sea water gave deposits of the evaporites gypsum and rock salt which are at their thickest in Cheshire. In contrast to the Old Red Sandstone of Devonian times the Permian and Triassic rock of Britain is sometimes called the **New Red Sandstone**.

At the end of the Triassic period most of Britain was invaded by the Jurassic sea (figures 6.39(a) and (b)). The Lower Jurassic (or Liassic) rocks consist mostly of dark mudstones with thin limestones deposited in deep basins in the shelf

6.38 (a) Distribution of Triassic rocks.

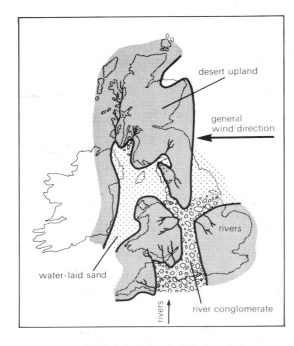

6.38 (b) Britain during the Triassic period.

rocks along with sandstones and mudstones. Deep-water sedimentation then returned to give the **Kimmeridge Clay**. After the deposition of the Kimmeridge Clay the sea began to retreat from Britain and the topmost Jurassic beds were laid down in deltas, lagoons and swampy lakes in the extreme south of England and on the edge of a retreating sea in Lincolnshire and Yorkshire.

At the start of the Cretaceous period the fresh-water lake in southern England was gradually filled in by deltas. These sediments are called the **Wealden Beds**; many of them are deltaic sandstones but there are also thin fresh-water limestones and mudstones. With the shallowing of the lake towards the end of this time, muddy sediments became dominant. While deposition took place in fresh water in the Wealden area marine sedimentation continued in Lincoln and Yorkshire. These two areas of deposition were separated by the upraised **London Platform** (figures 6.40(a) and (b)). Towards the end of the

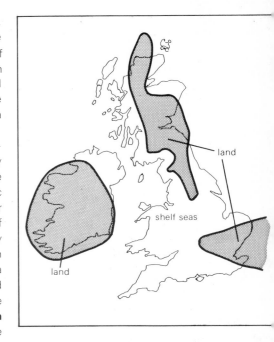

6.39 (b) Britain during the Jurassic period.

sea. The main basins were in southern England, Cheshire, Yorkshire and the Hebrides. Between the basins were stretches of shallow water called **swells** where the sediments are thin. Ammonites, belemnites and brachiopods are very common in Liassic rocks and marine reptiles are also found. In the Middle Lias (i.e. the middle of the Lower Jurassic period) the sea became shallower for a time and economically important, iron-rich limestones were deposited. Some of these limestones are oolitic and the iron in them was probably derived from the Triassic system. Upper Liassic rocks are similar to Lower Liassic rocks in that they were deposited in fairly deep water.

The Middle Jurassic system consists mostly of shallow-water, oolitic limestones, sandstones and mudstones. Ammonites are less common than in Lower Jurassic rocks but corals are common. The Middle Jurassic rocks of Yorkshire and Scotland were deposited in deltas. The Upper Jurassic system saw a return to deep-water sedimentation with mudstones (the **Oxford Clay**) again being deposited. Above the Oxford Clay came shallow-water limestones like those of the Middle Jurassic

6.39 (a) Distribution of Jurassic rocks.

Lower Cretaceous period the sea spread into th Weald from the south, breached the Londo Platform, and joined up with the sea to the nort The spreading sea deposited shallow-wat sandstone called the **Lower Greensand** which thick in the south-east of England but thins o just south of the Fens (figure 6.40(c)). After th the sea continued to spread rapidly until it covere the London Platform. Near the western shore the sea which ran north through Devon the **Upp Greensand** was deposited, while at the sam time the **Gault Clay** was deposited in deep water towards the east. The Upper Greensand w laid down as far north as Bedford while the Gau Clay reaches into Norfolk.

During the Upper Cretaceous period the s covered practically the whole of Britain. T Upper Cretaceous system is made up almo entirely of chalk. Chalk is a pure, white limesto composed largely of the skeletons of calcareo algae called **coccoliths** which floated in cle warm seas uncontaminated by land-derive sediment. Flint bands are common, particularly the Upper Chalk.

Upper Cretaceous (Chalk)
Lower Cretaceous

6.40 (a) Distribution of Cretaceous rocks.

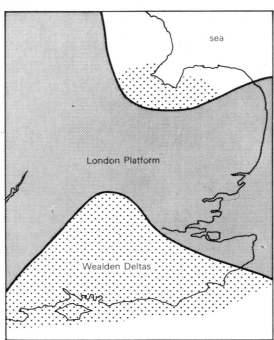

6.40 (b) South-east England at the beginning of the Cretaceous period.

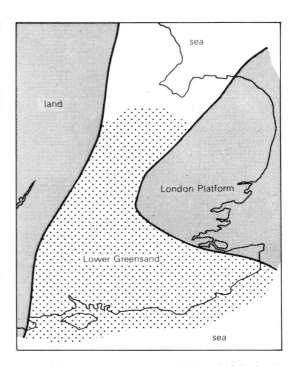

6.40 (c) South-east England towards the end of the Lower Cretaceous period.

e Cainozoic era

he Cainozoic era is made up of the Tertiary and aternary periods and it has lasted for the past 65 ion years. The Chalk sea which covered Britain ing the Upper Cretaceous period was a therly extension of the **Tethys Sea**—an ocean ich lay between Europe and Africa. During the tiary period the African Plate moved into the opean Plate, closing the Tethys Sea and hing up the Alps. At the end of the Cretaceous iod the sea withdrew almost entirely from ain so that during Tertiary times most of Britain fered deep erosion and Tertiary sediments are y found in the south of England. During the tiary period there was a great deal of igneous ivity going on in western Scotland and in th-east Ireland. During the first part of the aternary period the Earth's climate was very d and thick ice-sheets covered most of Britain. reat of the ice-sheets to their present polar sitions brings us into modern times.

n Lower Tertiary times the North Sea and the glish Channel remained as relics of the once widespread Chalk sea. The sea periodically invaded south-east England and then retreated again, so that the Lower Tertiary system shows a sequence of repeated marine and non-marine rocks. The marine rocks which were laid down tend to grade westwards into deltaic deposits laid down on the landward edge of the sedimentary basin. Lower Tertiary rocks are found in the **London** and **Hampshire Basins** (figures 6.41(a) and (b)). Although these areas are now separated as a result of folding caused by the distant Alpine orogeny, they were continuous while sedimentation was taking place. In the London area the first marine invasion ran in over a

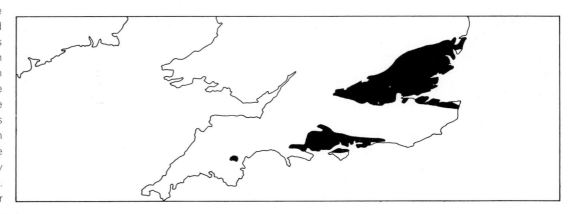

6.41 (a) Tertiary sedimentary rocks of southern England.

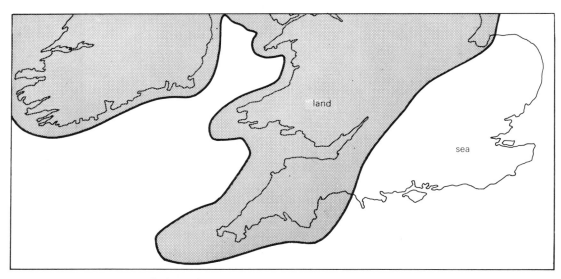

6.41 (b) Southern Britain during the Tertiary period. In these times the modern shape of Britain was beginning to emerge.

surface of deeply-eroded Chalk and laid down marine sandstones which were followed by logoonal and deltaic sediments deposited as the sea retreated. The second marine advance laid down the well-known **London Clay**—this deposit contains fossilized turtles and crocodiles and the remains of plants now found in Malaysia. These fossils clearly indicate the existence of a sub-tropical climate at this time. The London Clay is followed by non-marine deposits and then by marine sediments again (figure 6.42). The Hampshire area shows a sequence fairly similar to that of the London Basin; the sediments were also deposited by an advancing and retreating sea.

The igneous activity in western Scotland and north-east Ireland was related to the opening up of the northern part of the Atlantic Ocean. During most of the Cretaceous period Britain and Greenland were still joined, but about 70 million years ago a constructive plate boundary formed between them. (The south Atlantic Ocean had begun its formation about 30 million years before this.) What seems to have happened was that the initial Mid-Atlantic Ridge was a double or a branched structure, so that a ridge in addition to the one which now passes through Iceland developed down the west side of Scotland. This secondary ridge lasted from about 70 until about

45 million years ago when igneous activity ceased and the zone of crustal weakness died out. The Lower Tertiary igneous rocks are mostly basaltic lavas along with plutonic granites and gabbros (figures 6.43(a) and (b)).

At the end of the Lower Tertiary period Britain

was uplifted, the sea retreated to about its pres position and the general shape of Britain carved out by continued erosion. The U Tertiary period saw a general cooling from sub-tropical climates of Lower Tertiary tir Upper Tertiary rocks are represented only by a deposits of shelly marine sand in south England.

The climatic cooling which began in the Tert period reached its climax with the onset of **Pleistocene** (this is the name given to first part of the Quaternary period) about million years ago. During Pleistocene times ice-sheets spread from the poles and from h mountain ranges so that many countries wh now have temperate climates were covered by The ice advanced and retreated many times; periods of advance are called **glacials** and warmer periods of retreat are **interglacials**. In last 2.5 million years there seem to have been major glacials which may have included as m as twenty ice advances. The last glaciation Britain reached its height about 18 000 years and ended about 12 500 years ago. The glaciat before that was about 150 000 years ago; glaciation brought the ice nearly to London ar

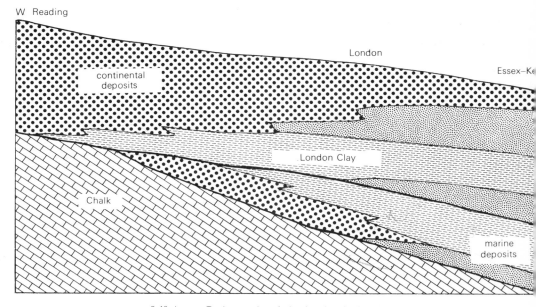

6.42 Lower Tertiary rocks of the London basin indicating deposition by an advancing and retreating sea.

basaltic lava | basic dykes
large intrusions | 100 km

6.43 (a) Tertiary igneous rocks.

When huge ice-sheets form, so much water is converted to ice that the sea-level falls. For example, during the last glacial the sea-level fell by about 150 metres. This meant that much of the continental shelf became dry land and Britain was joined to Europe. At this time the Thames ran into the Rhine before it reached the sea. The fact that the sea was lower is shown by the existence of peat on the floor of parts of the North Sea and the English Channel, and by the presence of submerged forests in places around the coast. Another effect of the ice was that its weight caused an isostatic depression of Britain. The rise of the land when the ice melted is shown by the raised beaches around our shores. When the ice melted the sea rose faster than the land, so that in places the sea reached far inland depositing sand, gravel and mud before being pushed back by the rising land. The best known glacial and interglacial deposits are found in East Anglia (figure 6.45). One of the lowest beds is deltaic or estuarine in origin and it contains the remains of elephant, rhinoceros, hippopotamus, deer and sabre-toothed tiger which lived in the area during a warm interglacial. Flint implements made by early man have also been found. Above this layer there is a boulder clay which contains rocks carried all the way from Norway.

As yet, we do not know what causes an Ice Age such as that of Pleistocene times to occur, and many theories have been put forward to explain the origins of major glaciations. For example, Ice Ages may be caused by decrease in the Sun's heat or by the movement of the Solar System through dusty patches of space. It has also been suggested that they are caused by periodic changes in the

...gue of the glacier, which stretched all the way ...oss the North Sea, even moved up the English ...annel. The limits of the last two ice-sheets and ...general directions of ice flow are shown in ...ures 6.44(a) and (b)).

The effects of glaciation in Britain are many and ...ied and they include both erosional and ...ositional features. The ice-sheets which ...vered Britain smoothed off the upland areas and ...posited boulder clay in the lowlands. Sands and ...vels were laid down around the edges of the ...ciers by torrential melt-water streams. When ...ice-sheets retreated, the ice in the mountains ...sisted as valley glaciers which formed many of ...landforms seen in the Scottish Highlands, the ...ke District and the Welsh mountains. All of the ...tures described in Unit 3 can be recognized ...en though the glaciers have long since ...appeared. The south of England lay outside the ...ciated area but here there are signs that the ...ound was permanently frozen.

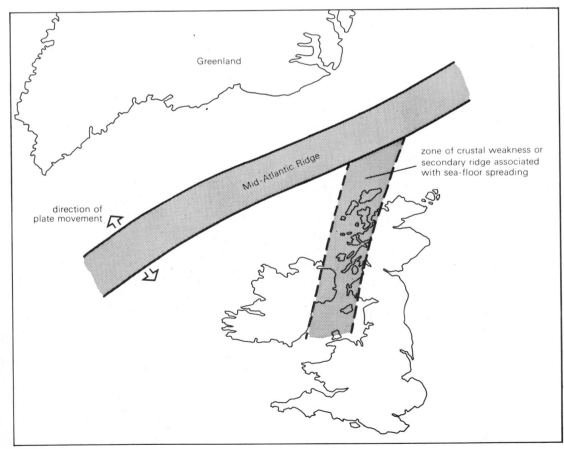

6.43 (b) 70 million years ago the North Atlantic may have looked like this

118

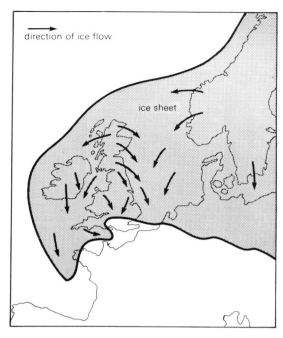

direction of ice flow

ice sheet

6.44 (a) The maximum extent of the European ice sheet during the Pleistocene period. This glaciation took place about 150 000 years ago.

Earth's orbit which produce variations in the amount of heat energy falling on the Earth. If the causes lie within the Earth then it may be that a great deal of volcanic activity could produce an Ice Age, because large amounts of volcanic dust could prevent the Sun's heat from reaching the surface of the Earth. It seems, too, that ice-sheets will only form if there is land or a partly enclosed sea at the poles. At present, Antartica lies at the South Pole and the Arctic Ocean is almost completely surrounded by land. It may be, therefore, that Ice Ages are caused by chance distributions of land and sea brought about by the drift of continents.

With the retreat of the glaciers to their present

positions about 10 000 years ago, we move into **Recent** or **Holocene** times. We may, of course, be living in an interglacial and Britain may one day again be buried by thick ice. Nobody knows when the ice will come back—it could be in 100 000 years or it could be within the next 1000 years. The post-glacial climate of Britain has not always been the same as it is now. We can get a good idea of how a climate has changed by studying the remains of plants and animals such as snails and beetles found in peat and other deposits formed since the last glaciation. For example, pine tree remains would indicate a fairly cold climate while the remains of oak trees would indicate a warmer climate. It has been found that in late glacial times

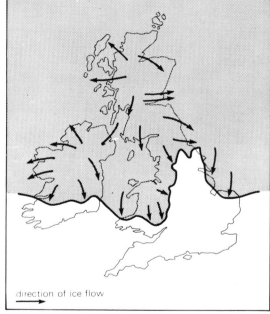

direction of ice flow

6.44 (b) The extent of the last major glaciation of Britain about 18 000 years ago.

6.45 Pleistocene deposits of East Anglia.

the climate was gradually getting warmer, and t about 7000 years ago it was warmer than it is present. A general cooling has been taking pla ever since with signs of expanding glaciers ab 6000 years ago and again about 3000 years a Even in historical times climatic changes ha been observed. In Britain there was a period cold climate from the middle of the fifteenth to middle of the nineteenth centuries which has be called the **Little Ice Age**. In this century glaci in the northern hemisphere have generally be retreating, but the Antarctic glaciers have n changed much in the last fifty years.

Table 6.3 summarizes the main events in geological history of Britain.

PERIOD (nos. indicate millions of years before present)	MAJOR EARTH MOVEMENTS	MAJOR EVENTS AFFECTING BRITISH AREA	HISTORY OF LIFE FORMS
Quaternary 2.5	Mid-Atlantic Ridge continues to spread	Retreat of glaciers to present positions. Widespread glaciation.	Modern man becomes dominant. Extinction of many large mammals.
Tertiary 65	Alps formed as Africa moves towards Europe. Opening of North Atlantic Ocean.	Temperate climate. Alpine mountain-building produces weak folds in southern England. Alternating marine and non-marine deposition in southern England. Sub-tropical climate. Igneous activity in north-west British area. Most of Britain above sea level.	Early man appears. Many large mammals become extinct. Rise of mammals. Grasses become common. Widespread forests. Spread of modern bivalves and gastropods.
Cretaceous 135	Opening of South Atlantic Ocean	Chalk deposited in clear seas. Deltaic then marine sedimentation in Lower Cretaceous period.	Ammonites and many large reptiles become extinct. Almost all belemnites extinct. Mammals still small. Flowering plants develop.
Jurassic 190	Pangaea breaking up.	Deposition in widespread shallow seas. Warm climate	Birds and first flowering plants appear. Dinosaurs common. Ammonites and belemnites abundant.
Triassic 225	Continued existence of Pangaea.	Desert conditions continue from Permian. Lake and river deposits. Hot climate.	Early dinosaurs and primitive mammals appear. First scleractinian corals. Spread of conifers.
Permian 280	Pangaea formed. Britain in arid region north of Equator. Gondwanaland at South Pole.	Rocks deposited in hot desert and in very salty sea, roughly in position of present North Sea. Variscan mountain building affects south-west England. Granites intruded.	Extinction of trilobites and rugose corals. Ammonites appear. Conifers appear.
Carboniferous 345	Britain crosses the Equator.	Coal-bearing rocks deposited in widespread coastal swamps. Limestones deposited in shallow seas. Deltas in central Scotland and north-east England. Volcanism mostly in Scotland.	Reptiles appear. Amphibians and insects become common. Non-flowering plants abundant.
Devonian 395	Britain in arid region south of Equator. Final deformation and uplift of Caledonian Mountains.	Continental deposition (except in south-west England). Caledonian Mountains deeply eroded. Igneous activity common. Warm climate.	Rapid development of land plants leads to appearance of first forests. Goniatites, amphibians and insects appear. Graptolites become extinct.
Silurian 430	Ocean closes as northern and southern continents collide.	Marine deposition but sea shallows towards end of period. Warm climate. Igneous activity ceases.	Fish abundant. Corals, brachiopods and crinoids common. First land plants appear.
Ordovician 500	Ocean closing as continents move together. Early stages in formation of Caledonian Mountains. Much folding and metamorphism.	Marine deposition continues. Widespread volcanism. Warm climate.	Graptolites and brachiopods common. Rugose and tabulate corals appear. Armoured, jawless fish appear. Spread of molluscs.
Cambrian 570	Wide ocean still exists between northern and southern Britain. Separate continents move generally northwards.	Sediments deposited in ocean between continents. Climate probably temperate.	Graptolites appear. Trilobites dominant. Appearance of many invertebrate groups with hard parts.
Origin of Earth 4600	Britain near South Pole? Continent breaks up 1000 million years ago. Northern and southern Britain lie on continents separated by ocean. Britain on continent along with Canadian Shield, Greenland and Baltic Shield. Oldest rocks 3800 million years old.	Cold climate. Gneisses succeeded by sediments — Torridonian, Moinian, Dalradian and Longmyndian. (Moinian and Dalradian metamorphosed during Lower Palaeozoic era.) Gneisses formed in north-west Scotland, Anglesey and Malvern Hills. Oldest British rocks 2900 million years old.	Many-celled invertebrates such as worms and jellyfish appear. Algae appear about 2500 million years ago. Primitive organisms similar to bacteria. Origin of life 3500 million years ago.

Table 6.3 A summary of the main geological events in the history of Britain.

UNIT
7
Earth Resources

Resources and reserves

The society in which we live depends heavily on the use of materials taken from the Earth. For example, we burn coal, oil and natural gas to provide us with energy, we extract metals for making tools and machinery and we dig clay to make bricks. The substances which we find useful are called **resources**. Materials such as coal, oil and natural gas which can be used only once are described as **non-renewable** resources while substances such as water which are not destroyed in use are **renewable** resources. The use of resources depends on factors such as their value, how easily they can be extracted and how far they are from where they are to be used. For instance, there is coal in Antartica and Greenland but it is impossible to mine. Also, we import oil from the Middle East but we would not import sand, because although sand is a very useful building material it is not valuable enough to justify the cost of transporting over long distances.

Resource materials still in the Earth are called **reserves**, and **extractable** reserves are those which can be profitably removed. For example, a coal seam 2 metres thick would be worth mining but a seam 10 centimetres thick would not be worth mining because the cost of the extraction would exceed the value of the coal. However, sometime in the future it may be worth using reserves which are not at present considered extractable. Why should this be so? Reserves can sometimes be assessed quite accurately. For instance, the thicknesses and extents of workable seams in a coalfield may be well known so the amount of coal available can be calculated. Often, however, a good deal of guesswork is involved in estimating reserves, and, as resources are used up or new discoveries are made the figures have to be changed.

Different countries consume resources at different rates depending on the size of their population and on how technologically advanced they are. In developed countries cars, lorries and machines are very common and their product and running requires the use of large quantities metal and oil. In developing countries there is lit heavy industry and few people own cars so le metal and oil is used. This means that, on avera someone living in a developed country consum a great deal more of the Earth's resources th someone living in a developing country. example, the average person living in the Unit States uses oil about one hundred times fas than the average person living in India.

Energy resources

Most of our energy comes from the burning the fossil fuels coal, oil and natural gas, while so electricity comes from nuclear and hydroelect sources. In places round the world geotherm tidal, wind and solar energy are all used althou these sources are not likely to contribute a gr deal to world energy supplies in this century. problem of energy supply is that as the worl

...ulation increases and as society becomes more ...hanized, the amount of energy required is ...stantly increasing. In fact, energy ...sumption for industrial purposes doubles ...y ten years. Britain's energy requirements are ...wing at the rate of 4 to $4\frac{1}{2}$ per cent every year ...re very fortunate in having enough coal to last ...or several centuries, but North Sea Oil will ...ably not last long into the next century. This ...ns that Britain will become heavily dependent ...oal again and inside the next hundred years ...vill probably find that most of our gas supplies ...be manufactured from coal, and that coal will ...sed more and more as a source of chemicals ...transport fuels. In the future, as fossil fuels ...ome depleted, we will come to depend more ...more on other energy sources and eventually ...t of our electricity will come from nuclear ...tors. Indeed, it has even been suggested that ...jenerating capacity of British nuclear reactors ...be increased by as much as forty times in the ...fifty years. Where conditions are locally ...urable, solar, geothermal, tidal, wind and ...aps ocean wave energy will be increasingly ...

...oal is formed from peat by a process called ...lification. When peat is buried by other ...ments it is compressed, and the deeper it is ...ed the more it is compressed. At shallow ...ths peat is changed to **lignite** or **brown coal**. ...ite looks quite like hard peat. At greater depths ...iminous or **house coal** is formed, while very ...o burial results in the formation of hard, shiny ...hracite. The main effect of compression is to ...ease the proportion of carbon in the coal ...hly as follows:

		bituminous	
at	lignite	coal	anthracite
% →	70% →	85% →	95%
bon	carbon	carbon	carbon

...percentage of carbon in a coal is described as ...rank of the coal. The heat-producing quality ...oal increases with its rank.

...oal has been formed several times in the ...ogical past since land plants became

established in the Devonian period. Most of the world's high-ranking coal is Carboniferous or Permian whereas Mesozoic and Tertiary coals are generally of low rank. British coal is nearly all Carboniferous. You will remember that during Carboniferous times thick forests grew on coastal swamps and deltas which covered most of Britain south of the Scottish Highlands. The peat which formed from these forest plants gave rise to our coal. Although coal was formed over a very wide area it is now found in coalfields which are separated from each other as a result of Variscan folding and subsequent erosion (figure 7.1). Where coal-bearing rocks come to the surface an **exposed coalfield** is formed, but where the Carboniferous system is covered by younger rocks a **concealed coalfield** results. The Kent

Coalfield is completely concealed (figure 7.2), as is more than half of the Yorkshire-Derbyshire-Nottinghamshire Coalfield. British coals are mostly bituminous, but high-ranking anthracites are found in South Wales and Kent where high pressures accompanied folding.

Before the mining of coal begins a great deal of work has to be done by the geologist. When coal is found in an area the type and quantity of coal present has to be assessed. The depths of the seams and the structure of the rocks also have to be worked out because deep mines are much more expensive to operate than shallow mines, and if the rocks are greatly faulted and folded mining will be difficult. All of these factors are taken into account when working out the costs involved to see if it will be worthwhile to open a mine.

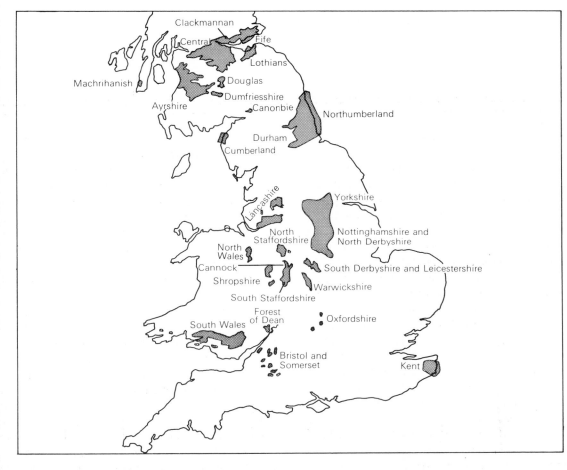

7.1 The major British coalfields.

SW   Tertiary   NE

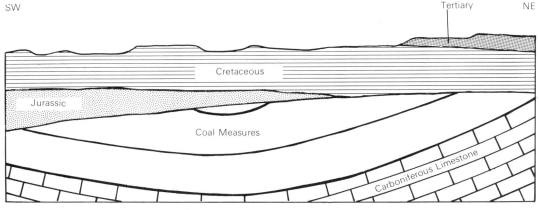

7.2   Section through the concealed Kent coalfield.

An opencast coal site showing a giant walking dragline operation.

Coal seams near the surface can most easily be worked by **opencast mining** in which the rocks above the seams (the overburden) are stripped off and the coal is removed down to a depth of about 200 metres by huge dragline excavators. At present, opencast mining in Britain produces about 10 million tonnes a year (a tonne is a thousand kilograms). The near-surface seams will probably be worked out by the end of the century. **Underground mining** is the only way of reaching deep coal seams. In this method shafts are sunk into the seams and the coal is removed by power loading machines which travel along the coal faces cutting the coal and loading it onto conveyor belts. Underground mining usually produces about 115 million tonnes a year. However, production figures change every year–figure 7.3 shows a graph of total coal production for the last twenty years.

In the future, coal production will probably rise and in the early part of the next century it may well be over 200 million tonnes a year. The National Coal Board has made plans to increase production by more than 40 million tonnes a year by 1985. This will be done by opening new mines, by increasing production at existing pits and by extending present underground workings. The main areas of expansion will be the development of mines at Selby in Yorkshire expected to produce about 10 million tonnes a year, and the extension of workings in the Midland and Durham fields.

Opencast production will be increased to about 15 million tonnes a year. Britain's coal reserves are probably somewhere in the region of 15 000 million tonnes so at present rates of production the seams which can easily be worked will last for more than a hundred years. However, the British coal mining industry will continue to operate for a long time after this by tapping resources not now considered economical. Eventually it may become necessary to mine far out under the North Sea, to reopen old mines, to extract thin seams, to mine below the present depth limit of 2 kilometres and to sink shafts into the 6000 million tonnes of coal known to exist under Oxfordshire.

More than half of the coal which is mined in Britain is burned in power stations to produce electricity. The other main use is for the manufacture of coke for the steel industry. Heat some coal in the apparatus shown in figure 7.4 until no more liquid or gas comes off. How has the coal changed? What kinds of liquid have you collected? The liquids given off during coke manufacture can be separated to produce many useful substances such as tar, creosote, benzene and ammonia. Coal is also used for heating factories, homes and other buildings. In the future, as oil reserves diminish, coal will be increasingly used as a source of oil and gas. To produce oil the coal can be liquefied by combining it with hydrogen under high pressure or by dissolving it in hydrogen-rich organic solvents. In the process of

gasification the coal can be heated with oxy and steam under high pressure, and g produced can, if necessary, be converted liquids.

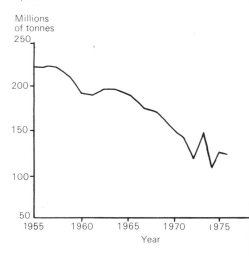

7.3   Coal production in Britain 1955–76

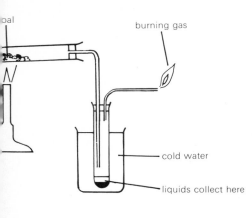

7.4 Heating coal.

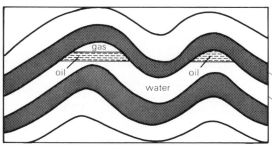

(a) Anticlinal traps.

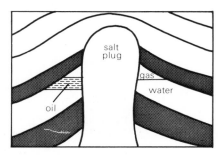

(b) Traps formed against a salt plug.

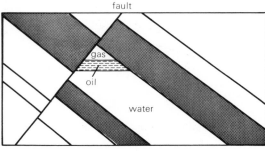

(c) Fault trap formed where impermeable and permeable rocks are brought into contact.

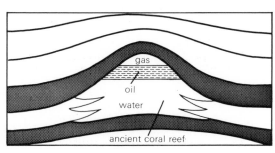

(d) Trap formed by a fossilized coral reef.

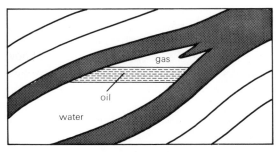

(e) Trap formed where permeable rock passes sideways into impermeable rock.

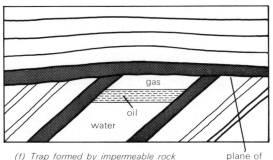

(f) Trap formed by impermeable rock above a plane of unconformity.

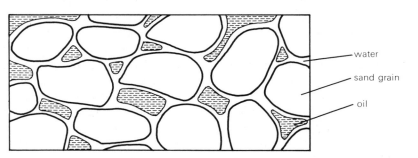

(g) Petroleum lying in the pores of a reservoir rock.

7.5 Traps: petroleum-bearing structures.

Petroleum

Petroleum is made up of natural hydrocarbons found in rocks. (Hydrocarbons are compounds consisting of the elements carbon and hydrogen.) Petroleum includes **crude oil**, **natural gas** (mostly methane) and **tar**, and is formed as a result of the decomposition of tiny, floating marine organisms. Most petroleum seems to have been formed from algae. When the organisms die their remains sink to the sea-bed and if they accumulate where there is a lack of oxygen they are partly decomposed by bacteria to form a black, organic mud called **sapropel**. Burial of the sapropel by other sediments increases the pressure and temperature acting on it and converts the organic remains to hydrocarbons. A rock in which petroleum forms is called a **source rock** and is usually a black mudstone. As the source rock is compacted after burial the petroleum is squeezed out and it moves or **migrates** upwards through the pores and joints in the overlying rocks. The oil or gas may escape at the surface or it may collect in porous **reservoir rocks**.

The most common reservoir rocks are sandstone and limestone. For the petroleum to remain in the reservoir rock it must be sealed in by an overlying layer of impermeable rock called a **cap rock** through which the petroleum cannot pass. The structures in which the petroleum is caught are called **traps** (figure 7.5). The commonest type of

124 trap is the anticline where the downward slope of the reservoir and cap rocks prevents upward movement of the oil and gas. Traps are also formed by faults and unconformities where impermeable rock lies above porous rock. Because of their low densities, salt deposits can rise up through the overlying sediments as **salt plugs**. The movement of the plug bends up the pierced rock layers, and where these are porous petroleum can accumulate against the impermeable salt. Petroleum is also found in traps formed by fossilized coral reefs. The petroleum in a trap can be oil or gas alone, or oil with the less dense gas above. Below the petroleum the pore spaces of the rocks are occupied by water.

Finding oil is much more difficult than finding coal because surface indications such as **oil seeps** are not common. Since the petroleum is generally hidden below the surface, indirect methods of search must be used to find structures which may form traps. After geographical maps of an unexplored area have been made, examination of the surface geology may show up the presence of possible reservoir rocks and trap structures. Geophysical methods are used to find deeply-buried structures. In a **seismic survey**, waves similar to earthquake waves are generated by detonation of explosives in shallow holes. The waves bounce off the underlying rock layers and when they return to the surface they are received by **geophones** and a record somewhat similar to a seismograph is obtained. The geophysicist can analyse these records and work out rock structures deep under the ground. In a **magnetic survey** slight differences in the Earth's magnetism are measured. This method is useful for finding the thickness of sediments lying on top of older igneous and metamorphic rocks. It is also possible to measure slight variations in the Earth's gravity. A **gravity survey** can show the presence of salt plugs because their low-density material produces a slight reduction in the force of gravity.

When a possible trap has been located the only way to find out if it contains oil or gas is to drill an **exploration well**. If petroleum is found, wells called **appraisal wells** are sunk round about so that the reserves and size of the reservoir can be assessed. If the oil or gas field is big enough for

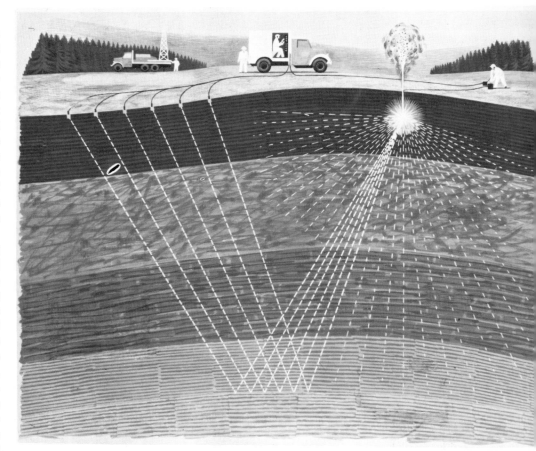

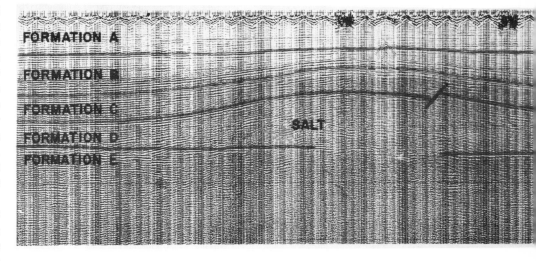

A seismic survey – the positions and forms of the rock layers can be determined by study of the shock wave record.

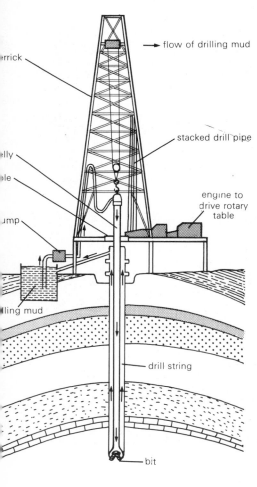

7.6   A drilling rig.

mmercial use the petroleum is extracted through
velopment wells.

Wells are drilled from **drilling rigs** (figure 7.6).
he base of the tall **derrick** there is a **rotary**
le which holds a square pipe called a **kelly**.
table is turned by an engine and the kelly and
ttached drill pipes rotate. At the bottom of the
l string is a tool called a **bit** which cuts
ugh the rock. As the rock is drilled new lengths
drill pipe are added to the drill string at the
ick. While drilling is in progress **drilling mud**
umped down the inside of the drill string and
k up between the drill pipe and the wall of the
. The mud lubricates and cools the bit, and
gs pieces of rock to the surface so that they can

be examined. The weight of the mud also holds
down any oil or gas which might be trying to
escape.

The rate at which petroleum can be extracted
depends on the permeability of the reservoir rock.
It will flow most rapidly from a highly permeable,
well-jointed rock. The most porous rocks are
usually the most permeable. Gas flows most easily,
and 'light', runny oils flow more readily than
'heavy', sticky oils. For oil to move through the
pores of the reservoir rock and into the well, the
pressure under which the oil is held must be much
greater than the pressure at the bottom of the well.
The pressure to push the oil out comes from two
main sources. Firstly, as the oil is removed the
underlying water expands and moves through the
pore spaces pushing the oil in front of it; and
secondly, gas above the oil or dissolved in it
expands and pushes the oil up the well. In a gas
reservoir the gas is pushed up by water drive and by
its own expansion. Eventually, as the reservoir is
depleted, the pressure exerted by the gas and water
falls away and the oil will no longer rise up the well.
When this happens the oil can be pumped to the
surface or the petroleum engineers can pump water
or gas into the reservoir to aid the natural water and
gas drive mechanisms. It is never possible to remove
all of the oil from a reservoir. If the oil is light and in a
highly permeable reservoir with good water drive,
80 per cent may be recovered. On the other hand, a
reservoir of low permeability with heavy oil may
yield only 10 per cent of the total. It is usual to
recover between 30 and 40 per cent of the oil
present in a reservoir.

The unit of volume in which crude oil is
measured is the **barrel**. A barrel is 42 US gallons
or about 160 litres, and in terms of weight 7.35
barrels are equivalent to one tonne. Estimating oil
reserves is much more difficult than estimating
coal reserves because the difficulty of finding oil
means that major strikes may still be made, and
because the supposed average recovery rate of 35
per cent may not be a correct figure. Known crude
oil reserves are about 700 000 million barrels.
More than half of these reserves are in the Middle
East while the North Sea has about 3 per cent of
the world's known oil. With estimates of
undiscovered sources added to known reserves

the world is thought to contain a total of about 2
million million barrels of oil, while natural gas
reserves may be about 300 million million cubic
metres. The leading oil-producing regions are the
Middle East (mainly Saudi Arabia and Iran), the
USSR and the USA. World production is about
22 000 million barrels of oil and about 1.5 million
million cubic metres of gas every year.

Other sources of hydrocarbons are **tar sands**
and **oil shales**. Large deposits of tar sand occur in
Alberta in Canada, and in Venezuela. In this sand
the tar forms the cement holding the sand grains
together. To obtain the tar the sand is mined and
heated with steam. The Athabaska Tar Sands of
Alberta are thought to have recoverable reserves of
about 300 000 million barrels, and similar reserves
may exist in Venezuela. Oil shales contain tarry
material called **kerogen** which is extracted by
heating the shale. It was from such Lower
Carboniferous shales that the British oil industry
began in 1851 in the Lothians of Scotland. The
shale mines were closed in 1962, but they may be
opened again some day if the price of oil continues

A drill bit seen in use on a production platform in the Brent Field.

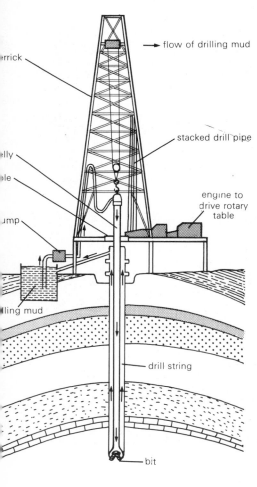

flow of drilling mud

errick

stacked drill pipe

ally

le

engine to
drive rotary
table

ump

lling mud

drill string

bit

to rise. Oil shales usually give about one barrel of oil per tonne of shale, so this oil is expensive to produce because of the cost of mining and heating the shale. In consequence, most of the world's reserves have been little used. Oil shales probably contain reserves of about 200 000 million barrels of oil.

North Sea Oil and Gas

In 1959 a major gas field was discovered at Groningen in Holland. The gas had formed in the Carboniferous Coal Measures and had migrated upwards to be caught in Permian desert sandstones capped by evaporites. Since these rocks were thought to extend across the southern North Sea, this discovery led to a reconsideration of the North Sea as a possible area for oil and gas production. Exploration began in 1962 and in 1965 the West Sole gas field was discovered. Oil was first found in 1967 in the Chalk off Denmark, and was found in the British sector in 1969 in the Tertiary rocks of the Montrose field. Since these early discoveries development in the North Sea has proceeded very rapidly with many oil and gas fields now in production (figure 7.7). Prospecting is going on in other parts of the British continental shelf such as the Irish Sea and the Celtic Sea (between Cornwall and the south coast of Ireland) but these will probably be much less productive than the North Sea.

Over much of its area the North Sea has been a sinking sedimentary basin since Permian times. If you look at the geological section in figure 7.8 you will see that thick sediments have been laid down from late Palaeozoic times until the present. The North Sea itself is made up of two smaller basins (figure 7.9). In the southern sedimentary basin which lies between England and Holland the fields are almost entirely gas fields. In most of them the reservoir rock is the Basal Permian desert sandstone, and the gas has come from the underlying coal. In the northern North Sea there is a thick sedimentary basin between Scotland and Norway which contains mostly oil fields. The reservoir rocks are of various ages but most of them are Jurassic and Tertiary. Most of the oil

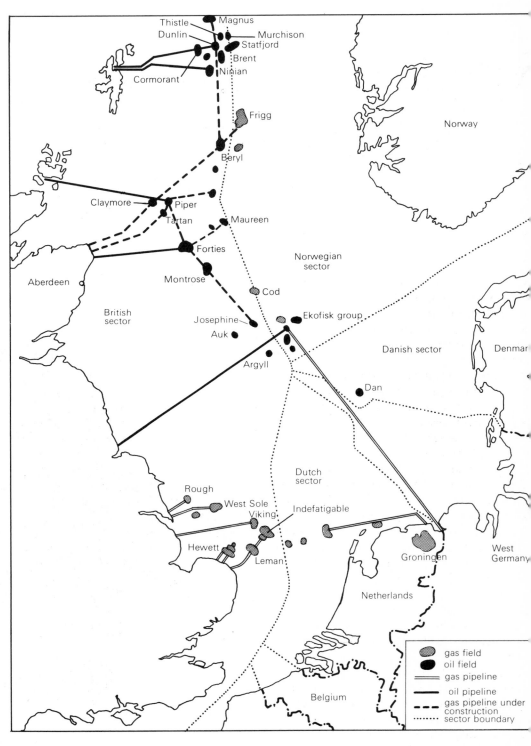

7.7 The main oil fields and gas fields of the North Sea

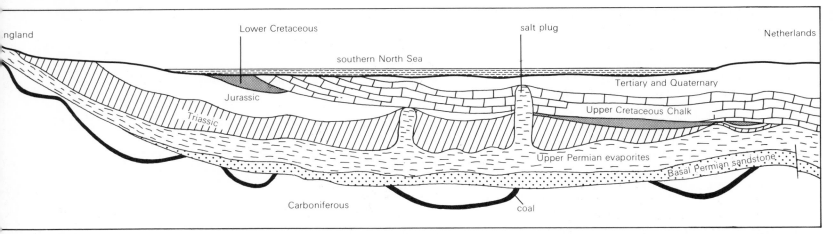

7.8　A geological section across the southern North Sea from England to Holland.

as come from source rocks composed
of **Kimmeridge Clay** (Upper Jurassic) and
Speeton Clay (Lower Cretaceous). Upper
Carboniferous shales may have been the source of
some of the oil found in the southern part of the
northern basin.

Since the rocks under the sea are not directly
accessible to examination, geophysical methods
must be used to find trap structures. In the North
Sea an airborne magnetic survey begun in 1962
showed that the sediments were thick enough to
contain oil and gas fields. Gravity surveys
conducted from ships showed the presence of
gravity variations which indicated the existence of
salt plugs. At sea, as on land, the seismic survey is
the most useful type of geophysical prospecting
because it allows rock structures to be accurately
worked out. Such surveys can be conducted very
rapidly because the geophones can be towed on a
cable behind a ship (figure 7.10). Also, the
explosive which is used to produce the required
sound waves can be detonated in the water
whereas on land the explosive has to be placed in a
shallow bore-hole. The use of computers allows
the collected data to be analysed very quickly.

Exploration drilling at sea takes place from ships
or from rigs mounted on platforms. In water with a
depth of less than about 50 metres the **jack-up
platform** has been most used. This consists of a
platform with legs which can be individually
moved up or down. After the platform has been

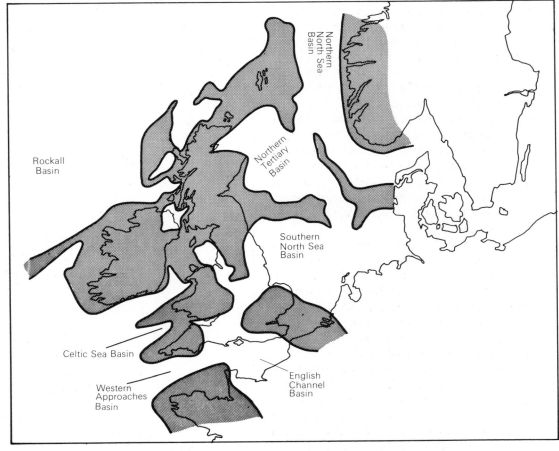

7.9　The main areas of oil and gas exploration around Britain.
The rocks of the shaded areas contain little or no petroleum.

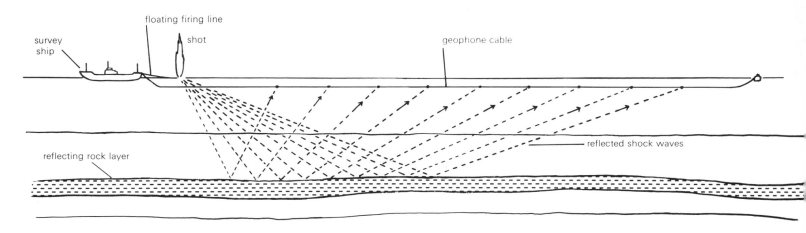

survey
ship

floating firing line

shot

geophone cable

reflecting rock layer

reflected shock waves

7.10 A seismic survey at sea.

towed to the drilling site the legs are lowered to the sea-bed and the platform is raised clear of the water. Jack-up platforms have only been used in the shallow southern North Sea. In deeper water anchored **semi-submersible rigs** are used. They are supported by submerged buoyancy chambers and can operate in depths of up to about 200 metres. Semi-submersible rigs are used in the northern parts of the North Sea. When drilling takes place in very deep water, **drilling ships** have to be used. These are specially designed ships with extra propellors which enable them to remain in a fixed position.

When an oil field has been located the exploration platforms are replaced by gigantic **production platforms**. These are steel or concrete structures placed on the sea-bed. Concrete platforms are becoming more popular than steel platforms, because whereas steel platforms have to be fixed to the sea-bed by piles, the weight of the concrete platforms is sufficient to keep them fixed. Concrete platforms also include tanks for storing oil. Up to about forty wells can be drilled at various angles from a production platform to tap a wide area of the field. Some of the wells are for extraction purposes while others are for injecting gas and water to maintain pressure. The oil from small fields such as Auk, Beryl, Argyll and Montrose is loaded onto tankers while larger fields such as the Forties field have pipelines laid to the shore.

Extraction of oil from the North Sea began in 1975 when the Argyll and Forties fields produced about 8 million barrels. Since then production has risen very rapidly indeed and in 1980 between 700 and 850 million barrels are expected to come ashore. Throughout the 1980s production will probably be maintained at between 750 and 1100 million barrels a year. Reserves of present oil fields are about 10 000 million barrels, but further discoveries in the North Sea and other shelf areas

The semi-submersible rig Stadrill *operating in the Brent Field.*

may bring Britain's total reserves to about 33 000 million barrels. At production rates of 1100 million barrels a year this means that our oil will last for about 30 years.

Gas was first extracted from the fields of the southern North Sea in 1967 and in 1975 these fields produced about 36 000 million cubic metres. With additional gas from northerly fields such as Frigg and Brent, production in the 1980s will probably be about 73 000 million cubic metres a year although it could be as high as 100 000 million cubic metres. Known gas reserves are about 815 000 million cubic metres while total reserves may be about 1 430 000 million cubic metres. With a production rate of 70 000 million cubic metres a year, British natural gas could last for another 20 years.

Before crude oil can be used it has to be treated in an **oil refinery**. Crude oil is a mixture of hydrocarbon molecules of various sizes, and the process of **fractional distillation** is used to separate the different parts or **fractions** of the mixture. The oil is heated and passed up through a **fractionating column** which produces heavy fractions such as tar, fuel oil and lubricating oil at the bottom and lighter fractions such as diesel oil, paraffin and petrol at the top. Because we need more short-chain molecules (such as petrol) than are contained in the crude oil, some of the larger molecules are broken up by a process called **catalytic cracking**. In Britain about 90 per cent of refinery products are used as fuel for power stations, transport and heating. The remaining products are mostly used in the manufacture of plastics, synthetic fibres, paints, detergents, cosmetics, fertilizers, insecticides and many other items.

Nuclear power

It is probable that the world's coal will be worked out in about 500 years and that crude oil will be used up in about 150 years. Since this is the case, future generations will not be able to depend on fossil fuels to the same extent as we do at present. The most promising area of energy production is the use of **nuclear power** from **nuclear reactors**. The energy given off by the nuclear reaction is used to produce steam which drives electricity generators. At present most reactors are **thermal reactors** which use as their fuel a form of the element uranium with 235 particles (protons and neutrons) in the nuclei of its atoms in the energy-producing reaction. In a thermal reactor one tonne of uranium gives off as much energy as about 50 000 tonnes of coal. Calder Hall was the world's first nuclear reactor and it began producing power in 1956. At present about 10 per cent of Britain's electricity is produced by thermal reactors at many sites in England, Wales and southern Scotland. Another type of reactor is the **fast breeder reactor** which is fuelled with a mixture of uranium with 238 particles in its nuclei and plutonium (which is produced in thermal reactors). In a fast reactor one tonne of uranium gives as much energy as about 2 million tonnes of coal. The fast reactor at Dounreay in Caithness was the first in the world to produce electicity for commerical use.

Since uranium 235 forms less than 1 per cent of all natural uranium, using thermal reactors alone would mean that easily extractable uranium reserves would be used up in about 50 years. However, use of the more common uranium 238 in fast reactors will allow reserves to last almost indefinitely. In addition, the fast breeder reaction produces more plutonium than it uses so this would again extend the future of nuclear energy production. The uranium in the world is capable of providing ten times as much energy as all the fossil fuels put together.

Uranium occurs most commonly in the mineral **uraninite** or **pitchblende** (uranium oxide). Uranium minerals are usually found in black shales or associated with granite. World reserves of easily extractable uranium minerals are probably about 6 million tonnes with the USA and Canada being the richest areas. All of Britain's uranium is imported; the reserves which we do have will not be worth extracting until the richer reserves in other parts of the world have been used up.

Amoco A, a gas production platform on the Leman Bank Field in the North Sea.

In future the electricity produced by British reactors will increase greatly. Production is expected to rise by about twenty times by the year 2000 as thermal reactors with improved designs are built. After the year 2000 fast reactors will rapidly replace thermal reactors, so that by 2030 well over 90 per cent of our electricity could come from nuclear sources.

Other sources of energy

In areas of igneous activity magmas are still solidifying in the Earth's crust. Ground water heated in the rocks above the magma may rise to the surface as steam or hot water from **geysers** or **hot springs**. If a bore-hole is sunk into the heated rocks, steam can be extracted to drive electric generators and hot water can be obtained for heating purposes. **Geothermal power** was first used at Larderello, Italy, in 1904. Since then electricity has been generated in places such as Japan, New Zealand and the USA, and about half the buildings in Iceland are heated by geothermal hot water. In Britain there are areas of Cornwall and Durham where the crust is warm enough at bore-hole depth for hot water to be obtained. Despite estimates that Cornwall could produce geothermal energy equivalent to 8000 million tonnes of coal, it does not seem likely that these resources will be used in Britain in the foreseeable future.

Energy can also be derived from the sun, from wind and from moving water. In Britain, **solar energy** will probably not contribute a great deal to our energy supply although its present use for heating buildings may be greatly extended. **Wind power** is, again, little used. It has been estimated that 10 000 large windmills or aerogenerators could produce enough electricity to save us about 5 million tonnes of oil a year. Such large-scale development is, however, unlikely in the near future and the main use of wind power will probably be domestic; houses may be fitted with small windmills to produce electricity which could then be stored in batteries. Although hydroelectric power stations produce about 2 per cent of our electricity, the energy of tides and waves has not yet been used in Britain. To generate tidal power, generators are built into a barrage across an estuary with good tidal flow. The movement of the water backwards and forwards drives the generators. A tidal barrage of this type is operating in the Rance Estuary of north-west France, but although Britain has many equally suitable estuaries it seems that such schemes do not produce enough electricity to justify the cost of construction. Wave power could be used in the future—the energy of the waves would be absorbed by specially designed floats called 'ducks' whose movements could drive generators. It has been estimated that a string of enormous 'ducks' 1000 kilometres long in the Atlantic could produce about half of our electricity. However, the considerable technical problems which would arise in building such a structure suggest that early developments are unlikely. Overall, even if these alternative energy sources are developed fairly quickly their contribution to our energy needs in the near future will be slight.

Metals

Most metals are found in the Earth's crust not as elements but in the form of compounds called **ore minerals**. Some ore minerals which you have already heard of are haematite, cassiterite and sphalerite. Which metals could be extracted from these? An **ore** is an accumulation of minerals which is valuable enough to be worth working. The **grade** of an ore is a measure of the percentage of metal in the ore. Ores with high percentages of metal are described as being of **high grade** while ores with low percentages of metal are **low-grade**.

Ore deposits are formed by both igneous and surface processes. A magma is made up of an enormous mixture of different substances, and when it cools it does not solidify all at once. Instead, the minerals separate out slowly and sink to the bottom of the magma chamber. Sometimes early-formed minerals such as magnetite or sulphide-rich and oxide-rich liquids sink through basic magmas and form layered ore bodies. This process of ore formation is called **magmatic segregation**.

The minerals which crystallize first from magma contain no water. This means that a crystallization proceeds, the magma become richer and richer in water, and the last minerals t form are therefore crystallized from a melt whic contains a lot of water. The presence of the wate allows the crystals to grow to enormous sizes s that a very coarse-grained rock called **pegmatit** results, especially in granitic magmas. Pegmatite may be injected into the rock around the intrusio or they may form veins in the upper part of th intrusion. Besides being rich in water, pegmatit magma is rich in metals which were not taken int the minerals formed when the main magm solidified. For example, uranium, zinc and ti minerals are often found in pegmatites.

A magma may give off hot water or it may hea up the ground water of the overlying rocks. Th hot water contains many dissolved minerals whic are deposited by the water as it rises towarc the surface through joint or fault fracture Such **hydrothermal deposits** are among th commonest and most important of all ore bodie and they include ores of copper, lead, tin and zin along with gold and silver. Hydrothermal deposit form **veins** (figures 7.11(a) and (b)) made up o ore minerals along with worthless **gangu minerals** which are often quartz and calcite. The are most commonly found associated wit granites, and there is a tendency for differer minerals to be found at different distances from th intrusion. Cassiterite crystallizes under the hig temperatures and pressures near the magm chamber, while further away from the magm chalcopyrite, sphalerite, iron pyrites, galena an haematite appear. In Britain, hydrothermal ores ar found in places such as south-west England, th Peak District, the Pennines and the Lead Hills c Scotland. These deposits are now mostly worke out. Hydrothermal processes also form low grad ores such as **porphyry copper** where the or mineral is finely spread out in small cracks throug a large volume of rock. At present, hydrotherma deposits are forming under the Red Sea and unde the Salton Sea of southern California. Can yo suggest why such deposits should be forming i these areas?

Magmas alter their surrounding rocks not onl

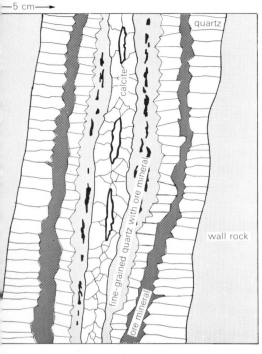

7.11 (a) An example of a hydrothermal vein.

magnetite, gold, rubies and diamonds. Placers are most often deposited by rivers so they consist of easily-worked sand and gravel. Where the gravel is buried to form a rock the ore mineral can be mined from the resulting conglomerate. The gold deposits of the Witwatersrand district of South Africa are found in Precambrian conglomerate which may have originated as a placer deposit.

Residual deposits are formed on the surface when ore is left behind after intense chemical weathering has removed most of the other minerals (figure 7.12). In tropical climates such weathering leaves thick soils called **laterites** which consist mostly of water-containing oxides of iron and aluminium. Laterite rich in aluminium is called **bauxite** and it is from this ore that virtually all of the world's aluminium is extracted.

Workable ore deposits can also be formed by a process called **secondary enrichment**. When a mineral vein outcrops, its top is subjected to weathering. The ore minerals may be dissolved in ground water which then carries them down and precipitates them in lower parts of the vein. Thus

the lower parts of the vein receive extra ore mineral and become enriched (figure 7.13). Removal of the soluble minerals leaves insoluble iron oxides on the surface which form a deposit called a **gossan** or 'iron hat'. The presence of a gossan may indicate the existence of the underlying vein. Deposits of copper sulphides commonly show secondary enrichment.

Now let us look at a few common metals:

Iron

The main ore minerals of iron are the oxides (magnetite, haematite, limonite) and the carbonate (siderite).

Magnetite deposits formed by magmatic segregation in gabbros are found in Sweden and South Africa, and deposits formed by contact metasomatism occur in Utah in the USA. However, sedimentary ores formed by the chemical precipitation of iron oxides are by far the most common sources of iron. Most sedimentary ores are the Precambrian **banded iron formations** which are made up of rapidly

y causing them to recrystallize during metamorphism, but also by adding material to hem in a process called **contact metasomatism**. Deposits formed in this way are most often found around acidic rocks especially if the rocks near the magma are reactive. For xample, limestone can easily be attacked and eplaced by fluids from the magma. Ore bodies ormed by contact metasomatism tend to be small ut they are often of high grade. They may contain xides of iron and sulphides of copper, lead and inc.

Sedimentary processes can form three types of deposit. Firstly, evaporation of sea water forms evaporites which contain useful salts of sodium, potassium and magnesium. Secondly, ore deposits can form by chemical precipitation. For example, oolitic ironstones contain iron minerals probably precipitated from warm tropical seas. Sulphides of copper, lead and zinc may also be precipitated from sea water under conditions where oxygen is lacking. Thirdly, **placer deposits** are formed by the accumulation during deposition of useful minerals such as cassiterite,

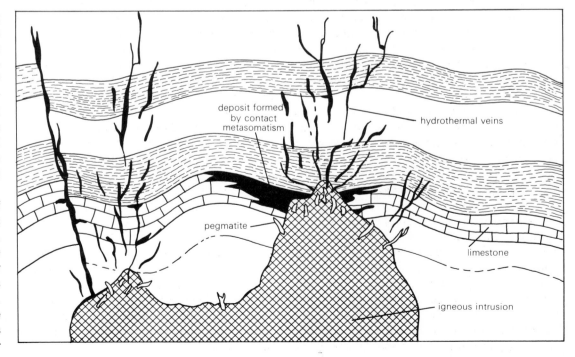

7.11 (b) Forms of ore deposit associated with a large intrusion.

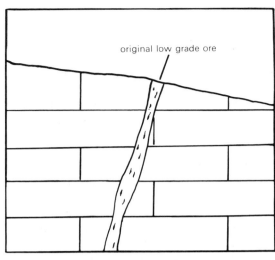

(a) Before weathering.

original low grade ore

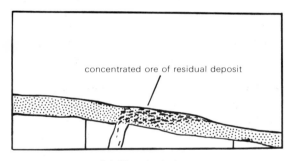

concentrated ore of residual deposit

(b) After weathering.

7.12 Formation of a residual deposit.

alternating iron-rich and quartz-rich layers. These deposits, which consist of 15-40 per cent iron, are found around Lake Superior and in Labrador, South Africa and Australia. Post-Cambrian sedimentary ores are not banded.

The chief source of iron in Britain is the Jurassic **ironstone** (iron silicate and carbonate) of Lincoln and Northamptonshire. Unfortunately these are low-grade ores (13-30 per cent iron) and although reserves are about 3000 million tonnes, they are extracted at a rate of only about 4 million tonnes a year because it is cheaper for the steel industry to import higher grade ore (62 per cent iron) and extract the iron more cheaply. In addition to the sedimentary ores, higher grade hydrothermal haematites in Cumbria and Glamorgan give about 170000 tonnes a year.

Iron is separated from its ore in a **blast furnace**. The furnace is loaded at the top with a mixture of ore, coke (a form of carbon) and limestone. The materials are fired and fanned to white heat by blasts of very hot air. The carbon reacts with the iron oxide to produce molten iron and carbon dioxide. The impurities in the ore join with the melted limestone to form slag which floats on the metal. The molten iron and slag are run out of the bottom of the furnace as more material is added at the top.

Iron is an extremely useful metal which is used in quantities twenty times greater than those of all other metals put together. The importance of steel is indicated by the fact that it forms the basis of the machinery for the manufacture of nearly all industrial products.

Aluminium

The main ore of aluminium is bauxite (aluminium oxide combined with water). As we have already seen, bauxite is a residual deposit formed in the tropics under conditions of activ chemical weathering. During weathering, solubl substances containing sodium, potassium calcium and magnesium are removed leavin behind a deposit rich in the oxides of aluminiun

World bauxite production runs at about 9 million tonnes a year with Australia and Jamaic being the main producers. There is no prospect o Britain ever becoming a producer of aluminium or so all our requirements must be imported as meta bauxite or aluminium oxide.

Bauxite is purified by heating it under pressur with sodium hydroxide. This produces pur aluminium oxide which is melted and broke down into aluminium and oxygen by passing strong electric current through the molten oxide

Aluminium is a very common metal and you wi have seen it at home used for items such a cooking pots, wrapping foil and milk bottle tops. is also used in overhead electric cables and its lo density makes it ideal for making parts of ships an aeroplanes.

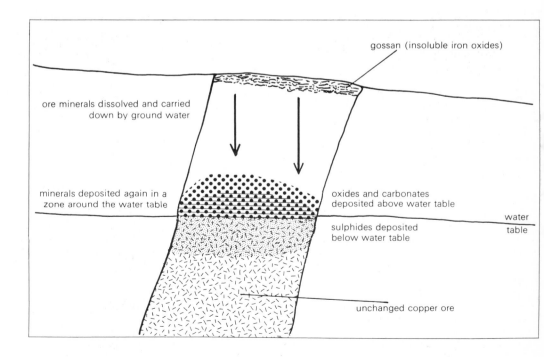

gossan (insoluble iron oxides)

ore minerals dissolved and carried down by ground water

minerals deposited again in a zone around the water table

oxides and carbonates deposited above water table

water table

sulphides deposited below water table

unchanged copper ore

7.13 Concentration of copper ore by secondary enrichment.

The main ores of copper, lead and zinc are the ulphides chalcopyrite, galena and sphalerite. ese ores are formed mainly by hydrothermal ocesses, by contact metasomatism, and by ecipitation from sea water. Copper ores are also mmonly formed by secondary enrichment. About half of the world's copper comes from w grade, hydrothermal **porphyry copper** posits. These usually contain about 0.5 per cent copper so they are usually mined in huge bulk opencast methods. The ore mineral (usually alcopyrite) occurs spread through fine fractures the crushed margins of intrusions of porphyritic neous rocks. Porphyry coppers are well veloped in the copper belts of the south-west A, Chile and Peru. Lead and zinc ores are not und in low grade hydrothermal deposits of the rphyry copper type. In the British Isles they cur in veins along with copper ores in places ch as Cornwall, the North Pennines and Eire. Copper, lead and zinc also come from sedi-

mentary deposits such as the **Kupferschiefer** of Poland and Germany. This is a thin shale less than 1 metre thick which is rich in sulphides of copper, lead and zinc precipitated on the floor of the Permian Zechstein Sea. The bottom of the Zechstein Sea must have been made up of black mud deficient in oxygen which was colonized by bacteria whose activities caused the sulphides to form.

World production of copper is presently about 8 million tonnes a year with the USA, the USSR, Chile, Canada, Zambia and Zaire being the main producers. There are no copper mines in Britain and since our requirements are about 750 000 tonnes a year this makes copper one of our costliest imports. It is not likely that copper will ever be mined in Britain because although low grade ores exist in the Snowdonia National Park, there are good environmental reasons for not mining them. It has been estimated that these ores might be able to supply about one-tenth of our needs for 25 years. In the past, rich copper ores were mined in Anglesey and in south-west

England, and tin mining in Cornwall still produces a small quantity of copper ore as a by-product.

World lead production is about 4 million tonnes a year with the USA and the USSR being the main producers, while zinc is produced at a rate of about 6 million tonnes led by Canada and the USSR. Lead and zinc are not mined in Britain, although some lead comes from fluorite mines in the Pennines and some zinc comes from the Cornish tin mines. In previous years lead and zinc were mined at many places including Devon and Cornwall, the Pennines, North Wales, the Lake District and the Southern Uplands of Scotland. There is a possibility that lead and zinc veins similar to those found in Ireland will be found in the British Carboniferous Limestone.

Pure metal cannot be produced directly from the mined ore. The first step in the treatment process is crushing of the ore to free the sulphide minerals from the gangue. Large lumps of ore are fed into a **jaw crusher** which breaks them into pieces with a diameter of about 15 centimetres. These fragments are reduced further in size in a **cone crusher**, and the last stage of crushing takes place in a grinder which produces particles about 0.1 millimetres in diameter. The powdered ore is then fed into **flotation** tanks in which the different sulphides are separated by being collected in chemically produced froth on the tops of the tanks. In this way **concentrates** of copper, lead and zinc sulphides are obtained. The concentrates then go to **smelters** where the metal is extracted. At the smelter the sulphide concentrates are roasted to convert them to oxides which can then be treated in furnaces to produce the metals.

The main use of copper is as an electrical conductor. It is also used for making water pipes and boilers and is the main component of brass (copper-zinc alloy) and bronze (copper-tin alloy). Lead is used in car batteries, as sheathing for electric cables, for ammunition and for making paints. Zinc is used extensively as a coating for steel to prevent rusting and its alloys are used in the die casting of components for cars and machinery.

Tin

The ore mineral of tin is cassiterite (tin oxide). It is found adjacent to acidic igneous rocks as the

An opencast copper mine at Morenci in Arizona, USA. The mine is about 3 kilometres across and 500 metres deep.

134.

earliest mineral deposited in hydrothermal veins or in deposits formed by contact metasomatism. Since cassiterite is a very hard mineral it can easily survive weathering and transport so it is commonly found in placer deposits.

World production of tin is about 225 000 tonnes a year with Malaysia, Bolivia and Indonesia being the main producers. Cornish tin mining produces between 3000 and 4000 tonnes a year which gives us about one-fifth of our needs. These mines may eventually produce greater quantities.

The main uses of tin are in the manufacture of tinplate for the food canning industry, and in the production of solders.

Some other useful minerals

Minerals have many uses besides that of metal extraction. For example, the chemical industry requires huge quantities of sulphuric acid which is manufactured from **sulphur**. Some pure sulphur is obtained from active volcanoes but most of it occurs above salt plugs around the Gulf of Mexico. Here it has been produced by the action of bacteria on calcium sulphate. Sulphur can also be extracted from hydrogen sulphide in petroleum and from the roasting of sulphide ores.

Fluorite (calcium fluoride) is used in steel making and as a source of fluorine chemicals. It is abundant as a gangue mineral in the hydrothermal veins of the Pennines. British production of fluorite at a rate of about 200 000 tonnes a year is more than enough for our needs.

Asbestos is the name given to more than one type of fibrous silicate mineral. Its resistance to heat and chemicals makes it very useful for items such as insulators, roofing tiles, fire-fighting equipment and brake linings. The main producers are Canada and the USSR.

Diamonds are formed under very high pressure at great depths in the Earth. (Diamond is a form of carbon). They reach the surface through volcanic pipes contained in a rock called **kimberlite**. The indestructible nature of diamonds allows their accumulation in the placer deposits from which most diamonds are obtained. The world's leading producers are South Africa, the USSR and Zaire. The main uses of diamonds are as abrasives,

cutting tools and drills. Only about 20 per cent of diamonds are of sufficient quality to be used as gems. Industrial diamonds can now be made artificially.

Resources and plate tectonics

There is a marked tendency for ore deposits to be found in distinct geographical areas called **metallogenic provinces**. For example, tin occurs in belts in Malaysia and Indonesia, in Bolivia and across Europe from Cornwall to Italy (figure 7.14); porphyry coppers are found in zones in the south-west USA and in Chile and Peru; and lead and zinc deposits occur across the central USA. Distributions such as these suggest that the origins of ore deposits may be related in some way to plate movements.

Since plate boundaries are the sites of igneous activity, it would seem reasonable to suggest that ores will be formed here by igneous processes. For example, in the Red Sea, which lies on a constructive boundary, sulphides of iron, zinc, copper and lead are being deposited in the sea-floor sediments by rising hydrothermal solutions. Also, samples of sediment from oceanic ridges are often found to be enriched in metals such as iron, copper, lead and nickel. Beneath oceanic ridges the hydrothermal solutions probably deposit mineral veins, while deeper still magmatic segregation of ores may take place in gabbro magma chambers. Such deposits have, in fact, been raised from the sea-bed in Cyprus. Here there are sediments rich in iron and manganese, lavas with hydrothermal copper and gabbros with magmatic segregations of chromium ore.

At destructive plate boundaries igneous activity is more acidic than at constructive boundaries, so pegmatites and deposits formed by contact metasomatism occur along with those formed hydrothermally. For example, the copper belts of the USA and South America seem to have formed above Mesozoic subduction zones.

Constructive plate margins in their early stages of development also provide good sites for petroleum formation. Organic matter can collect and decay in the narrow sea which is first formed,

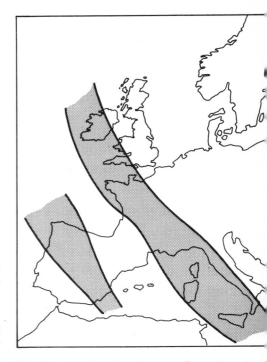

7.14 Metallogenic provinces in western Europe. Deposits of minerals are found in two well-marked belts.

and the evaporites deposited in such areas v form salt plug traps. Later widening of the oce will leave these petroleum deposits on 1 continental shelves on each side of the oce Island arcs near destructive boundaries can h petroleum formation by restricting wa movement with the open sea so that organ matter can accumulate.

Away from plate boundaries ore deposits su as the chemically precipitated ironstones a sulphides will be formed. Coal also seems to fo on level continental margins away from pla boundaries.

Trying to relate the possible positions resource materials to plate movements may help to decide where to look for new resources. F example, the continental shelves of the Atlan may contain many oil fields besides those alrea discovered, because deposits could have form when the Atlantic was in its early stages development. Figure 7.15 shows some possik sites on plates for the formation of ores, petroleu coal and evaporites.

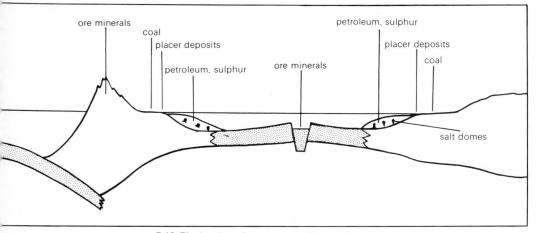

7.15 The location of resource materials on plates.

ulk materials

Many materials including sandstone, limestone, anite, dolerite (whinstone), slate, gypsum, sand d gravel are used in the building industry. owadays natural stone is not much used in ilding, and has largely been replaced by bricks d concrete. Slates are being replaced by anufactured tiles and curbstones are now made m concrete. Look at the older buildings in your vn and see if you can identify the rock types ed. You may be able to visit the old quarries from hich the building stones came. On newer ildings you may find ornamental fronts made m a type of rock not occurring locally. In Britain out 100 million tonnes of rock are quarried every ar. Most of this is crushed for use as aggregate in ncrete and for road building. Find out the rock ed for road making in your area. There is a good ance that the quarries which produced it are still use—try to visit them and find out how the rock extracted and treated for use.

Sand and gravel are used in even greater bulk an stone. About 120 million tonnes are used in itain every year, with gravel production usually ing about twice that of sand. Sand and gravel n be quarried from various sources including er, glacial and beach deposits. Soft sandstones n also be used for sand production. Sand and avel are mostly used to make concrete.

Of all natural materials **limestone** (calcium rbonate) has the greatest number of uses. It accounts for about 90 per cent of the rock quarried in this country with an annual rate of production of about 90 million tonnes. About three-quarters of the limestone is crushed for use as aggregate in the construction industry. It is also used in iron smelting, glass making, water and gas purification, salt and sugar refining, in agriculture, and in medicines, toothpaste, candles and paint. (These are only a very few of its uses). In cement manufacture limestone is roasted with clay or shale in a kiln. This drives off water and carbon dioxide, and changes the composition of the mixture into cement. When water is added to the cement the ingredients react to form new compounds which set in a hard mass of interlocking crystals. British production of cement is about 20 million tonnes a year.

Besides its use in cement making, clay is used to make bricks and pottery. In brick making the clay is ground, damped and moulded into shape. The bricks are then fired in kilns. Firing produces silicate glass which binds the unfused particles together. The best brick-making clays such as the Jurassic Oxford Clay contain small quantities of carbon which burn during firing and greatly reduce fuel costs. Clay can also be fired to produce pottery. White **china clay** (kaolinite) is formed by the hydrothermal alteration of feldspar in granite. China clay associated with the granites of south-west England is used to make china and as a coating for paper.

Plaster is made by heating gypsum. This drives off most of the water contained in the gypsum and forms **plaster of Paris**. When plaster of Paris is mixed with water it forms a hard mass of gypsum crystals. Plaster is used for coating walls, for filling cracks and for making plaster board.

Glass is made by heating a mixture of sand, powdered limestone and sodium carbonate. This produces a liquid made up of the silicates of calcium and sodium which on cooling forms the common type of glass used for making windows, bottles etc. Different types of glass can be made by using different materials with the sand. For example, glass for cut-glass tableware is made using lead oxide, while 'Pyrex' glass is made by mixing borax and aluminium oxide with the sand. Glass can also be coloured by adding oxides such as those of iron, cobalt, copper and chromium.

The resources which we have mentioned in this section are all easily and cheaply produced, and Britain has reserves of all of them to last for a very long time.

Water

Water is probably our most valuable resource. It is essential for the maintenance of the life processes of plants and animals and its industrial and domestic uses are numerous.

On the surface of the Earth there are about 1500 million cubic kilometres of water. Of this, about 97 per cent is in the oceans and seas and a further 1.9 per cent is frozen as ice. Most of the remainder occurs as ground water with a small quantity in lakes and rivers. The Earth's water goes through a continuous series of changes called the **water cycle**. Water passes into the atmosphere as water vapour formed by evaporation from water surfaces and from plants. (Evaporation from plants is called **transpiration**). The water vapour in the atmosphere is condensed by cooling to form clouds, and the water is returned to the Earth's surface as rain or snow. The combined processes of evaporation and transpiration (often called **evapotranspiration**) return about 60 per cent of the precipitation on land to the air. The remaining water soaks into the soil and rocks or forms lakes and rivers, eventually making its way back to the sea. During the water cycle, the sea loses more water by evaporation than it gains from rain and snow. On the other hand the land receives more water as rain and snow than it loses by evaporation. The excess water is returned to the sea by rivers and glaciers and as ground water.

In general, Britain receives enough rain to meet its water demands though problems of supply were highlighted by the exceptionally dry summer of 1976. Unfortunately, however, most of the rain falls on the mountainous west side of the country away from the main centres of population, and while the Highlands of Scotland have more than enough water the south-east of England has barely enough to meet its needs. The variation in rainfull from place to place means that water sources may vary. In Scotland, surface sources such as Loch Lomond are adequate and there is little need to extract water by sinking wells into water-bearing strata (these are called **aquifers**). In many parts of England, on the other hand, large natural reservoirs are absent and about 15 per cent of the water used comes from aquifers such as Chalk, Triassic sandstones and Oolitic Limestones.

Most of the 17 000 million cubic metres of water used every year in Britain is taken by industry. About 40 per cent is used in power stations for steam generation and cooling while other major users include the chemical, steel and paper industries. About one-third of our water goes into the public water supply. Can you think of the many uses to which this water is put? At home the average person uses about 140 litres a day, mostly in the toilet and for washing. Some water is also used in agriculture for such things as spray irrigation.

The demand for water rises continuously at a rate of about 3 per cent a year. Since our rainfall will probably remain relatively constant into the foreseeable future, we will never have any more water than we have at present. The only way in which we can meet the extra demand is to use our resources more effectively. We could store more water in new reservoirs or behind barrages built across Morecambe Bay, the Wash and the Dee and Solway Estuaries. We could also store water by pumping it back into our seriously depleted aquifers. In addition, water could be piped from Scotland to England and some fresh water could be obtained by the removal of salt from sea water.

More economical use could be made of water by using it again and again with repeated purification, or by designing toilets which use less water in flushing. Also, water consumption could probably be cut if it was metered like gas and electricity and paid for in the same way. Since water purification is expensive we may someday have two water systems – one containing pure water for drinking and cooking and the other with impure water for toilets and washing. Other less likely schemes to obtain extra water have also been suggested. These include using ships to tow icebergs or huge plastic bags full of fresh water, and making rain by seeding clouds with crystals of silver iodide.

Geology and engineering

When major engineering projects are planned the geologist can often help the engineer by advising him of the best places in which to build. Buildings, bridges and dams have to be very strong so careful site investigation must come before construction to find out whether the underlying rocks will provide good foundations Since dams must be watertight the valley rocks should be impermeable so that water will not leak out under and around the dam. Dams should not be sited where the rocks are heavily jointed or faulted because such rocks are both weak and permeable. However, small areas of fissured rock can be consolidated by injecting liquid cement in a process called **grouting**. Care must also be taken not to build on sand and gravel because these materials are extremely permeable. Water can also leak out through the weak rocks on the hinges of anticlines, whereas the hinges of synclines are strong. In the early stages of investigation, estimates of sedimentation rates might also be made because reservoirs often become silted up quite rapidly. For example, the Hoover Dam in the USA has had its capacity reduced by a half since 1937. When a dam is built the water table rises and the water may lubricate rocks on the valley sides; this may cause them to slip into the reservoir. The danger of large-scale landslides is illustrated by the Vaiont Reservoir disaster which took place in Italy in 1963 (see page 33). In general, the best

sites for dams are in deep, narrow valleys becau these provide reservoirs with small surface areas that water loss by evaporation is minimal. T valley rocks should preferably be igneous metamorphic since these are strong and nea impermeable.

Geological knowledge can also be usefu applied to tunnelling. For example, when a tun strikes a fault it may be flooded by water coming from the shattered rock along the fault plane. If t positions of faults can be worked out beforeha suitable precautions can be taken to avc disaster.

Conservation

The very rapid rise in population and indus has meant that our demands for resources from t Earth are constantly increasing. This is illustra by the fact that energy consumption doubles ev ten years. More coal has been used since 19 than in all the time up to that date and sir significant oil production began in 1880 the use oil has increased at a rate of about 7 per cent ev year. The extraction and use of materials a leaves its marks on the environment. Quarryi and mining change the landscape, produce sp heaps and cause subsidence; industry pollutes air and water; and the building of dams floc parts of the countryside.

Of course, we must use the Earth's resources order to survive and this causes unavoida depletion of fuels and ores. We should, howev use them as sensibly as we can and with as li waste as possible. To make better use of resources we could, for example, use more oi the chemical industry instead of burning it power stations. We could also re-use materi more effectively. Steps have been made in t direction, as shown by the fact that a good dea steel in Britain comes from scrap and about on third of our lead comes from old car batteries. can also use substitute materials such as plastics replace metals whenever possible.

The limited resources of the Earth and delicate environment are all too easily abused. should treat them with care — after all, we o have one Earth.

INDEX